A CONCISE
ECONOMIC HISTORY OF
BRITAIN

T0312057

A CONCISE ECONOMIC HISTORY OF BRITAIN

FROM THE EARLIEST TIMES TO 1750

BY

SIR JOHN CLAPHAM

CAMBRIDGE
AT THE UNIVERSITY PRESS
1966

CAMBRIDGE UNIVERSITY PRESS
Cambridge, New York, Melbourne, Madrid, Cape Town, Singapore, São Paulo, Delhi

Cambridge University Press
The Edinburgh Building, Cambridge CB2 8RU, UK

Published in the United States of America by Cambridge University Press, New York

www.cambridge.org
Information on this title: www.cambridge.org/9780521046633

First edition 1949
Reprinted 1951, 1957, 1963, 1966
Re-issued in this digitally printed version 2008

A catalogue record for this publication is available from the British Library

ISBN 978-0-521-04663-3 hardback
ISBN 978-0-521-09216-6 paperback

EDITORIAL NOTE

From 1908 to 1935 (with a short interval after 1917) Sir John Clapham lectured in Cambridge on English Economic History. Among generations of undergraduates, his lectures were famous; and out of his lectures this book grew. It was the work of his last years, written month and month about with the third volume (completed, but not yet to be published) of his *History of the Bank of England*. It should have told the story, as his lectures did, from prehistoric times to our own. At the time of his death, on 29 March 1946, Books I and II were written and typed, and the manuscript of Book III was in the typist's hands; Book IV had scarcely been begun. Therefore the story breaks off in 1750. Professor W. H. B. Court has undertaken to complete it, but since his continuation will not be ready for some time to come, the Syndics of the University Press have decided to publish Sir John Clapham's work now, and to publish the continuation as a companion volume at a later date.[1]

At the request of the Syndics, I have prepared Sir John Clapham's text for the printer. I have tried to verify quotations, and names, dates and other matters of fact; but I have not succeeded in tracking down all his far-ranging knowledge to its sources. In particular, there remain some quotations from modern works which I have not traced, and have therefore been unable to acknowledge, as he intended, in footnotes. The few alterations I have made (they fall chiefly in Book III, which he did not live to revise in typescript) have been designed to secure the accuracy on points of fact which he would have wished. On matters of judgement, I have been careful to allow his opinion to stand.

Lady Clapham has very kindly relieved me of the task of making the index, for which I wish to thank her. I am responsible for the Table of Contents and for the titles of books, chapters and sections, and I have added the footnotes on pp. 30, 32, 80, 85 and 257.

Many have helped me in the work of verification, and to them all my grateful thanks are due: to Lady Clapham herself, to Professor Helen Cam, Miss I. F. Grant, Miss J. M. C. Toynbee, Professor F. E. Adcock, the City Archivist of Bristol,

[1] The continuation (W. H. B. Court, *A Concise Economic History of Britain from 1750 to Recent Times*) was published in 1954.

Dr G. H. S. Bushnell, the Reverend M. P. Charlesworth, Professor G. N. Clark, Professor H. C. Darby, Professor Bruce Dickins, Mr C. R. Fay, Professor S. R. K. Glanville, Mr H. J. Habakkuk, Mr W. F. Haslop, Professor M. C. Knowles, Colonel R. S. Manley, Mr Christopher Morris, Dr J. H. Plumb, Professor M. Postan, Mr E. E. Rich, Mr F. R. Salter, Mr A. F. Scholfield, Dr R. C. Smail and Mr C. H. Wilson.

This book is not the text of Sir John Clapham's lectures, for he did not write them out; not is it an expansion of the brief notes from which he gave them. It is a new work. Yet much from his lectures went to its making, in substance and in phrase. I believe that those who knew and heard him will sometimes hear again, as they read, the tones of his voice. For me this book echoes, as few others, the sound of its author's spoken word.

KING'S COLLEGE   JOHN SALTMARSH
CAMBRIDGE

May 1949

In the second impression of this book, issued in 1951, a few slips and misprints were corrected, and alterations of substance were made on the following points: the Roman roads (p. 34); early fulling-mills on the Continent (p. 154); estimates of population in the eighteenth century (pp. 186 and 189). I also added note 2 on p. 156. Nearly all these alterations were based on work published after Sir John Clapham's death. In this third impression, besides correcting a few further slips, I have added note 4 on p. 27, since it is now clear that the Roman made more use of water-mills in Britain than Sir John Clapham believed. On pp. 154–5 I have revised his account of the numbers and distribution of early fulling-mills in England in the light of recent discoveries; and on p. 158 I have deleted some figures derived from the unreliable ulnagers' accounts. Sir John Clapham also made use of the ulnagers' accounts in his description of the distribution of the cloth industry in the late fourteenth century on p. 191; but for the reason given in note 1 to this page I have allowed his words to stand. I have to thank Professor E. M. Carus-Wilson, Professor T. S. Ashton, Professor D. V. Glass and Dr G. H. S. Bushnell for help in making these corrections.   J.S.

KING'S COLLEGE

CAMBRIDGE

16 April 1957

CONTENTS

Chapter III

SAXONS AND NORMANS

page 39

BOOK II

From A.D. *1100 to* A.D. *1500*

CHAPTER IV

AGRICULTURE AND RURAL SOCIETY

page 77

CHAPTER V

TRADE AND INDUSTRY; PUBLIC POLICY
AND ECONOMIC DOCTRINE

page 125

BOOK III

From A.D. *1500 to* A.D. *1750*

Chapter VI

BRITAIN IN THE EARLY MODERN PERIOD

page 185

Chapter VII

AGRICULTURE AND RURAL SOCIETY

page 194

CHAPTER VIII

INDUSTRY, GILDS AND TRADE CLUBS

page 225

Chapter IX

TRADING COMPANIES, FINANCE AND PUBLIC POLICY

page 262

INTRODUCTION

Of all varieties of history the economic is the most fundamental. Not the most important: foundations exist to carry better things. How a man lives with his family, his tribe or his fellow-citizens; the songs he sings; what he feels and thinks when he looks at the sunset; the prayers he raises—all these are more important than the nature of his tools, his trick of swapping things with his neighbours, the way he holds and tills his fields, his inventions and their consequences, his money —when he has learnt to use it—his savings and what he does with them. Economic advance is not the same thing as human progress. The man with a motor-car may have less imagination, and perhaps a baser religion, than the men who frequented Stonehenge. But economic activity, with its tools, fields, trade, inventions and investment, is the basement of man's house. Its judicious structure and use have, in course of ages, provided, first for a privileged few and then for more, chances to practise high arts, organise great states, design splendid temples, or think at leisure about the meaning of the world; though a lone shepherd in a poor society may also have time to think. The economic basement may be dull, but need not be. A patch of earth dug level, a right stroke with a felling axe, a neat bit of welding, a locomotive brought smoothly to rest, even a tidy balance sheet or a quick calculation in forward exchange, all yield the craftsman's, not to say the artist's, satisfaction. Most sports of leisured people are variants of old economic activities —or of warlike ones. Men first hunted the deer to get his flesh to eat or his leather skin to wear; they first climbed mountains to save the sheep or kill chamois. As most men and most ages have had little leisure, it is a comfort for the economic historian to remember that the sun has seldom completely failed to get into this basement of his.

Book I

FROM THE EARLIEST TIMES
TO A.D. 1100

Chapter I

Prehistoric Britain

FLINT, COPPER AND BRONZE

'*When* Britain first at Heaven's command arose from out the azure main' is not easy to say: the region where it lies has in fact done a great deal of rising and sinking. Certainly men of a sort were here long before it finally—as we suppose—became an island, not so many thousand years B.C. Its last link with the continent, geologists now hold, was a marshy belt across the shallow southern part of the present North Sea. Until that was cut, land migration into 'Britain' was possible; but the fact and its date are not important; for primitive men have often managed to cross narrow, and even wide, water barriers. With stone tools and fire they have made dug-out canoes. Coracles of wicker and hide have done some astonishing voyages. That such vessels seem small for population movements is no obstacle. All primitive populations, even when fairly advanced, are almost incredibly thin. One or two tens of thousands, or even less than one, may well have been the total population of Britain when it was new: the whole vast North American continent is thought to have held not more than a million three hundred years ago. Little family or tribal groups can move in a few canoes; and such groups are all that we need picture.

The savages of the new island were probably in what is now called the Mid Stone (mesolithic) stage of technical development. They were wanderers who looked for game and collected wild vegetable foods—in summer on high ground where their camp-sites have been traced, in winter probably from caves. Those who frequented the coasts knew how to catch even deep-sea fish: we have their bones. Like the Eskimo, they made bone harpoons and other implements; but their best cutting-tools were of flint. They had brought the dog to heel, but they had no cattle. They could make fire, but they had no pots. They were almost helpless against the forests which were spreading and growing denser as a result of climatic changes; for to fell even a single tree was a long and heavy task. But low and brutal as their life must have been, there was high skill in their flint-chipping and bone-carving. They must have understood barter: flint was used far from the sites where it can be picked up or dug. This was almost certainly 'imported', though some of the flints that we find may have been brought by wandering hunters from flinty to flintless sites. We know that when flint was very far away more bone was used. But some of the better flints are found almost everywhere.

The crafts, the way of life, and, so far as we can tell, the physical type of these 'mesolithic' savages had been much the same all over northern Europe before the isle of Britain rose or the North Sea bottom sank. We have probably inherited some few things from their bones and their brains.

For, at each stage of migration into Britain, there is reason to think that new arrivals absorbed, perhaps enslaved, the natives, as and when they met them, both teaching them and learning from them when there was anything to learn. Those who began to arrive from a date which scholars now fix round about 2400 B.C. had not much to learn. For they brought what has been called the New Stone (neolithic) economic revolution. The improved stone implements, from which (by an accident of archaeological language) the new arrivals get their name, are for the economist far less important than other things that they brought—a knowledge of agriculture and of managing cattle. These arts had spread from the Near East, where great civilisa- tions already flourished; and they had spread rather rapidly because primitive agriculture without fertilisers or rotation of crops exhausts the soil—except in Egypt where the sacred river restores fertility—and obliges the cultivators to move on; and because, as men moved on north-west, the sites and soils fitted for their sort of agriculture were limited.

This was specially true of Britain when the first farmers crossed a narrower Channel into a country just like the one they were leaving in 'France'. Lowland Britain was then mostly covered with 'damp oak' forest—oak and hazel, bramble and thorn, thorn, thorn. Valleys were waterlogged and marshy. Great parts of the drier ground were also stocked by nature with well-grown oak and ash, beech, birch and yew—hard to clear with stone axes. Forest or scrub probably spread over the dry chalk and limestone ridges—the Downs, the Cotswolds and such. But the vegetation there was more open and had some natural gaps. These you could extend and your goats would nibble down the seedlings: there is nothing like a goat for stopping the spread or revival of forest. In any case, it is on such ridges from the Sussex Downs westward into Devon that ten or a dozen settlements of these first farmers have been examined. They were mainly cattle keepers; but they also kept goats, sheep and pigs, and they cultivated little plots of wheat, probably using some sort of digging stick to turn the ground or a pick made of a deer's antler to furrow it.

Their known settlements include fortified camps with trenches about them in concentric circles, for defence and to keep the cattle in, enclosing a maximum area of ten to fourteen acres. They dug pits to get good flint: surface flints are often damaged by weathering. On the Norfolk chalk, when a society similar to that of the southern Downs was established, they learnt to mine with deer-antler picks, ox-shoulder-blade shovels, and miners' lamps of chalk. And where they mined they 'manufactured' flint axes and other weapons and tools—often in the rough—for 'export'. There must have been specialised flint-workers, perhaps professional flint pedlars.

How their contacts began with the handfuls of earlier, non-agricultural, lower-grade flint-using people we can only guess. Perhaps it was through these better flints. The hunting savage who hears of a better tool or weapon will always do his utmost to get hold of it—give slaves or skins or wild-honey or whatever he has in barter. At first the immigrant farmer, looking for the high dry land and living on his stock and his wheat, can hardly have heard of men who lived by snaring and hunting and fishing and gathering berries and fruits in the thick woods and along the rivers and the sea-coasts. The different societies may have lived apart in their several ways for centuries: they almost certainly did, just as Dr Johnson's friends and crofters of the Hebrides lived apart four thousand years later. But gradually some of the older stock learnt from their distant neighbours the use of better-made tools and how to make pots, with all that this implies.

Meanwhile a far more highly developed civilisation was affecting Britain, and all the British Isles, from the South and West—immediately, we may assume, from Brittany, ultimately from the Mediterranean. It is classed as neolithic, but once again to the economist its weapons and implements—apart from the fact that they were of stone—were much the least interesting thing about it. Archaeologists call it the Big Stone civilisation, because they have been able to trace its spread by its monuments of big stones, stone tombs usually covered by great mounds of earth, barrows, standing stones and stone circles. It came up from the Mediterranean, by way of Malta, Sardinia and the Balearic Islands, round the coasts of Spain and Portugal, across central France from the Mediterranean coast to Brittany, and so north and north-about Scotland to the Baltic. The tombs are common in the Scilly Isles, well known from Cornwall to Wiltshire, found in many other places, and very common in Ireland. For some of the tombs 'big stone' is a misnomer: tombs of the same sort were also made with smaller stones; and there are places where even this is difficult, to which, nevertheless, the 'Big Stone' men may have penetrated. That, however, does not prevent our recognising quite clearly the lines along which the religion spread that certainly inspired them. It was a sea-borne faith and its followers—or men who served them—must have been fine seamen. Like the religion of Egypt, it was an aristocratic faith: big tombs and great barrows are not built for common men.

The economist is more interested in these social divisions, in the organisation which the handling of the great stones required, and in the seamanship and shipwrights' skill without which the voyages were not possible, than in speculation about a shadowy 'megalithic' doctrine of the dead. 'If indeed their ships instead of their tombs had been made of indestructible material',[1] it has been said, historians might talk less about that doctrine and more about the splendid voyages.

There is no need to suppose that voyages were made from the Mediterranean direct. No doubt the Big Stone civilisation spread gradually. But the crossing from Portugal, or even from Brittany, is not child's play; and the route north-about Scotland, through the tides of the Pentland Firth towards the Baltic, is for fine seamen only. What brought these adventurers to Britain, and 'always a little further' to Denmark, and further still? The spreading of their religion? The search for those isles of the sunset to which their great dead had 'gone west'? Search for the gold of Ireland, that 'prehistoric El Dorado', and for the amber which, as the Mediterranean world knew, came from somewhere in the misty North? Lust of conquest and the urge to colonise? Mere accident and the drive of south-west winds off the Atlantic? Likely enough this last

[1] H. O. Hencken, *The Archaeology of Cornwall and Scilly* (1932), p. 17.

was the beginning, and then men came back with their travellers' tales.

Anyhow they came. The pioneers from the Mediterranean were a comparatively tall long-headed race, maybe from Crete. But there was conquest, conversion, blending of populations and sometimes adoption of habits and modifications of crafts from whatever natives were found. The newcomers, or the arts and beliefs learnt from them, can be traced along the coasts and islands and inland to those sites, especially those south-western sites, where all primitive half-civilised men mainly settled—the chalk and limestone downs or ridges and the easily worked gravel soils. Their agricultural life differed little from that of the first farmers known in Britain, some of whom perhaps accepted them as chieftains or tribal priests.

Somewhat later, it is believed, than the long-headed sea-farers from the West, other men, mostly with rounder heads, were making easier crossings from the East. (We are about the date 2000 B.C.) Archaeologists call them 'Beaker Folk', from a certain style of pot that they had in common; but to the historian their pot or 'beaker', not being the first of all pots, may be a convenient label but is not of great interest. He cares more for the arrows tipped with barbed flint, the flint daggers, the stone battle-axes, the copper daggers, with which they hunted and fought. Stone and metal are competing and will compete for centuries. The working of the easier metals had long been understood about the Mediterranean, and had spread to central Europe. The long-headed tomb-builders had found copper as well as gold in Ireland—just possibly gold-smiths too; though these in all probability came in their train. Certainly in the second millennium B.C. Ireland exported goldsmiths' work, with weapons, tools, utensils and ornaments of copper and of bronze. The 'round heads' got metal daggers from Ireland; for the continental sources from which presumably they drew their first daggers of copper were further away.

They were well armed and resolute fighters who 'imposed themselves as overlords on older stocks and mingled with or absorbed these'.[1] Their life seems to have been that of migratory herdsmen, with a subordinate agriculture, like that of the historical Welsh and Irish. As pastoralists they followed their various predecessors on to the more open, drier ground. They have left plenty of splendid graves, like the 'Big Stone' men,

[1] V. G. Childe, *Prehistoric Communities of the British Isles* (1940), p. 97.

but few if any known settlements. They had cattle, some of which they may have ferried over from the continent, pigs and sheep and goats. As would be expected with such people, so equipped, they were great hunters.

What primitive group or type of men designed and organised the erection of the greater stone circles such as Avebury and Stonehenge, or to what extent these were designed in stages by different groups of rulers or priests, at different dates, is a technical problem. But it is agreed that they come from the age about 2000 B.C. and from the frontier of the eras of stone and metal—though there is no proof of metal having been used in their construction: it had not yet got down to mason's tools, or it may be that the gods, being old, had in any case to be served in the old way. What the technician admires at Stonehenge are the handling of the enormous upright blocks nearly thirty feet high; the skilful shaping and tenon-and-mortice attachment to them of the curved horizontal blocks; the knowledge of perspective effects shown in making these horizontals wider at the top than at the bottom; and the whole lay-out in relation to the sunrise at midsummer.

The building suggests organised servile labour, directed by men of high intelligence, from a society whose upper strata at least were rich—rich through their flocks and herds, through trade perhaps, through pillage no doubt. The most amazing bit of organisation was the transport of the inner ring of much smaller but yet massive 'blue stones' to their present site. Plenty of the great stones occur locally, or did, for they have been much used up in some four thousand years: they are worked blocks of the weathered sandstone, 'sarsen-stones', which lay about on the chalk of Salisbury Plain. But the blue stones, it is now certain, were brought, as treasured or sacred things, from Pembrokeshire—by sea and probably river, and then no doubt by rollers overland.

Was it in fact servile labour from some relatively dense population that did this—like pyramid-building in imaginative pictures? Second thoughts pass to medieval cathedrals, often built leisurely over long years, with a comparatively small labour force. A cathedral of some kind Stonehenge certainly was; it may have been built slowly; and it may not have been necessary to set up more than a couple of uprights and a single carefully worked cross-lintel in a year—a great feat of skill, but a job that need not have employed sweating crowds.

Yet only crowds can have heaped up many of the huge funeral barrows: the hugest is nearly six hundred yards long. Here the pyramid analogy seems more appropriate. Perhaps a herd of prisoners of war was driven to honour the great dead man who had subdued them; or perhaps the whole tribe turned out as a religious duty. In any case, there are highly and perhaps brutally organised labour activities among these shadowy tribesmen who have left such durable monuments; who spoke what language or languages we do not know; whose needs, or perhaps only their greed and their superstitions, were served by seamen who could risk bad weather off Land's End with ugly cargoes of stone; by metal workers in Ireland and other distant places; by potters nearer home; by spinners and weavers, no doubt at home, among the sheep of Salisbury Plain. There was also a certain amount of agriculture as before, and evidently some of that division of labour of which Adam Smith was to write.

It is possible that the so-called Beaker Folk spoke a primitive Celtic dialect; but languages and skulls hardly concern the economist. The patois of the generally round-headed mountaineers of Savoy contains many Celtic words. There are round and long skulls among the German-speaking mountaineers of the Bernese Oberland. Economic conditions were, and are, much the same at Grindelwald and Chamonix.

Most of the waves of invaders in the second and first millennia B.C. were no doubt of Celtic speech. Some were more agricultural than others, and archaeologists have connected with the invasion of a 'land-hungry peasantry'[1] an undoubted increase of population and of land under the plough in lowland Britain that began in the eighth century B.C. But even nearer the Christian era than that, the country as a whole may be pictured as pastoral with a subordinate agriculture—as so much of it still was in Caesar's day. There were marked variations from region to region, variations which survived into medieval times, when great parts of Wales and Scotland were still essentially pastoral.[2]

For all the years between 2000 and 100 B.C., what little is certainly known about agriculture can be set down on a page or two. Wheat was grown from the first, and barley. Oats and rye have been traced, but no more. The Romans regarded both

[1] V. G. Childe, *Prehistoric Communities of the British Isles* (1940), p. 187.
[2] See below, pp. 55–6, 87–8, 103.

as weeds that spoiled the better grains; though they knew of oats as a fodder crop. However, as oats have been found in continental lake-dwellings of the second millennium B.C., and as the Romans had heard that Germans made oatmeal porridge, there seems fair reason to think that it may have been eaten here. But we do not know.

Nor do we know when a plough drawn by oxen first came into use. It was here when men had learnt to work iron—perhaps earlier. Ploughshares of bronze have not been found; but as the primitive plough was certainly made of wood with a grubbing-point hardened in fire, this does not prove that it was not known. After digging-sticks, and perhaps picks made of deers' antlers, may have come that foot-plough (*caschrom*) to turn the soil and get a rough furrow which is still known in the Hebrides. The total amount of land worked with oxen was no doubt trifling before the first century B.C., and the plough was a light rather inefficient thing—a primitive version of the Roman *aratrum*, without wheels or coulter, made of a convenient bough for handle and part of the stem from which it grew for base and grubbing-nose: so ╱ . There are men living who have seen an Alpine peasant mount his mule with such a 'plough' over his shoulder. Being of wood, prehistoric ploughs have rarely survived; picks and hoes of wood must also have rotted away with most of the early foot-ploughs and ox-ploughs.

The survival of the *caschrom* is a reminder that, though the existence of Celtic ploughed fields in some districts favoured for settlement can be proved, and can no doubt be assumed in others, it is most likely that more primitive ways of preparing the patches of corn were really far more common.

Air-photography has recovered from the remote past the outlines of some of those patches. We see small irregular or roughly squared fields, surrounded with banks, lying round the site of the farmstead or hamlet—forerunners of many that we can see to-day, only with banks bigger and more overgrown, in Wales and Cornwall and the West. We must suppose that either these fields, being small and near, were kept fertile by the manure of the beasts, or that some fields were cropped until they were tired and left to recover fertility while others were ploughed up. Naturally we know nothing at first hand about prehistoric manure, but cattle-keepers may learn its use from observation—though often they do not. Some of these early

Britons may well have advanced to the stage of agricultural technique at which successors of theirs in Scotland and elsewhere remained for many centuries—'infields', such as we can trace, kept fertile by a good head of cattle, and an occasional 'outfield' somewhere in the waste, used until tired and then left to revert to rough pasture.[1] Such 'outfields', if they existed, might escape even the eye of the flying camera.

In the little fields, we picture rude ploughs drawn by a couple of tiny oxen scratching up the light chalky or gravelly soils on which alone we can yet prove that such permanent agriculture had developed. In rougher places you might grub up a bit of ground by hand and foot, and take what crop off it you could get. You reaped it with a light sickle, first of flint, then of bronze, last of iron.

How the stock of beasts was herded and handled we must guess: we only have their bones to show that they were eaten. There was no sacred cow as among those other pastoralists who invaded India, speaking languages akin to Celtic.

Industrially and commercially the second millennium B.C. and the first quarter of the first is the age of bronze. Then iron comes, but not effectively here until about 500 B.C. There is no sharp division of 'ages'; and, from one aspect, we might speak of an age of gold. Flint long overlapped bronze. Men using iron swords might have bronze shields and every sort of ornament and utensil of bronze, more workable and much more beautiful. It has been suggested that some of the remoter Britons whom Agricola fought may still have been armed with bronze weapons only. Iron swords were not for everyone. We know from the far later sagas the value that the northern fighting-man put on his iron sword: it had a name and sometimes it talked. This half-sacred giver of death was never a thing easily replaced.

Before bronze there was copper. Ireland had the copper but no tin to blend with and harden it. There was copper in Anglesey and in Cornwall; but most Cornish copper lies deep and inaccessible. Some that occurs in small quantities near the surface may possibly have been worked; but of this we have no proof either for prehistoric or any other ancient time. Nor can we prove the working of the Cornish 'tin-streams'—water-made streaks of soil with tin washed into it—before about 400 or 500 B.C.; but there is every reason to think that they were

[1] For 'infields' and 'outfields', see below, p. 48.

tapped much earlier. The method is a form of washing like that for alluvial gold. It was by washing that the primitive diggers got gold in the Wicklow Hills. The Big Stone civilisation which they certainly shared was well established both in Ireland and in Cornwall. It seems, therefore, as certain as anything can be in these misty ages, that the splendid Irish bronze industry was based on early working of Irish copper and Cornish tin by linked groups of prospectors and bronze-smiths.

The trade connection between Ireland and Cornwall we know to have been constant and intimate in the early Bronze Age. Besides her bronze wares Ireland exported her gold. A favourite ornament of this period was one of flat gold, shaped like a crescent moon: it was worn no doubt at the neck. These 'little moons' have been found abundantly in Ireland; on the continent here and there from the Danish islands to south of the Loire, but most in the Cherbourg peninsula. In Britain they have nearly all been found in central Scotland or in Cornwall— that is on northern and southern trade routes from Ireland to Europe.

Later, it has been supposed, there was a decline in navigation, the two serious voyages from Wicklow to North Cornwall and from South Cornwall to 'Cherbourg', or the still more serious voyage round Land's End direct, being abandoned in favour of easier crossings to Wales or Scotland. The ground for this is the rarity of later types of gold ornaments in Cornwall and the South-West, and their relative abundance in some other parts of Britain, especially Wessex. The rich lords of Wessex may well have attracted the gold—raw or worked—and so side-tracked Cornwall.

It is also thought that the demand for Cornish tin may have slackened at the same time. There are continental sources of the metal from which supplies may have been drawn; but we are here in the realm of speculation.

The active trade of the age of bronze, especially of the late Bronze Age, say 1000 to 500 B.C., is not a matter of speculation. Of course the total amount of it was trifling. But the things that men most coveted—ornaments, good weapons, good tools, rare utensils, especially the big bronze cauldrons that Homer's heroes thought so precious—were moved over great distances in a way that may be traced with almost absolute certainty. Almost, because in some cases we cannot be quite sure that some article of a type that originated, say, in Ireland was not imitated in other places where it has actually been found. But if the other places had not the materials, as usually they had not, this is unlikely. And as copper and tin were mined only at a few scattered points in western Europe, either the finished goods must have been traded in, or the raw materials. In discussing the importance of trade, it does not much matter which it was. When we see a type that originated in a place where copper is handy, modified in a place where it is not, we may perhaps assume that the trade was in copper ingots, not in swords or knives or whatever it may be. But in any case we have trade.

There is an early type of Irish bronze axe produced, it is said, before 1500 B.C. An archaeologist's map of Ireland[1] is dotted almost all over with finds of these axes, here and there with so-called 'hoards', that is, small stocks of them and other bronze articles; and in a few places there have been found the moulds in which they were made. The dots are thickest in the North-East. From Ireland, they run across central Scotland and thicken again in the Scottish North-East. There also, moulds prove a local manufacturing industry. Another was in Northumberland. Except for one in North-West Wales, no moulds have yet been found south of the Tees; but there are several 'hoards', and single axe-heads in considerable numbers wherever settlement was fairly dense. There is a big element of accident in these finds; but the picture, as it now stands, can be interpreted with some confidence in terms of manufacture and trade routes. The Irish did most manufacturing; the part of Wales nearest to Ireland and to copper—there is copper in Anglesey—did a little; North-East Britain did a good deal; the rest of Britain was supplied by trade. No copper or tin was ever mined near where the moulds are found in North-East Scotland; so either metal ingots were imported or old axes and bronze 'scrap' were remelted. We get a faint, but not for that reason untrustworthy, picture of trade in raw materials and in finished goods. As there had been a trade in flints for thousands of years, this was a perfectly natural development.

'Possession of copper and tin and geographical advantages made the British Isles manufacturing countries, producing for a world market when bronze was the principal industrial metal.'[2] If not quite a 'world', certainly a 'European' market. Types of bronze weapons from the British Isles have

<hr/>

[1] Sir Cyril Fox, *The Personality of Britain* (1943), Plate VI.
[2] V. G. Childe, *Prehistoric Communities of the British Isles* (1940), p. 163.

been found so far afield as Hungary and the neighbourhood of Danzig. The influence of foreign on British styles and patterns suggests migrations of metal-workers, or at least 'international' relations among them. Archaeologists speculate about groups of travelling merchant bronze-smiths who collected the 'scrap' and delivered the new finished goods. The collection of the scrap is proved for the late Bronze Age. Stocks of old worn articles have been found, and with them sometimes the moulds, ingots and metal-workers' tools. The migratory groups of skilled men outside the life of the tribes whom they served are only assumed; but the assumption is probable. The smith often appears as an outsider in legend. When he is a god, as in Homer, he is a rather second-rate god. In northern legend, Wayland Smith was an unpleasant character; and the dwarf smiths also were unpleasant, greedy, unscrupulous folk whom anyone might cheat or rob. This suggests times before iron was in general use, and the blacksmith not yet a friendly character from among your own people.

Whether migratory outsiders or not, the smiths of the late Bronze Age were very highly skilled. They had a whole range of tools for their own use—hammers, chisels, tongs, gouges. They made weapons and ornaments of every sort; the round shields of which Achilles' shield was an idealised memory; and those treasured cauldrons. Carpenters got good bronze tools. There were general-purpose knives; there were razors and sickles.

Important, essential as they were, these bronze-smiths were a mere handful among the cattle-keepers, corn-growers, and women spinning and weaving at the homes of the tribes with whom they dealt.

THE EARLY IRON AGE

For Britain the age of iron, of some iron, begins very near to historical times, about 500 B.C. or a little earlier. (The first written account of Britain was given by the Greek traveller Pytheas, about 325 B.C.) Egypt had known iron, but not iron tools or weapons, before 1000 B.C. For Europe, effective and economical iron-working seems to have developed first in Styria and about the Alps between that date and 700 B.C. It was a revolution comparable with the discovery of steam, of cheap steel, or of the internal combustion engine. An axe of flint or bronze is a poor thing at best for a woodsman; but with an axe of iron or steel he can 'go up against the thick trees'. Iron swords made conquerors of men; iron axes began that conquest of the forests, with which Europe was occupied for nearly two thousand years, a conquest which the American axe took over savagely after an interval of some centuries. An axe of iron or steel: the difference is only that of a tiny percentage of carbon, and for fine steel the presence of a scrap of some metallic alloy, until very recent times generally manganese. The right carbon percentage may easily get in by accident; and it is believed that the rise of regular local steel industries much later can be traced to the occurrence of manganese with the iron ores. The primitive heroes' wonderful swords may well have been of such 'accidental' steel, and no doubt some felling axes were also, though they remained nameless.

Iron is not only better than bronze for cutting: its ores are very much more common. There was wood for charcoal in abundance everywhere. Very likely, during the first iron-using generations, the sword-smiths were specialists who came in the train of conquering chieftains, such as those chiefs of the Parisii—the tribe that gave its name to Paris, *Lutetia Parisiorum* —who overran the East Riding of Yorkshire in the third century B.C. But very early the smelter and the blacksmith—at the start probably the same person—spread over the country and utilised most of the various sorts of iron ore in which Britain south of the Forth and Clyde abounds. In Ireland and the Highlands iron is rarer; and with the Iron Age the great metallurgical days of Ireland close.

How truly it was an Iron Age is seen by the adoption in South Britain—from Devonshire to the Thames and from the Isle of Wight to the head-waters of the Warwickshire Avon—of wrought-iron bars as currency. They were in use when Caesar came, and had been in use for perhaps two centuries before that. They are properly graded by weight. We can work out the unit on which bars of the six known grades were based. A great convenience they would be both for traders and black-smiths; for the blacksmith could forge his iron money into knives or horseshoes, just as a Victorian goldsmith at Birmingham melted a sovereign to make a wedding ring.

Iron and bronze and flint long lived side by side; but bronze and flint were steadily ousted as materials for weapons, implements and tools. Bronze survived for utensils and orna-ments and horse-trappings; there was never much demand for iron bowls or iron brooches. Besides, under primitive conditions, they would have been very hard to make. But the swords and axes and knives, the sickles, bill-hooks and light shares to be fitted to the nose of the plough, all came to be made of iron. How many people used an iron-shod plough we cannot begin to guess: we only know that there was such a thing.

Even in the 'civilised' South, South-West and North-East, where the iron currency circulated or the Parisian chieftains were buried in their chariots with iron-tyred wheels and fittings of bronze, we must think of little by-passed groups of early populations in forest and fen and remote valley, living whole 'ages' back, perhaps in the 'bronze', more likely in the 'stone' style; for the economic organisation of the Bronze Age was crumbling as the demand for bronze declined. Caesar's informants told him that life in Britain became more primitive, more dependent on cattle or on the chase, as you went north and north-west; and there is every reason to think that they were right.

The connection between Britain and the continent had always been close. It became closer still in the late prehistoric 'Iron Age'—the two centuries before Caesar. Populations, fashions in art and industry, the actual manufactured goods, moved with comparative ease among the Celtic-speaking tribes of Gaul and Britain, constantly at war with one another though they were. That Breton tribe of navigators, the Veneti, whose oak-built merchant fleet Caesar brutally destroyed, must have known well the ports on both sides of the Channel; one can never be sure that some fine bit of bronze work was made anywhere near the site where it has been found. The tribal wars that regularly interrupted trade explain the building of the very many hill-top forts of Britain: there was a special outburst of such buildings in the third century B.C. with a formidable invasion from Gaul. A normal hill-top fort is a place of refuge, usually with room for the cattle; but the remains often suggest some amount of permanent residence, something rather like a town. Yet the fortress-hill in Britain very seldom became a centre of population for later times, as it so often has become in Italy. Possible exceptions are Edinburgh and Stow-on-the-Wold.

There must have been gatherings of people at some of the ports at which traders arrived. It is hard to believe that London, with its Celtic name and splendid site, was of no importance before the conquering Romans made it their supply base and road centre in the first century A.D. But until about a hundred years before that, we cannot prove the existence of anything even faintly resembling what a modern economist means by a town—a place most of whose inhabitants are engaged not in agriculture but in administration, industry or trade.

Faint approaches to the economist's town-life come, as do several other forward moves in economic civilisation, with the conquest of South-East Britain by the Belgae about 75 B.C. This invasion is historic; Caesar records it. Our knowledge of it is, however, almost all 'prehistoric', based on finds. These Belgae were a tribe, or series of tribal groups, from northern Gaul, reputedly mixed Celt and German. Their politics were getting beyond the mere tribal stage. In Britain they built up 'kingdoms' with 'capitals'. Kent was first occupied; but by Caesar's time the kingdom of Cassivellaunus also covered Hertfordshire and Buckinghamshire and stretched towards the Fens. His first 'capital' was a hill fort of about a hundred acres above Wheathampsted; his next Verulam. Before the final Roman conquest, Cunobelinus (Cymbeline) ruled the kingdom from Colchester, beyond the great forests that have dwindled to Epping Forest, on low ground and near the sea. Perhaps after all it was the Roman eye for a good site and centre for communications that selected London, where we have as yet no proof of any important Celtic settlement. Cassivellaunus and Cymbeline must have seen the hill by the Thames; but they had chosen sites better protected by forest. However, their capitals had size, and Colchester had a situation fit for the 'economic' towns that were to come.

The fact that it was the Belgic princes who first struck coined money in Britain points toward trade and intercourse and a more developed economic life. Coins were issued not only in the eastern kingdom but in a second Belgic state whose centre of gravity was in Hampshire and its frontier in Somerset— a state whose existence is known mainly from these coins. Perhaps the striking of them was an act of policy in the first instance, an assertion of kingship. But as Gaulish coins had arrived in Britain two generations or more before local minting began, it may be assumed that their economic utility had been recognised. That British coins have been found well beyond the frontiers of the Belgic kings—in Norfolk, Lincoln, even Yorkshire—shows that they circulated, though perhaps long after

they were struck. Gaulish or British, they all ran back to one
model—a coin of Philip of Macedon, father of Alexander the
Great. Of this, many of them were most inferior imitations.
The coiners soon lost interest in, or skill to imitate, the Apollo's
head on one side and the chariot on the other: these were
conventionalised into whorls and blobs, though something like
a horse survived. British types all date from the years between
Caesar's raid and the regular conquest in 43 A.D. Some of them
bear in Roman letters the King's name, the tribe, the capital.
By this time Britain was in regular contact with what was now
Roman Gaul; traders from the Empire had easy access; the
inscriptions suggest that craftsmen also came. 'Cymbeline'
must have been in much the same relation to the Roman
Empire as some rajah just across the frontier has often been to
British India.

The relatively higher political and social organisation of the
Belgic states was certainly connected with a denser population
and a better agriculture than had before existed. When Caesar
raided Kent there was plenty of corn for his men to loot. These
Belgae are specially fascinating for the economic historian
because they have been claimed as pioneers of that agricultural
revolution which, by a thousand years later, had replaced in so
much of Britain the little Celtic fields by those big open fields,
ploughed in long strips, which made the familiar patterns of
medieval and early modern times. It is worth while to set out
the argument and evidence: there is so little to relate that this
is easy. First, long furrows go with a heavy plough; though
a heavy plough need not produce a pattern of strips. They go
with it because of no quality of the plough except its weight: if
your plough is heavy and cuts deep, you want to turn it as
seldom as possible. A heavy plough was known to Gaulish
tribes in north Italy and the Alpine regions about the beginning
of the Christian era; and this plough had wheels. It is thought
to have been invented in the open parts of central Europe. It
may have been invented many years B.C.; but that we do not
know. This wheeled plough has been connected by some historians with the long furrows and the strips. It may be so; but
you can have strips and long furrows without wheels on your
plough. There were wheelless ploughs in England all through
the Middle Ages. There are still. The case of wheels versus no
wheels was being discussed in the reign of Henry VIII. The
plough in use about Paris when William the Conqueror was

living had no wheels: at least, a contemporary list of its parts does not mention them. The old Scots plough was a heavy cumbrous wheelless affair. And in all these cases the land was usually ploughed with long furrows.

The connection of the Belgae with this plough argument rests on the discovery of one or two large ploughshares and a large coulter at a Belgic site in Kent; which do suggest a heavy, though not necessarily a wheeled, plough. There are some big coulters from the Roman era in Britain which also suggest a heavy plough; and there is air photographic evidence for long furrows near Roman-British buildings.

It seems highly probable that some of the owners of the wide fields attached to country-houses in Roman Britain would adopt the heavy plough, wheeled or wheelless, that made a deep furrow suited to the soil and climate of Britain. The ownership or tenure of land in strips is quite another story; and there is no shadow of evidence for anything of the kind either in the Britain of the Romans or in the little kingdoms of the Belgae that the Romans absorbed. The only thing that can be said wisely of the Belgae and agriculture then is, that perhaps they may have been in a few places users of a heavy plough and ploughers of that long furrow, the furlong, which in the end settled down at two hundred and twenty yards—a thing quite unknown to the little, enclosed, lightly scratched, so-called 'Celtic' fields.

Chapter II

The Roman Era

THE ROMAN ECONOMY IN BRITAIN

The Roman era in Britain, as long as that from the death of Henry VIII to the present day, gave time enough for economic change, but in one sense at least there was very little of it. For, at the time of the conquest, the economic life of the home provinces of the Roman Empire had reached a stage beyond which it did not pass and below which it not infrequently fell. Romans of the first century A.D. were superb civil and military engineers: they had systems of fortification, road and bridge systems, systems of water supply, of town planning and town building, of drainage and of central heating for cold climates which—in the absence of further invention—could not be improved upon; and were not improved upon until the nineteenth century. Their agricultural technique did not change in any essential. Nor did their industrial or commercial technique, so far as we know: certainly the manufactured goods of the first century were not bettered; and there is no reason to think that the business methods were.

Yet important social changes were taking place above that almost unchanged groundwork of production and exchange. Society was always based on slavery; but when Rome ceased to conquer, the slave population could not be maintained at its former level. In industry the free craftsman, in agriculture the *colonus*—bound to the soil by custom and economic fact, before in the fourth century he was bound to it by law—became relatively much more important elements: considerable importance they had always had.

What we watch in Britain is the partial introduction into a half-civilised society, which had already been in political and commercial contact with Rome, of that Roman economic equipment of the first century which was never bettered. From the third century, with the increasing political instability of the Empire, the equipment shows signs of wearing out at various points: there is decline in the easy commercial intercourse of the Empire's great days; a retrograde movement towards the local self-sufficiency of an earlier political and economic stage; decay in Romano-British towns. In the fourth century the dykes about outlying provinces of the Empire are threatened. In the fifth they go down. To the ignorant invaders the mysterious Roman buildings become 'giants' work', the still more mysterious products of earlier conquerors and organisers the work of devils.

Of written contemporary evidence for events in Britain there is singularly little after Tacitus's *Agricola*, and although Tacitus is believed to have known northern Gaul—*Gallia Belgica*—there is no proof that he ever crossed the Channel. In any case, he was a poor economist even in his *Germania*. Many things that interest us did not interest him at all: he had a proper classic indifference towards, or contempt for, traders, money-lenders, the 'base mechanic arts'; though he had the inherited Roman eye for agriculture. We must rely mainly on the work of the archaeologists. Casual references in poor chronicles, in imperial laws, in lives of the saints, help us now and then; but an economic account of Roman Britain that had to rely on these would be most meagre and inaccurate.

It is not always easy to date a Roman structure, still less easy to date a manufactured article; we may be able to say that buildings suggest partial 'Romanisation' of such and such a district, or that potsherds indicate this in such another district, without being able to give more than approximate dates. But men in Roman Britain managed to drop, hide away, or bury such an astonishing quantity of coin that this difficulty can often be overcome. We can at least say that this building or that rubbish heap is associated with coins of such and such emperors; or that no coin hereabouts is later than such another. For example, no coin excavated at Caerleon-on-Usk, the headquarters of the Second Legion, is later than A.D. 296: the legion was moved or broken up. No coin on the Wall is later than the reign of Gratian, who died in A.D. 383; it had been abandoned. And some inscriptions give close dates, as when at Wroxeter (*Viroconium*) the '*civitas*' of the Cornovii built a forum in honour of the Emperor Hadrian. Broadly speaking, the Roman Britain which the economist can try to interpret, and of which accurate maps can be made, is Britain from Hadrian to Aurelian (A.D. 117–275), after the difficulties of the original conquest had been surmounted, the frontiers more or less determined, the social system set, the towns raised to the highest level of importance and prosperity that they were to reach. And the 'country-houses' of a comfortable and internally peaceful age become as numerous and luxurious as they would ever be.

The population of Britain was mixed, but by the end of this period, fairly well blended. Anthropologists claim to recognise a Romano-British type. Rome, even Italy, would not supply an important element. The legionaries came from all over the Empire and so did some traders. The strangest gods were worshipped on the Wall. From the second century Emperors themselves were rarely Italians. No doubt the main inward movement would be from the province of *Gallia Belgica*, which had supplied immigrants and conquerors for Britain before it was a province. The survival of Welsh and Cornish in regions conquered but not fully romanised suggests that the country-folk may have long retained their Celtic dialects. We know that in other provinces of the Empire—Syria, Spain—the decline of the local language was very slow. But the urban language was Latin; the language of literature, the law courts, the army, and, when it came, the Church, was Latin. Inscriptions are all in Latin—and so are the few things we have found that workmen scribbled on bricks and tiles—*satis*, 'fed up'; *puellam*, 'my girl'. Latin was also the language of the mint and the 'country-houses'. Latin words were apparently used to describe things with which the natives were not very familiar: in Welsh a bridge is *pont* and a window is *fenster*. So it is possible that, by the end of the period, Celtic speech had been driven back into stretches of forest, lost valleys and fens, and the regions where it survived when Rome had fallen.

In attempting to estimate the total population at its maximum, including the troops and their camp-followers, we have guidance from the known sizes of the legions and the towns, of a great number of country-houses, and of many hundreds of 'village sites'—places where people lived in small groups. Estimates or guesses, based on this knowledge, have led to the suggestion that the 'more or less romanized inhabitants of Britain'[1] may have been so many as half a million. At the number of the rest it is better not even to guess.

[1] R. G. Collingwood and J. N. L. Myres, *Roman Britain and the English Settlements* (1936), p. 180.

Naturally more is known of the country-houses, great and small, from huge palace-like villas to small but substantial buildings in the Roman style, than of the 'villages' of what were no better than huts. About the 'villas' and their durable contents modern Englishmen have always been curious: the search for humbler remains is a recent thing and can never have more than partial success—yet upwards of seven hundred inhabited sites are already known.

The geographical distribution of the country-houses shows that the 'Romans', that is the romanised ruling class of whatever blood, had definite tastes in sites, tastes sometimes determined by considerations of safety and what may be described as congenial society, more often by considerations of soil. The forests had not yet been mastered, and forest sites, generally speaking, did not attract the 'villa' resident or give him scope for the agriculture needed for his maintenance and that of his staff.

Political conditions, combined with the roughness of the country, explain the complete absence of these 'Roman' houses between the east border of modern Devon and Land's End—except for a single rather mysterious discovery at St Ives. There are barely half a dozen known in all Wales—chieftains' houses, maybe. There is none at all known north of Swaledale or north-west of the upper part of Wharfedale. Beyond that we enter the region of forts, very permanent or temporary, which stretches to the Wall and far up the east coast of Scotland into Aberdeenshire. It is a land of military rule or campaigns; and so are the southern Pennines. Though the 'waters' of Buxton had given it its Latin name, the Peak was not a 'residential' district.

But *Aquae Sulis* (Bath) was. A fantastic picture of Roman Britain might show the houses of the well-to-do radiating from that health resort. But their location is explained by Bath's situation as a road centre—the villa is seldom far from a road—on the great 'Jurassic' belt of rock and soil that curves through England from the Dorset coast to the Humber and beyond, and contains all England's best stone—Portland, Bath, Cotswold, Northamptonshire. Bath is also near to the butt of the chalk that from Salisbury Plain stretches a short finger south-west into Dorset, and then long fingers, one to Beachy Head, one to Dover, and one—the longest—right through England once more, to the Wash, the Lincoln Wolds, the Wolds of the East

Riding and Flamborough Head. Remove all the Roman villas
from the map along these five belts of country—and from Wight
which also has chalk—and not very many would remain. The
chalk Wolds of the East Riding are the most northerly district
in which a fair number of country-houses have been found.
Like their prehistoric forerunners, 'Romans' liked the south,
what sun was to be had, and dry open sites. Those were still the
sites favoured for agriculture.

Oddly enough, the butt of the chalk, Salisbury Plain where
the prehistoric monuments crowd so thick, has hardly any
country-houses—but it has a crowd of village sites. There, and
in other places, the village of huts does not shelter under
'the hall', as the modern mind might perhaps expect. There
are village districts, on and sometimes off the five villa belts,
and there are villa districts—much as in South Africa you may
find a district of white men's farmhouses and one of black men's
kraals.

The villa, large or small, was not a mere residence: it was
a unit of agriculture, sometimes of industrial activity. In its
outbuildings there was room for the working staff of the estate:
there is nothing to suggest that these came in, as black men
do in Africa, from the kraals. No doubt they were mainly or
exclusively slaves, native or imported. Celtic society was
perfectly familiar with servitude of various sorts; though as the
Celt had not the Roman capacity for businesslike organisation
we hear more of servile villagers in Celtic society than of
organised working staffs of slaves. It is for the servile villager
and the peasant farmer (*colonus*) that one naturally looks in
Roman Britain. No doubt the servile villager existed, and in
large numbers. We meet him much later in the early Welsh
Laws: he does not so much work for his lord as feed him.[1] But
our present state of knowledge suggests that the villa system of
Britain did not depend on him but on real slaves, however
things may have been in wilder parts. Perhaps, before the
villa system vanished, something like him came into existence.
All over Europe one of the transition types from ancient slave
to medieval serf was the 'hutted' slave (*servus casatus*) who was
given a bit of land and told to keep himself—and work for his
owner in return. We meet this sort of *servus* with land in
Domesday Book, when that transition was going forward in
England.[2]

[1] See below, p. 56.   [2] See below, p. 50.

As for the peasant farmer, the *colonus*, a single reference to *coloni* in Britain is all that we know at first hand of him. Perhaps the term was applied to the free cultivating tribesmen; or perhaps in some districts the more commercial landlord-and-tenant system which the tenure implies had come into being. Of *coloni* on the land of the villas we have no evidence; but that does not prove that they did not exist.

Round the villages, wherever they have been carefully examined, we find the old pre-Roman agricultural life going on—the little irregular, squarish fields, divided by their banks, which could be tilled with a hoe or a light two-ox plough. What the tenure was we can only guess, but nothing suggests that it was communal; for the agriculture of these little enclosed fields pretty obviously was not. The guess that suggests itself is a system of food-rent, or produce-rent of some kind, payable to a chieftain or sub-chieftain of one of the tribes who, like the Cornovii of Wroxeter, retained their regional existence under Roman rule. We may imagine, if we will, a romanised chieftain of Salisbury Plain with a villa near Bath and a market there for his rents in kind.

In no case have the little enclosed fields been found about a villa. It had something bigger, better adapted for the cultivation that had to maintain a great household. Just what its fields were like and how they were cultivated we do not know. Our only representation of a Romano-British plough is a queer little statuette of a very primitive light *aratrum*. We have those few big coulters which suggest the use of heavy ploughs;[1] and we know that the Romano-British smiths could easily turn out any sort of metal-work. We have shears, turf-cutters, excellent scythes, spuds, hoes, all kinds of knives, and a few iron tyres which might be for the wheels of a plough but were just as likely for those of a cart. It is hard to believe that these competent smiths did not regularly fit up good ploughs: the coulters point to this; but that is all.

The crops were those we know. The villa arable fields, we should assume, were cultivated on a two-course rotation: corn, fallow; corn, fallow. We should assume it, first, because that was the classical Roman rotation, and, secondly, because it was a rotation very widespread in England at a much later date, and remarkably persistent on such light, often stony, upland soils as those on or near which so many of the villas stood.

[1] See above, p. 19.

Villagers were in a position to get the good tools and good utensils, if they could afford them. Nothing is more remarkable in the life of the Roman Empire than the widespread production and distribution of such things and of all manufactured— hand-made—goods. Industry was carried to as high a level as it can possibly be without the use of power and machine tools. In the first century there was a mass export of artistic metal wares and all kinds of luxuries—fine linens, perfumes, jewels— from Italy itself, Etruria and Campania. From Italy organised manufacture spread to the provinces. A whole group of pottery firms at Lezoux in Auvergne, south of Vichy, sent the so-called Samian ware all over the Empire. The ware of one Italian firm of 'Samian' potters has been found 'from Carthage to Carlisle'. This particular type of pottery was not much made in Britain, so far as we know;[1] but many other types were. The Celts were excellent potters and had used the wheel for two centuries or more before the Romans came. Celtic imagination sometimes affects the classical restraint of decorative designs. Glass was much used; but it is not quite certain that glass-ware was made here—window glass was; it is certain that much was imported from Gaul. Of metal every sort was worked, and every kind of useful, ornamental or superfluous article made, for the common people or the well-to-do, from whole ranges of carpenters' tools and chains and locks to bracelets, amulets and hair-tweezers. Among articles not of metal are engraved gems and fine stone stamps with which doctors or quacks marked their medicines—including that for the 'invincible' eye-ointment of Titus Vindex Ariovistus, surely a trade name to make it sell.

Luxury articles are naturally most often found in villas and towns. Useful goods were traded far into the hinterland of the settled and peaceful provinces of the South-East and South. At Traprain Law, near the coast of East Lothian, was a settlement whose way of life was mainly native Celtic. For a time it was nominally within the Empire, though far from any road or fort; but it remained subject to 'Roman' influence long after the legions had fallen back to the Wall (towards the end of the second century A.D.). 'Roman' pottery continued to drive out the native ware. Even glass was in use. Some people there knew enough of the Roman alphabet to scrawl its letters on

[1] Kilns for decorated Samian ware have been found at Colchester. *Antiquaries Journal*, vol. XIV (1934), p. 236.

potsherds; and from the finds it is confidently inferred that Roman coins were 'in circulation as ordinary currency from the first century onwards'.[1]

Economic historians used to write about the transition from a so-called 'natural economy', in which money is not known .or not used for buying and selling, to a 'money economy' in which it is. Clearly there must have been such a transition at some time in every civilisation. But primitive societies have often been quick to hit on media of exchange and measures of value—cowries, wampum, gold rings, iron bars. All northern Europe knew the coinage of Macedon in the two or three centuries B.C. and the British Belgae had imitated it.[2] Then came the widely circulated and exceedingly abundant coinage of Rome. Here, at Traprain Law, we find unconquered Celts learning and retaining its use. Whether the fall of Rome made people in Britain forget or abandon the use of money has still to be discussed.[3]

It is a chief puzzle in ancient economic history that the Romans, superb craftsmen and civil engineers, never took to the use of natural power. Throughout their empire there was no lack of water, but as nearly as possible no use was made of it as power. In Britain they had the sense to use the coal they found to warm their houses with hot air in a highly scientific fashion; but they never raised steam. Querns, the mills at which two women might be grinding, are found everywhere, including many made of a volcanic rock brought from Andernach on the Rhine. But there is nothing to suggest a water-mill, though the water-mill was at least known to the ancient world. It was when these expert Romans had gone that the lumbering Anglo-Saxons, with other northern tribes, took to water-mills.[4] An historian of Britain need not attempt an explanation of this blind spot in the Roman technical eye.

That the accomplished metal-worker of Roman Britain was well served by mining prospectors and mine managers is evident. For thousands of years the metallic wealth of the British Isles had been known. They were far better endowed than Italy or southern Gaul. That, according to Tacitus, on this point a good witness, was one reason why they were

---

[1] Sir George Macdonald, *Roman Britain, 1914–1928* (1931), p. 34 (British Academy Supplemental Papers, no. VI).

[2] See above, pp. 17–18.   [3] See below, pp. 41–2.

[4] See below, pp. 67–8. The Romans made rather more use of water-power than is here suggested. Roman water-mills are known on Hadrian's Wall and elsewhere in England. [J.S.]

conquered. All these metals had been worked less or more from prehistoric times, including lead. The 'Big Stone' men had known lead in Spain; so perhaps they first hit on it in Britain, as well as on the copper and gold of Ireland. Romans were great plumbers—we have their lead water-pipes—and there is silver mixed with the English lead. The speed with which the mines were developed suggests good information and anxiety to make the conquest pay. In Roman practice, mines such as these belonged to the state, and might be worked direct or leased out as concessions. We have a Roman dated lead ingot from the Mendips of A.D. 49, six years after the invasion, and another from Flintshire of A.D. 74. That is quick work, and there is no need to suppose that the first ingots cast have survived. For the mining no doubt slave labour was used and used up. The most refined peoples of the ancient world always worked slaves out in the mines; the Athenians did in their silver mines at Laurium.

Romans sampled all the other chief lead-bearing regions of England, especially where the lead is argentiferous, as in the Mendips—in Shropshire, in Derbyshire, on Greenhow Hill above Pately Bridge, in the high valleys of Durham. For copper they went to the once rich deposits of Anglesey—finally worked out by the Amlwch Copper Company in the late eighteenth and nineteenth centuries—and to one or two other points in North Wales. Iron was worked a little everywhere, but especially in the Weald of Sussex and in the Forest of Dean, at the north end of which stood what has been called a little town of smiths, *Ariconium* (Weston-under-Penyard). There was nothing of that kind in the Sussex Weald: not a villa, and hardly a village, has been found anywhere near the iron workings. It looks as if they may have been of a type well known in later centuries—little furnaces and forges moved from site to site.

Cornish tin the Romans at first neglected. The trade had fallen into decay and other sources of supply had been developed in Spain. Indeed there is very little evidence of early Roman interest in Cornwall, besides a few coins which point to intercourse by sea. But from about A.D. 250 the interest was evidently greater, though never great. There are four rather crude and mysterious Cornish milestones, connected with no known road. There is the solitary known tessellated pavement in the county, in a district rich in tin streams. And there are other rather scanty remains that point to a revived intercourse with the rest of Britain and a better market for Cornish tin. But there is no evidence of organised workings. Probably the tin was washed by natives and traded east in small quantities.

Mining when organised under the state was, it has been assumed, usually based on slavery. If iron was in fact melted and forged by migratory groups, these groups must, however, have been made up of free men. What the division between slave and free labour was in the other industries we do not know. In big Roman industrial concerns in the home provinces gangs of skilled or unskilled slaves had often been employed; but with the decline in the slave supply during the second to the fourth century this became less easy. Nor have we reason to think that big manufacturing concerns, such as those of Etruria and Campania, were ever reproduced in Britain. We do not hear of slave craftsmen among the Celts, whose pottery and ironwork and other crafts were the basis of those of Roman Britain. The suggestion then is that the craftsman was normally a free man, native or immigrant. A solitary scribble by such a man on a London tile suggests this. Note that this early Cockney was literate. What he scribbled was 'Au[gu]stalis goes off on his own every day for a fortnight'.

Of trade organisation among craftsmen we must not think. The only type of organisation which the imperial authorities allowed and approved approaching that was the *collegium*. This was a club or gild of people who had some interest in common —religious, like a medieval Corpus Christi gild; social or convivial, like that of the 'late drinkers'; economic, like the solitary British *collegium* of this class of which we have definite evidence, the smiths' 'college' at Chichester.

No doubt other 'trade colleges' existed from which inscriptions have not survived; but there cannot have been very many, because the number of towns that may have contained economic groups big enough for collegiate life was limited. A *collegium* was primarily a friendly society, social always even when it had a trade basis. It would have a patron god or saint, and it saw to it that members were buried with the proper rites: the burial club, which to-day is the state, has an ancient pedigree. Social as a *collegium* was, is it reasonable to suppose that the smiths when drinking together never discussed the prices to be charged for ironware?

COMMUNICATIONS, TOWNS AND TRADE

All this industrial life, like the commercial life and the whole government of Britain, depended on those roads which were better aligned and better made than any that would traverse the island for another fourteen hundred years. Indeed, the road history of those centuries is mainly a record of how what the Romans left deteriorated into the rutted and pot-holed tracks that Arthur Young[1] cursed. Excellent as the roads were, few came up to the full standard of solidity and permanence at which the Roman road-engineer aimed, and which on the continent he often reached. But they were twenty to twenty-four feet wide and would carry the four-wheeled Gaulish type of waggon which no doubt was used in Britain. The campaigning roads were naturally light. There were some in Wales, and two or three pushed into the rough country beyond the Wall and came to what look like rather purposeless ends among the hills. Others were more solidly constructed. It was perhaps only when Englishmen returned to road travel in the present century that they learnt to appreciate properly the excellence of the alignment, as they drove through the heart of the country along Watling Street; or along the straight of the North Road up to Catterick Bridge; or turned left with the Romans at 'Scotch Corner' along no 'rolling English road' but one of Roman directness over Stainmore to *Luguvallium* (Carlisle); or perhaps passed the Corner and crossed the Tees at Piercebridge on to another noble straight which forty years ago was neglected, the merits of whose alignment the twentieth-century road engineer has recognised.

One, but only one, of the main points from which Roman traffic radiated has lost all economic importance. From *Calleva Atrebatum* (Silchester, six miles north of Basingstoke) five main roads set out. No traffic centre had more—not *Venta Belgarum* (Winchester); not *Corinium Dobunorum* (Cirencester); not *Ratae Coritanorum* (Leicester); not *Londinium* itself, from which the roads branched much as the railways do to-day. But *Calleva* died; its roads went out of use; the lanes in time twined about it; and the whole parish of Silchester into which it fell had thirty-nine households when Domesday Book was compiled— or thirty-two if the seven slaves 'lived in'—and 311 inhabitants in 1801. Fortunately for the historian, the village grew up just

[1] Farmer and author, 1741–1820. [J.S.]

outside the old town boundary, so that the spade has revealed the complete ground-plan of a Romano-British provincial town, besides turning up quantities of things made or used there.

Calleva Atrebatum and *Viroconium Cornoviorum* (Wroxeter) may serve to introduce the most numerous, though not the most important, group of the Roman-British towns, a group of about a dozen places. Without a town, in ancient thought as in etymology, there was no civilisation. The great emperors of the second century—Trajan, Hadrian, Antoninus Pius—were encouraging the creation of towns in outlying and un-civilised provinces, as a matter of considered policy. In the Mediterranean region towns existed already; but in central and northern Gaul or in Britain they had to be made. The sites usually settled themselves. Tribes had those fortified 'cities' of refuge to which they could retreat in bad times, perhaps with their cattle, and in which some permanent population tended to accumulate. At *Calleva*, and other places, the area so enclosed was appreciably greater than that adopted by the town-planners of the second century. This suggests cattle; for the Roman boundaries proved more than ample. It is the tribal name attaching to cities of this class which recalls the Atrebates at Silchester, the Parisii at Paris, the Treveri at Trêves. Where the town became a permanency, its ultimate name may come from the tribe as at Paris or from the original first-name, presumably of Celtic origin, like the *Corinium* which appears in Cirencester. The town was to have the conveniences and attractions of a small provincial capital, *forum* and temples, baths and perhaps even a theatre; and the tribal district around it, we assume from the analogy of Gaul, became an *attributa regio*, not exactly its property, but, as you might say, its county, the region throughout which officials from the 'county town' superintended justice and taxation. This, for Britain, is hypothesis, but it is reasonable hypothesis.

For the town itself, in the case of *Calleva* and some others, there is no need for hypothesis: we know that whether the town enclosure was rectangular or not—in this towns varied—the site was cut up, so far as the lie of the ground permitted, by parallel and cross roads into square 'city-blocks', 'islands' (*insulae*). In a densely populated Italian town these might be entirely built over with tenement houses or public buildings. But in *Calleva*, and similar 'country towns', this was not so. The central block, with the *forum*, was fully utilised. Near to it were other blocks fairly well covered with buildings, but quite irregularly—buildings of all sizes and uses. There was much unbuilt space—gardens, one supposes. Some of the blocks nearest the *Calleva* town-wall were almost empty, and in the corners of the enclosed area, which was an irregular octagon, were considerable spaces without roads in which houses were scattered anyhow. There were some fine public buildings, religious and administrative, appropriate to a 'county capital'. There were some shops, some few evidences of industry; but the whole impression is that of an administrative and 'residential' centre. From the size and number of the houses, a population of from 1000 to a maximum of 2000 has been inferred. The modern parallel is that smallest of county towns, Appleby.

Yet *Calleva* had urban amenities if few urban industries. As it was well-placed, early laid out, and had a long life, it is fair to assume that it had reached something like the highest level of development for which such a tribal centre might hope.

These tribal towns were all of the second rank. A first-grade Roman provincial town might be a colony (*colonia*), of retired soldiers settled on the land, Roman citizens; or a municipality (*municipium*), a local centre promoted to this rank and given a regular municipal constitution. Britain, so far as we know, never contained more than one *municipium*, Verulam, and four *coloniae*, Colchester, Lincoln, Gloucester and York.[1] Their foundation-dates as colonies all fall—it is believed—between A.D. 50 and 160. Generally, perhaps always, but this is not sure, they were at or near an old tribal centre—as Colchester and Verulam were. A colony usually began as a military camp with a native 'bazaar' outside it. By imperial edict it received later its status, its privileges, its boundaries. These included the lands assigned to its ex-soldier citizens and a 'region' 'attributed' to it—whose inhabitants had certain rights in it and duties towards it, but were not citizens. The same was true of a *municipium*.

Our knowledge of these constitutional facts all comes from outside. Of Britain we are so ignorant that we should not even know that Lincoln had been a *colonia* but for the finding of a Lincoln citizen's tombstone at Bordeaux. There has been much discussion about whether the lands outside the walls were laid out in true Roman squares. Outside 'colonies' in

[1] London was not a true *colonia*, but was given honorary colonial status at a late period of the Roman occupation. [J.S.]

Italy they certainly were: the lines are on the Italian maps to this day. Some evidence faintly suggests the same here. But only two points in the matter interest the economist: first, that the 'colonial' square of land, if it ever existed here, was ample for a long furrow, if anyone wanted to plough that way; second, that if the squares did exist they were most completely washed out after Roman times. Of Roman-British 'colonial' or 'municipal' agriculture we know only one fact beyond our scanty list of facts known about Roman-British agriculture generally, namely, that the 'colonist' was given land to live by: he was meant to be a farmer-citizen of the traditional Roman sort.

As Lincoln, Gloucester and York have remained city sites like London, we can only learn about them piecemeal, here a little and there a little, sometimes aided by recent 'enemy action' which opened up foundations. But St Albans did not grow up on top of Verulam. The first 'Roman' Verulam, as modern excavation has shown, was a wooden town with a typically native life and industries. Boadicea burnt it. It was laid out afresh, rectangular in plan, eventually covering 200 acres—to Silchester's 100 acres—with the proper straight streets. Gradually, governors and emperors encouraging, stone and brick replaced wood, as in every rising town; you got a *forum* with shops and a *basilica*, 'a municipal centre'; public baths, a water supply for the baths and perhaps for fountains, to supplement the private wells; temples; and a theatre, but this last not before A.D. 125. If a town had no theatre, it might have an amphitheatre outside the walls, seats banked up from which thousands could watch the 'games'. The troops were naturally keen on this: there was a big amphitheatre at *Isca* (Caerleon-on-Usk), where the Second legion was so long quartered.

As at Silchester, not by any means all the enclosed area at Verulam was built over. Again, as at Silchester, the larger houses are 'residential'. The smaller are only in part those of an industrial population. These leading British towns were not specialised industrial centres, as Lezoux[1] was, though some smaller ones, like *Ariconium*,[2] may have been. They had the essential urban craftsmen, masons, bronze-workers, blacksmiths, carpenters, and the rest. But trading centres all the towns certainly were—places in which the men of the *attributa regio* might sell produce; places from which a few things made on

[1] See above, p. 26.   [2] See above, p. 28.

the spot and other things made in the various industrial centres of the Empire might be procured for the villa or even the village; places through which the imperial coinage, sometimes struck in Britain but normally at one of the various continental mints, passed into circulation, reaching the Wall and beyond it to Traprain Law and other remote places, just as sovereigns paid out at Johannesburg pass to very remote African tribes.

London stands apart. It was certainly bigger than any other town, and it is supposed that in the end it became the head-quarters of the government, which were originally at Colchester. It had its bridge about where London Bridge now stands, and its massive walls which have been assigned to all sorts of dates and are just at present credited to the period A.D. 100–150. They enclosed more than 300 acres. To speculate about its population is unwise: we do not know the plan of the streets nor how much, if any, of the 300 acres lay open. But specula-tions have been risked freely, of which the last is 'possibly not more than 15,000'.[1] That it was the hub of the road system we know. That it was the prime distributing centre for imports and for government we believe. The strength of its walls testifies to the importance attached to its safety; and the finds made from time to time beneath the modern city confirm the impression of considerable wealth. That it had a mint late in the third century proves little. The Empire had been in chaos; conti-nental mintage had declined; Britain and other provinces had relied on inferior local imitations; and the man who started the mint was the local pretender to the empire, Carausius. It was not even his only mint, but it at least suggests London's importance, if it does not prove any great wealth.

That importance was evidently based on the city's function as a distributing centre, a function to which the roads testify. From the ports of the Kentish coast—Reculver, Richborough, Dover and Lympne—they all met in the first of the tribal capitals, *Durovernum* 'of the men of Kent' (*Cantiacorum*), Canter-bury; thence ran the great single route through Rochester to London Bridge. Between Lympne and the Great Harbour (Portsmouth) other branching main roads fanned out from London towards the sea; others again left London for the West, the Midlands, East Anglia, and the North. What London distributed were troops, military supplies, officials

[1] R. G. Collingwood and J. N. L. Myres, *Roman Britain and the English Settlements* (1936), p. 198.

before these were recruited locally, and no doubt considerable quantities of civilian goods—wine and oil, luxuries and utensils. How much traffic came up-river we do not know; but it seems possible that landing was often made at Rochester, through which the great road passed. The higher reaches with their shallows and sandbanks were not easy to navigate. We know that the Kentish ports were busy. There was an important 'villa population' to be served along the North Downs. The imported goods were mostly of the bulk and value that will stand transport; you had to unship and take to land carriage at some point, and the road and the bridge were there. The very existence of the bridge is significant in this connection: traffic called for it and it made more traffic.

Much that was imported we know because we find it—the *amphorae* for the wine and the oil, the metal-ware and pottery and durable luxuries of all sorts, often stamped with their makers' names or easily identifiable as imports by their style. As might be expected, certain classes of imports slacken off when Britain learns to serve herself in the Roman fashion. Most ordinary tools and utensils, and a great many of the cheaper ornaments, of the second century and later, were British-made. The tools were wonderfully good. A bricklayer, mason or carpenter had much the same equipment as he had in the nineteenth century—foot-rule, plane, leaf-shaped trowel, chisels, and plumb-bob.

No doubt there were luxuries imported that have left no trace—silks and dried or preserved foods of various kinds; perhaps some furniture of perishable wood. No contemporary had occasion to 'list' such things.

Exports were occasionally listed, in a vague rhetorical way; but we are fortunate to have lists at all, as so many of the exports were perishable. We have all heard of the oysters and the pearls—bad pearls, it must be added, and now extinct. There were the cattle and hides, the slaves, the sporting dogs and the iron that Strabo mentions in the first century. He also mentions corn; and there is a good deal of evidence, from the first century to the fourth, which suggests a fairly regular export trade, at least during parts of this long period. But we are inevitably ignorant of the size of the trade.

THE LAST DAYS OF ROMAN BRITAIN

This has been a scanty account of the external trade of four centuries, but no more can be given. Besides, it is to be remembered, first, that long-distance trade was, at its maximum, a very subordinate element in the life of Roman Britain, and second, that from the troubled times of the third century trade most certainly declined. The Empire could no longer be governed effectively from Rome. It had to be subdivided, and claimants to the subdivisions fought one another. From about A.D. 275 the Channel and the southern waters of the North Sea, where order had once been kept by the *Classis Britannica*, based on Boulogne and Dover, began to suffer from Frankish and Saxon piracy. We come to the fortification of the 'Saxon Shore', from Brancaster, just outside the Wash, to Porchester, on the Great Harbour. The two names with their *castrum* termination suggest the process.

The story of Richborough (*Rutupiae*), possibly the most important of the fortified sites, has its economic implications. Now two miles and a half from the sea, throughout Roman times *Rutupiae* was the leading cross-channel port. At the Claudian invasion it was roughly fortified as a base camp. Before the end of the first century it had become a busy little port town, with a huge concrete platform in its centre on which stood— what? Not a lighthouse, it is believed, but something monumental; gilded bronze fragments and bits of Italian marble have been found near it; parts of a conquest group perhaps. For a century and a half *Rutupiae* remained a 'peaceful commercial port'.[1] Then, about A.D. 250, fortification began—after a piratical raid, it is guessed. Finally, between A.D. 275 and 300 the massive wall now uncovered was built, a defence 'of extraordinary solidity'.[2]

Administration had weakened: trade had slackened and been interrupted. Trade and administration made the life of British towns. Besides there had been fighting. There had been debasement of the currency and that pitiless fiscal pressure on well-to-do townspeople which crushed them all over the Empire. Imperial revival under Diocletian and Constantine did much to restore order but not prosperity; and there was no easing of fiscal burdens.

---

[1] Sir George Macdonald, *Roman Britain, 1914–1928* (1931), p. 58.
[2] *Ibid.* p. 60.

With the well-to-do less prosperous, perhaps ruined, the urban crafts which existed mainly to meet their needs could not but decay. The villages met most of their own needs. If Samian pottery was no longer easily distributed, there were local-style pots to be had everywhere. The part-romanised or hardly touched Celtic populations had not forgotten how to work metals well enough for ordinary needs. They may have been helped by refugee recruits from towns, when consumer demands were slackening, but not those of the tax collector. The village women could always spin and weave.

There was no serious internal trouble from the end of the third century until late in the fourth, though there was piracy, and raiding on both coasts. Any local revival of town-life that the improvements in administration from Diocletian onwards may have brought about was short-lived. It used to be supposed that Romano-British towns perished by violence in the fifth century. Perhaps a few did. But all the archaeological evidence now available points to slow and drawn-out decay through about a century and a half, between A.D. 275 and 425. 'By the middle of the fourth century...the greater part of Verulam was uninhabited, a waste of empty land and ruined houses. Here and there squatters lived among the ruins. The theatre had become a rubbish-tip, and its orchestra and auditorium were silted up beneath foot upon foot of domestic refuse.'[1] Silchester, Wroxeter and Caerwent (*Venta Silurum*) in Monmouth tell much the same story. Sometimes, as at Caerwent, it is the blocking-up of a gate or some new bit of fortification that suggests growing dangers and falling traffic. Sometimes there is no suggestion of fear, but unfinished or ruined buildings register continuous economic decay. *Calleva*, it would seem, decayed and died quietly; became, like many other places in Britain, what Angles or Saxons called a 'ruined chester', but gave half a name to the little village of Silchester which came into existence just outside its no doubt ghost-and-devil-haunted ruins.

But while the towns had decayed, the villas—many of them at least—had not. They show evident signs of economic activity in exactly those closing centuries of Roman rule during which all the towns whose history we have been able to trace were going downhill. It has been suggested that people

[1] R. G. Collingwood and J. N. L. Myres, *Roman Britain and the English Settlements* (1936), p. 206.

withdrew to their villas. That is possible. Perhaps imperfectly romanised and urbanised Celtic tribal magnates did go back to the land. What is certain is that the villa estate, like the humble village, was self-sufficient in essentials; and with a little trouble might be made more completely so. If it was not fought over—and as has been seen there was reasonable security during that century and a half of town decay—its equipment could be kept up, even improved. The more self-contained it was, the less it was affected by currency debasement. With towns decayed, the villa was in much the same self-sufficing position as early medieval estates before the towns had revived. There is no reason to suppose, as has sometimes been suggested, that Saxon invaders took over such villa estates as going concerns—though some Frankish and other continental conquerors almost certainly did. It is a case of like conditions producing similar results; but before this occurred for the second time in England, many social refinements, technical accomplishments, and capacities for economic organisation had been lost. The master of a villa admired mosaics and knew where to find men who could lay or repair them. He understood central heating. He could read and write and keep accounts. No chieftain, thane, or king between Hengist and, shall we say, Henry III was so fortunate; and Henry III did not understand central heating.

Long before urban decay and the accompanying need for villa self-sufficiency had done their work, Roman Britain had become a nominally Christian country which—as the story of St Patrick, kidnapped from a villa by raiders, shows—could nourish great Christian characters. The Church had spread in the British Islands beyond Rome's jurisdiction. Churches had been built, to be destroyed in the Diocletian persecution. Traces of some later ones have been found. In the fourth century, British bishops attended Councils on the continent; Pelagius from Britain became scholar enough to be accused of heresy in the fifth. The argument that economic conditions had much to do with the spread of Christianity in the Empire deserves every consideration; but the story of Roman-British Christianity is not full enough to be of much use to those who consider it. Nor can we trace economic influences radiating from the Church in these last obscure centuries of Roman rule.

Chapter III

Saxons and Normans

THE EVIDENCE AND ITS INTERPRETATION

Conquests are not always of great significance in economic history. It is very easy to overrate the strictly economic importance of that of A.D. 1066. Even the long-drawn-out and piecemeal conquest of A.D. 450–600, or thereabouts, shifted nothing like all the economic landmarks of Britain—hardly any of them in Wales or the Highlands of Scotland. But in England and East Lowland Scotland it was not merely a conquest, but a colonisation that changed language and place-names, law and some agrarian customs; so the economist must be on the look out for new things at every turn, though sometimes he may find the old ones.

His materials, at first scanty, gradually increase until, for the close of what we still call Anglo-Saxon times—in spite of the 'Old English' of our philologists and the 'Anglo-Celtic' of reforming historians—they are, in many ways, far the best available for any country of the eleventh century. There is nothing like Domesday Book, the record from which, for the East Anglian counties, we can report on the farm stock for A.D. 1086–7 with more accuracy and detail than the published statistics allow us to do for to-day. From A.D. 600 we have an unequalled series of early laws and charters. We have a Chronicle, for later centuries contemporary. We have the Venerable Bede, not an economist but the greatest European historian of the so-called Dark Ages. We have in Alfred that rare thing, a king who wrote books; and we have the most abundant national literature of any which, for that period, have survived.

But all this needs interpretation, and in that the economist would not get very far without help from the archaeologist, from the scholar who works back from the known to the unknown, and from the man who studies economic institutions comparatively. Among these helpers, the archaeologist is hampered by the Saxon habit of building most things of wood—houses, 'palaces', churches, town walls. To fortify was to 'timber'; and we even hear of the worm-eaten walls of a cathedral. Not only did the Saxon build in wood, but he built almost exactly where his descendants have been building ever since. Roman and British sites, especially those of villas or groups of huts, were generally deserted; Anglo-Saxon sites have, as nearly as possible, never been deserted. Where 'Trump' and his men settled down in A.D.—what shall we say?—there Trumpington stands to-day, with its stone church presumably where the wooden church was, if it had one. Not only did Anglo-Saxon huts and houses rise, decay or burn where we now live, but with them perished their 'furniture' and their wooden platters and spoons. The Saxons' metal-work, their money, and what pottery they used we know; and sometimes archaeologists have luck with bone, leather and wood-work. But Britain is short of the preservative soils which, on the continent, have kept a few ships and even one or two men from those centuries for us to see.

ANGLO-SAXON ENGLAND: SETTLEMENT AND AGRICULTURE

With the help of archaeology and the study of place-names, the story of the actual conquest has been to a considerable extent rewritten in recent years. We no longer suppose that Port landed at Portsmouth; we wonder whether a couple of fighting leaders really were called the Stallion and the Mare; and we realise the immense importance of the Humber estuary, with its river system, and of the drainage area of the Wash, in giving access to the heart of the country for the light boats of invading and colonising parties. We have always known how slow the conquest was, and how constantly the various conquering and colonising groups clashed with the natives and with one another. Much more than this the strictly economic historian does not need to know.

But he does well to remember that the conquering war-bands and the colonising groups and clans who accompanied or followed them came from peoples not all at the same stage of economic development, peoples who had been, some, for a time at any rate, in fairly close contact with the northern provinces of the Roman Empire, and some who knew no more about it than they, or their fathers, may have learnt on a piratical raid. That they all spoke Teutonic dialects our language proves. Some of them may have come direct from marshy islets on what are now the North German and Frisian shores, where they had lived on scraps of ground raised laboriously above tide-level—had their predecessors learnt to do this while the shore of the North Sea was sinking? Others had passed through, and probably for a time occupied, parts of the Roman provinces of *Germania Inferior*, bounded on the north-east by the lower Rhine, and *Belgica* farther to the south-west, with their towns and broad fields. So the 'Anglo-Saxons' must have entered Britain to conquer and colonise with varied economic backgrounds and impressions.

But certain things they had in common besides the elements of language. If they had seen Roman provincial towns, all their later history bears out the old opinion that they neither understood them nor liked them—except as places to loot. None of them had been in close enough contact with Rome to make them get their own customs set down in Latin, as some Teutonic tribes did while the conquest of Britain was in progress. When they began to set them down, about a hundred and fifty years after the traditional date of 'Hengist and Horsa', they did it in English. They were pugnacious and well-armed—their general name of Saxons probably means the men of the long knives—adequately provided with tools and implements, and with ships. Certainly they had mixed trading with their piracy, and had been familiar with the trade that had existed in northern Europe since distant prehistoric times. Money they knew, if only as part of the loot. Numismatists are disposed to think that during the dark century and a half of conquest (about A.D. 450–600) Roman copper circulated 'whether surviving in currency or dug up as treasure'.[1] And, at the end of that dark age, the laws of Kent are full of fines and estimates of social value in money. As such rules in primitive societies are of slow growth, it is likely that the Kentish men at any rate reckoned in money of some sort for certain purposes from the beginning. Maitland used to say that the oldest English Law runs—'If one man strike another with the fist on the nose, 3 shillings.' Not long after that law was written down, the Kentish kings began to strike money of their own—copying Merovingian, Byzantine or old Roman types already familiar.

[1] George C. Brooke, *English Coins from the Seventh Century to the Present Day* (1932), p. 2.

But knowledge of money does not mean its general use, and such a word as circulation may mislead. There was something arbitrary and sacred about these money valuations of crime: they are forerunners of '6*s*. 8*d*.' and 'not exceeding 40*s*.'. They may have been paid not in money but in money's worth, which again might be arbitrary: a Wessex law, of a hundred years later than these first laws of Kent, contains the clause 'an ewe with her lamb is worth a shilling until a fortnight after Easter'. Yet presumably you could haggle about it three weeks after; and the very next law deals with buying and selling of beasts, and what is to be done if a blemished animal is sold, without any reference to prices. As to payments in kind, there is a long list of food supplies in these Wessex laws—honey, loaves, ale, oxen, sheep, geese, hens, cheese, butter, salmon, fodder and eels—to be paid as a rent or tax from each area of a certain size. That Wessex king who issued them, Ine, had many Welsh subjects; and such food rents were more universal and lasted longer among the Celts than among the Saxons; but they survived in England down to 1066, and indeed much later.[1]

The conquerors formed a graded society: men of noble blood, from whom leaders and kings were chosen; common free men (*ceorls*, churls); slaves. In the Kentish law we meet another grade, *laets*, who appear to be freedmen, but they are not of economic importance. What is interesting in that law is the grading of the slaves: a man paid 6*s*. if he seduced a freeman's domestic slave girl, but below her were two grades of slaves whose chastity was less valuable. (Above her were the more expensive nobleman's and King's maids.) The distinction suggests that between the domestic negroes and the field-hands in the old American South. And note that it was so natural even for ordinary freemen to have slave girls that a law about their seduction was worth while.

The kings and noblemen may have had considerable servile households: we know that the Kentish kings had slave women grinding at the mill. But in simple societies there is no place for the plantation, or the mining, or the manufacturing slave-gang. Tacitus had been told, about A.D. 100, that the German male slave generally had his own hut and bit of land—'just like a *colonus*'. That was the easiest way of keeping him. But a curious early Kentish law about a slave being fined or whipped if he 'eats on his own authority' (*ete his sylfes ræde*) suggests the

[1] See below, pp. 70, 98–9.

working gang, or, perhaps more likely, the big rationed household. It also suggests that even a slave was supposed to be able to pay a fine, though he probably got a whipping.

And who were the slaves? Various ways of sinking into slavery appear in the laws, but the main source of supply was no doubt capture in war with the natives or in tribal wars among the conquerors. There are no early accounts of enslaved Britons, but in the Northumbrian literature of the eighth century appear Welsh slave herdsmen and Welsh slave women working in tan-pits or carrying buckets, products of border wars with the Celtic kingdom of Strathclyde or Cumbria. There must have been many such people in the early days of the conquest: in slave-owning societies conquerors, however savage, keep at least some of the women.

Before raiding, and then conquest, from Denmark and Scandinavia set in (A.D. 787 and later), most of the sites of existing villages and hamlets, from the Firth of Forth to the Channel and westward to the frontiers with the Welsh, had been occupied and named by 'Anglo-Saxons'. This the study of place-names shows. Whether there had been named settlements on all the sites whose present names are Danish or Norse we do not know; but the change of name at Whitby (originally *Streonæshalch*) suggests that generally there had. In Yorkshire we can trace pure Anglian names, a few Celtic ones from the pocket of independent Welshmen that survived until about A.D. 625 round Leeds, Anglian names modified after conquest from the East, a mass of pure Danish names in the East Riding, and a thick sprinkling of Norse names in the Dales where incomers settled down who had pushed across the watershed from Cumbria after A.D. 800.

At various dates between the original settlement and the time of Edward the Confessor, groups of villagers must have hived off to make what in Domesday book is called 'another' So-and-So, now generally Little as opposed to Great So-and-So; or an extensive area dominated at first by a single settlement might come to contain several, often named in Christian times from their churches. And there are Newtons and Newhalls in Domesday, obviously not primitive sites. But in any part of the country surveyed by the Conqueror's commissioners there are singularly few names on the map to-day which are not in Domesday, and which were not centuries old when the Domesday inquiry was made.

The original settlements must have been small—sometimes only a group of huts and, if the very few which have been excavated on rare deserted sites are any guide, rather wretched huts. But most sites never were deserted, and these few wretched huts may not be in any way representative. Many sites no doubt contained substantial buildings of timber, yet not at any time, least of all in the earliest times, many people. Even in the eleventh century it was a very substantial village that had thirty households; though a few here and there were much bigger. A village with a church might well have only ten or even less; and villages or hamlets with from two to six households were exceedingly common, especially in wooded or rough country—the Essex forest-land, Devon, or the Yorkshire Dales, for example. The place-name termination '-ton' does not always mean 'village', but often just 'enclosure', 'settlement', or 'farm'. A king can have a '-ton'. So can a man of noble birth. So can a group of churls. So can anyone. In the earliest Kentish law the fine for being the first to break into a man's '-ton' (*mannes tun*) is six shillings, only twice the cost of hitting him on the nose. The low price implies quite ordinary and limited 'premises'. If you killed a man in the King's *tun*, it cost you fifty shillings, as much as for seducing one of the King's slave girls.

It used to be supposed that places with the usual terminations -ingham or -ington were settled by groups of blood-relations. Perhaps some of them were. But it is now held by philologists, besides being intrinsically probable, that the original Paddington or Wilmington or Pocklington was just the place of Padda, Wilma or Pocela—or whatever the names were—and his family, perhaps a slave or two, perhaps if he were an important man a few freemen whose leader he was. It is evident that usually the really important man had his own *tun* and that groups of freemen had theirs—the Charltons and Chorltons, churls' places. And it is fair to assume that many settlements, especially the small ones, which did not acquire the tell-tale name, were also churls' places. Maybe Padda, Wilma and Pocela were just freemen.

That the average man had a lord of some sort there is no doubt; but we do not know the ratio of men to lords. There is little doubt that freemen would give presents to their lord and do various jobs for him—harvesting, wood-cutting, driving the game perhaps—besides, of course, fighting under his leadership, either to snatch land from the natives, to defend it when once settled, or to snatch from another English tribe, Middle Angles from East Angles, Dorset-men from Somerset-men. By Ine's time (about A.D. 700) there was a law in Wessex that if any one moved away from his lord without leave and went into another 'shire', when found he had to come back and pay a fine. That rule may have been made to meet some special cases of migration: Ine, or his predecessors, had conquered a good deal of land from the Welsh in Somerset, and his great men may have wished to check a drift of Wessex frontiersmen to occupy it. We know from Domesday that even in the eleventh century there were still a few men so free that they could leave their personal lord, and could transfer their land, that is the lord's economic advantages from it, to someone else. The whole flavour of Anglo-Saxon society is one of lordship nevertheless; but the immediate pre-Conquest lords, judging by Domesday, were relatively few, and great.

That King Ine of Wessex was worried about migration is suggested by other laws of his which show him making grants of land not to ordinary freemen but to his noblemen, in order to get it developed. If a man has twenty hides—a considerable 'estate'—he must show twelve settled, and that implies worked and used, when he wants to move on (*he faran wille*). There were similar rules for men who had ten or three hides.

A rule follows which shows curiously 'modern' and well-considered relations between these rather restless noblemen and the free tenants whom they might settle on the land: 'if a man takes a yard of land [no doubt, as later, a quarter of a hide] at an agreed rent and ploughs it, if the lord requires work as well as rent he need not take it if the lord does not give him a house'; and so on. What 'work' the lord might have asked for we are not told, nor what sort of rent it was; but we see informal relations between lord and freeman being regularised, and that with considerable regard to the freeman's position: if I am to do any job for you, you have to find me a home. We see also a mobile, colonising, frontier sort of population, such as must certainly have existed in those earlier generations when the very irregular frontiers between the incoming English and whatever Roman-Britons they may have met lay much further east than Ine's frontiers did in A.D. 700. Yet another law of the same series illustrates the restlessness of these noble pioneers and throws some light on their households: 'if a nobleman moves on (*gif gesithcund mon fare*), he may take with him his reeve, his smith, and his children's nurse'. He must not take away the 'settled' men, evidently. The lawyer will ask, how would that rule be enforced? The economist surmises that these three people, so easily taken about, were servile or at least semi-servile; and he notes that a Wessex lord may be expected by this time to have a smith in his *tun*, or attached to it.

As for that word the hide, there is general agreement that its original meaning was the amount of land needed to support a family, almost certainly not a family in the modern sense but a big primitive family of two or three generations living together. It is first met in a queer document which seems to have been compiled for one of the kings of Mercia at some time in the seventh century or the eighth. The document gives the 'hides' for the various tribes and sections of his kingdom or overlordship, in round hundreds and thousands—the men of the Peak have twelve hundred, the men of Kent fifteen thousand. This is not a land survey: it is a rough and ready basis for levying tribute or raising troops—the Peak must provide so much or so many. Bede says more than once that such-and-such a district is, 'by the English way of reckoning', of so many families. He is using a recognised description. There would, of course, be some relation between the figure for hides and the size, fertility and populousness of the region: Kent was known to be wealthy. When tribute had to be paid or men raised, there would have to be some local interpretation of a hide. Probably there were pretty clear primitive local notions of the number of 'families', and of how much land would carry a family.

That amount would vary with the quality of the soil and the method of using it. As time went on, the hide began to be thought of as 120 acres, with its quarter the yardland or virgate; but there is evidence for much smaller hides, as one might expect. And what is an acre, and how many of the acres were ploughed? There were six different customary acres in eighteenth-century Lancashire, and the Cheshire acre was twice the statute acre. The question of how many were ploughed leads straight to that of early Anglo-Saxon agriculture, and of Anglo-Saxon agriculture generally.

What is known of it with absolute certainty? That men ploughed with oxen and ploughed long furrows; not much more. They knew the four grain crops, wheat, barley, oats and rye, but made most use of the last three and in particular of the rye, which dominated the countryside for centuries—'the acres

of the rye', 'coming through the rye'. Primitive North
Germany, from which the invaders came, was not a good wheat
country, and Germans have always lived largely on rye bread.
Wheat growing was no doubt encouraged by the Christian
missionaries who came from wheat-using countries and wanted
fine bread for the sacrament; but for the people at large any
corn would do; and no doubt like their later medieval descendants they grew and ate mixtures of the two autumn-sown
crops, rye and wheat, and the two spring-sown, oats and barley.
Barley will ripen farther north than any other grain, which
may explain why outlying hamlets and bits of cornland were
known, especially in the north, as berewicks, barley-farms.

About the oxen there is no doubt. We cannot prove that
a horse was never harnessed to a plough, but there is no
evidence the other way. Anglo-Saxon England had horses
enough, and men rode to hunt or to fight. If Hengist and
Horsa never existed, it was a horse-loving people that invented
them. The early laws are full of horse stealing and horse riding.
The horses of East Anglia are all registered in Domesday book;
and there were plenty of them. But there is nothing anywhere
suggesting a plough-horse, though no doubt horses might be
used for pack-work about the farms. The ox, the plough-ox,
is everywhere.

In trying to picture the early fields, we have to bear in mind
that some at least of the invaders had almost certainly not got
beyond that phase of primitive agriculture in which the
ploughed land is changed every few years, worked until it is
declining in fertility, and then left to recuperate. That is easy
where land is plentiful, though the breaking-up of fresh land
means heavy ploughing, especially if it has been grown over
with thorns or briars or bracken, as it probably has. This, with
the heavy ploughing which was still necessary even in more
developed forms of agriculture, no doubt helped to establish
the strong and persistent tradition that a full plough-team
contained eight oxen. It is known that in Germany the eight-ox
team was normal only for breaking up fresh ground (*Neubruch*),
and that at a later date in England the two- or four-ox team
was normal for the ordinary working especially of light soils.
'One *villanus* is there ploughing with two oxen', an unusual
sort of entry in the Domesday of Yorkshire happens to tell us.
In Scotland, where regular breakings up of 'outfield' remained
part of the farming tradition, the eight-ox and even the twelve-ox

team—with a terribly heavy, cumbrous, and wheelless plough—survived until the eighteenth, even the nineteenth, century.

Scotland, in fact, rather than Norman or Plantaganet England, supplies the best aids when reconstructing in imagination the course of events on the land; Scotland and places in England where we can spell out the agrarian history of small settlements. For Scotland retained the small settlement—the clachan. Scotland's traditional system of agriculture was adjusted to it; and East Lowland Scotland was Anglian enough, as Edinburgh's name and its dialect show. We are not, that is to say, dealing with a purely Celtic system when studying old Scottish agriculture, though systems about small settlements—Celtic or Anglian—are likely to develop common features.

The ancient Scottish system is not known to us at first hand from any primitive, or indeed any medieval, century. But its character plainly points to the next stage beyond that of constantly shifting arable fields. The field nearest the clachan, the infield, was permanent. It was cut up into long strips, usually held alternately by different tenants; and it got most of the manure. Beyond it lay grazing land from which semi-permanent 'outfields' were ploughed up at intervals, perhaps given a little manure, and cropped till they were tired and needed a rest, just as in primitive agriculture. The breaking-up of an outfield that had gone back to rough pasture for ten years or so would always be a heavy job. When broken, it would be doled out in strips to the tillers of the infield, whose oxen had done the work.

This system of in- and outfield was practised in Scotland about single farms, as well as about clachans; traces of it survived into the late eighteenth century both in the Anglo-Danish East Riding of Yorkshire and in Celtic Cornwall, and elsewhere besides; there can be little doubt that, if we knew medieval England completely, we should meet plenty of it.

But that in much of England, and especially about its bigger and more important villages, arable fields had become permanent things to whose features and boundaries you could refer, the Anglo-Saxon land charters that became fairly numerous after A.D. 700 show. If outfield agriculture is being practised, it is being practised within the known bounds of a village or group of hamlets. These bounds will normally include arable, or potential arable, meadow, waste land and woodland, all essential to the life of the community. Rights over wood, waste and meadow go with the land held in the arable fields. There is no trace of communism, no scrap of evidence that the arable was reallotted periodically among the villagers. If you have shifting fields or outfields you must allot as you plough.

The earliest written reference to fields and their management comes, like so much else, from a law of Ine: 'if churls have a common meadow or other shared land to fence, and some have fenced their share and some not, and the crops or the grass are eaten [by cattle, or maybe deer], then' those who have failed to fence must compensate the others. The situation is simple. Churls, ordinary freemen, have this land. It is not a 'manor' with a lord to issue instructions. The land is so much theirs that a royal order is needed to make the obstinate man who delays fencing his part, because that is his affair and no one else's, compensate those whom his obstinacy has hurt. It is shared land (*gedálland*, what the Scots much later called 'rundale') that lies open until haymaking or harvest gets near, and, the outer fence once broken, the sheep may be in the strips of meadow or the cows in the strips of corn.

Nothing is clearer than that we have here, about the year 700, some early kind of open-field agriculture—and in a community of plain freemen, controllable only by the king.

But lords and other great men, lay or (after the conversion) clerical, also had *tuns* and had households to feed. The lord's 'town' was certainly sometimes distinct from the churls' 'town' (Charltons). Perhaps in the beginning the lord, when not a very great man, did some work himself—though Tacitus believed that a gentleman German usually idled or talked public affairs when he was not fighting. Certainly he would have some slaves: the slave plough-man remained a familiar figure in English society in A.D. 1000 and A.D. 1066. 'Bitter hard work it is, bitter hard work it is; because I am not free', the ploughman says in Aelfric's picturesque dialogue, written to teach boys Latin about A.D. 1000. He is not just anyone who ploughs, but the slave who is kept for that purpose. In Domesday Book the number of a lord's own plough teams constantly agrees with the number of slaves recorded on his 'manor'.

If the churls have not a distinct *tun*, their land and the lord's land may lie mixed up 'in rundale'. They may pay him a food-rent; or if he has found the house as well as the land—land assigned to him abundantly at some early tribal conquest, or granted later by such a conquering and colonising king as Ine

—in that case, by Wessex law, he may demand some work from them.[1] What sort of work, or how much, the earlier Anglo-Saxon records never say. From the end of the period there have survived, probably from Wessex or south-west Mercia, some precise notes in Latin of the obligations of various named classes of men. But we do not know their authority, and there has been a great deal of indecisive discussion about the meaning of the names, and to what classes they correspond, if to any, in earlier or later times, or in other parts of England. They do at least suggest that the gap between Wessex rural society before and after the Norman Conquest was not very great: the strictly economic gap, there and elsewhere, was narrower still

There can be no doubt that lords with slave ploughmen or other slaves often found that it saved trouble, instead of feeding and housing them, to let them have a bit of land and run up a hut of their own. Slaves with bits of land are mentioned in Domesday Book. And long after Domesday Book, we some-times meet a type of villein, as he was then called, with very heavy labour-services to perform but very little land: he looks like a descendant of this 'hutted slave' type.[2] It may be a primitive type. In view of what Tacitus learnt about Teutonic slavery,[3] perhaps the able-bodied male slave in England usually had his bit of land. With the slave girl or woman it was different: she could work about your *tun*, serve as your concubine, or perhaps in time be married off to the ploughman.

Where the hamlet was very small, and there were innumerable such places in Scotland, the North of England, the West and South-West, on the 'greens' (Walham Green) of forest clearings, and at the -ends (Ponder's End) in many counties, there fields might be open, but no complicated system of strip holdings could grow up. At Kexbrough, near Barnsley, in 1086 a man called Swan had a plough-team and two tenants who shared a team: there was meadow, and plenty of oak woodland for the pigs. At Great Slamseys (*Slamondesheia*) near Braintree in Essex, a certain Roger held fifteen acres from the Bishop of London: there seems to have been no one else there. Seven hundred years later, there lay near the hamlet of Appleton, in South Lancashire, an 'Appleton Field' which was divided into 'about four' plots 'all bounded by mere-stones' (boundary stones). There were other fields at Appleton in 1794, but this

---

[1] See above, p. 45.   [2] See below, p. 102.
[3] See above, p. 42.

evidently ancient one with the hamlet name suggests what fields in places with three or four households may have been like in the beginning.

The lie of the land in the North and West often favoured hamlets: there might be no room, or no big enough stretches of good land, for villages with extensive fields. In such regions many Celts and Scandinavians had learnt to settle in hamlets, or almost solitary halls. Danes in the open country of Jutland, and settlers in what is now southern Sweden, developed in course of time big villages with their wide unenclosed fields. So did Celto-Romans in Gaul. In many open, sandy or chalky regions, such as northern France, the North German plains or eastern England, the number of good springs is limited: population tends to accumulate in rather big blobs along the watercourses. In rockier western Britain there are springs nearly everywhere. There are stones too, which have to be cleared and heaped into boundary banks or walls before agriculture can even begin. 'Gather out the stones.' On such land the hamlet with its small roughly enclosed fields is the obvious form of settlement.

Just how the conquering armies of Northmen took over the land, when they occupied and partly colonised what came to be the Danelaw, we do not know. But it was not merely a change of the ruling class, though it was certainly that. There was also a strong infusion of free fighting men who seized on old village sites or perhaps chose new ones. Harewood, at the mouth of Wharfedale, was held in 1066 by Thor, Sprot and Grim, obvious Danelaw names. No one else is mentioned there; though as this Domesday entry is condensed there may have been a few thralls to help them and their families with the five ploughs reported. Swan of Kexbrough sounds like a Scandinavian, and so does his neighbour Haldene of Worsbrough. To the east, in Lincolnshire, not only the men, when mentioned in Domesday, but a high proportion of the villages to this day have their Danish names. The agrarian and social life of the Danelaw was much freer than that of Wessex at the time of the Norman Conquest, and so remained. The Scandinavian type of personal name survived into the thirteenth century, and working peasants long after the Norman Conquest had land that they could give away to monasteries.

Gifts of land to the Church had played a great and not always a wholesome part in the evolution of Anglo-Saxon society and law; but the direct influence of the Church or of churchmen on agriculture and village life was limited. The Church certainly taught barbaric kings how to grant away their rights over land by charter—by landbook. The Church became a landowner on a huge scale: by the eleventh century it held a third of Kent. Grants to laymen followed grants to the Church; and all this was very important in the evolution of what has sometimes been called 'Anglo-Saxon feudalism'. On the material side, missionaries coming from Italy or the Mediterranean, like St Augustine and Theodore of Tarsus, must have known about many crops and agricultural methods which would be new to the English. Their successors for a long time had continental contacts. Some fruit trees and vegetables may have been brought in by, or for, them: the few and rather unhappy vines of England certainly were. Reasons of luxury and old habit as well as of religion probably led immigrant churchmen to encourage wheat growing: we find chapters and monasteries eager to get all the wheat they can after the Norman Conquest.[1] And it is possible, though on this point there is no scrap of first-hand evidence, that churchmen may have encouraged better use of the land and improved rotation of crops.

This is possible because it seems certain that churchmen had a good deal to do with that more systematic organisation of village life in the interest of the controlling powers that can be noticed in the later Anglo-Saxon centuries. The cleric could read and write: he could keep accounts: he could record contracts and obligations. When the time came, from A.D. 991, for paying Danegeld, a tax heavy enough to crush down whole classes of society, church lands were often exempt; and where others may have sunk economically, the corporate ecclesiastical landlord might rise. The Church never died, never had its lands confiscated, though in the Danish wars they were often ravaged just as monasteries were regularly pillaged. But everyone's land was open to ravage.

The proper organisation and maintenance of what in Anglo-Norman times came to be called the demesne, that part of the estate by which the lord, or lords, lived, were of special importance to monasteries, and were certainly watched over with a continuous care which few great laymen could match. Moreover, the great laymen were always changing: a large

[1] See below, pp. 80-1.

part of England was held in 1066 by members of the house of Godwin—new men.

If, therefore, one is looking in the eleventh century for big, rich, highly organised 'estates', one turns to the lands of the Archbishop of York or to those of the Abbot of Glastonbury, or rather of St Peter or St Mary. St Mary held all Glastonbury, a very large village. It was tax-free: *nunquam geldavit*. There were twenty-one first-grade tenants (*villani*), thirty-three second-grade (*bordarii*, literally cottagers), and no less than seventeen slaves. (It was Aelfric, a churchman, who had described the slave ploughman as a normal, if unfortunate, type about the year A.D. 1000.) St Mary had a big demesne, enough for five ploughs; and the slaves, her slaves, are entered immediately after the ploughs. There are two remarkable entries before the very remarkable valuation of Glastonbury at £20—a rentable not a capital valuation, if such modern terms may be used. They are '8 smiths and 3 arpents of vines'. On these few words imagination has to play; as it may on islands in the Glastonbury marsh where St Mary had more vines and some fishermen.

Near London the influence of commerce, and what without anachronism can be called business methods, make themselves felt on Church lands. At Westminster the 19 *villani* include one very substantial man who is said to hold, that is be taxed as for, a whole hide. (Some of the others held what was a very normal full holding for a *villein* later, a virgate, a quarter of a hide apiece; the rest held half-virgates.) But the most interesting group at Westminster are forty cottagers who all told pay 40s. 'for their gardens'. Who were they? Thames boatmen? London labourers? Hangers-on of the abbey?

At Willesden business methods obtrude. St Paul, in the persons of his canons, has abandoned demesne altogether—*in dominio nil habet*. The *villani*, who here must certainly be translated by 'villagers', not by the later Anglo-Norman *villeins*, have taken it over and pay rent for it. It is held at farm (for a fixed payment, that means) of the canons—*ad firmam canonicorum*. The villagers will of course have their own holdings too. The demesne in any manor, it may be added, as we know it later, might be either a separate area—as St Mary's vineyard was—or a set of strips in the fields, or a mixture of the two. Whether a village had a single lord or not, there would naturally be land, garden and paddocks about the hall or halls,

or in the case of an absentee about his barns and farm buildings.
Most Saints were absentees.

It has been suggested that clerical managers of land may
have had something to do with forward steps in the use of the
arable land and the crop rotations which took place at some
date between A.D. 500 and 1100. The classical rotation of the
Roman Empire had been two-course, crop and fallow.[1] This
was partly because in most Mediterranean lands spring-sown
crops are seldom a success. Early missionaries from the South
can hardly have taught the English to grow them. Spring
sowing as a general practice must have begun in the moister
North. An old popular legend credited the three-course rotation of crops on the continent—winter corn, spring corn, fallow
—to the Emperor Charlemagne (A.D. 800). We know that
this rotation was practised, though we do not know how widely,
in England after A.D. 1100; and there is no sufficient reason to
suppose that it was then a novelty. We also know that in
thirteenth-century England, and indeed much later, the two-
course rotation was widespread;[2] and other more primitive
ways of cropping, from one of which the later Scottish system
certainly evolved, must—we have argued[3]—have been more
widespread than we can prove. Welsh evidence suggests that,
among the mainly pastoral people that the medieval Welsh
were, the most primitive system of all long survived—that in
which the cornfield is not a permanent thing, but is ploughed
up from the wide grazing land that a pastoral tribe requires,
and then allowed to revert to pasture, the tribe perhaps
moving on.

Crop-rotation is independent of the lay-out of the fields.
There can be a two- or three-course rotation in big village
fields or on the two or three fields of a solitary farm. But in
village fields, whether two or three, a man must have about the
same amount of land in each, if he is not to starve at intervals.

The Charlemagne legend suggests, and continental documents confirm, that the three-course rotation spread in
north-western Europe from 'the vast well-organised demesnes
of the crown and the great abbeys of Northern Gaul', during
the eighth and ninth centuries.[4] Probably it had spread to

---

[1] See above, p. 25.   [2] See below, p. 80.
[3] See above, p. 48.
[4] Charles Parain in *The Cambridge Economic History of Europe*, vol. 1 (1941),
p. 130.

England before A.D. 1000. What makes one suspect the influence of the Church is the difficulty of picturing any re-adjustment of cropping in village fields except where there was some strong and far-sighted directing authority. That the Church was. True, in a small village of free churls, with plenty of land in reserve, where one field had been divided, say between rye and oats, and one left fallow yearly, a village meeting can be imagined deciding to make a small new field on the waste to grow more of one of the crops, and then deciding to extend it year by year until it matched the others. The division of all the big shared fields, when we come to know more about them, into sections—the furlongs or shots— whose strips often ran in different directions, suggests such a gradual adding of section to section. But it is easier to imagine an Abbot of Glastonbury, or one of those managing reeves whom Ine's law allowed lords to take about with them, issuing instructions about field lay-out to tenants obliged to do some work for a lord who had provided them with log-cabins. Easiest of all if he were a colonising lord, or one trying to bring back into cultivation land laid waste in a Danish raid or some campaign. For that there was ample opportunity between the reigns of Alfred and Canute.

All this is speculative: we know of open fields and strips, but we have not absolute proof of any three-course agriculture in England before A.D. 1100. It may conceivably have come first with Normans who knew those 'well-organised demesnes' across the Channel; and no doubt in some cases it did. But the high probability is that it was here already.

THE ECONOMY OF SCOTLAND AND WALES

Of Scotland before the eleventh century we are infinitely ignorant, for lack of documents; on early Wales we are better informed. We know that in time the Scottish infield and outfield agriculture became common both to the Anglian Lothians and to the Celtic West and North: it was a product not of racial instinct but of economic environment. We know that Celtic life was tribal, the land held by tribe or clan, and the mainstay of life the cattle. We suppose that agriculture in Scotland long remained at the primitive stage in which some of the tribal land is broken up for crops yearly, or from time to time, and then allowed to go back to pasture. We expect that where the non-tribal Scandinavians came in by sea—to Caithness, the Hebrides and some other places—a more individual and settled agriculture must have been practised about those scattered homesteads that appear in the Icelandic sagas. We need not be told that the main crops everywhere were oats and barley, with very little wheat.

Welsh society is clearer, although there is difficulty in dating the earliest Welsh laws. It also is dominated by the herds and flocks. The prince is a great rancher, with his winter and summer pastures. His freemen are the same on a smaller scale, living not in villages but in scattered halls, '*quasi solitarii*', just like hermits, as Gerald of Wales wrote in the twelfth century. It is the servile people, no doubt of conquered tribes, who live in hamlets: below them are the absolute slaves, of the prince, of the freeman, or even of these servile '*taeogs*'. In Wales we know that virgin soil was broken up from time to time, as in a predominantly pastoral society we should expect. But since parts of the country—Anglesey, the Vale of Clwyd, the Vale of Glamorgan—were famous for their corn (Bede knew of the Anglesey crops), in them probably a more permanent agriculture developed early. It is for some of these servile villages that there has survived an elaborate set of rulings about how the ploughed land is to be divided up among those who supply the various oxen of the team and the plough itself: you must have some such rules or understandings when you are breaking up virgin soil co-operatively, and humble men must co-operate. 'There is nothing to suggest that a system of co-tillage existed...among the free tribesmen.'[1] Perhaps they did not need to till at all; for the servile hamlets paid them rents in food. Or perhaps, like Swan of Kexbrough, each substantial free tribesman had his own team, and a slave or two to manage it. The only *taeogs*, serfs, who held their land for labour, not for a food-rent, were groups settled close to the prince's 'court', his wooden palace, and controlled by an ill-sounding official, the 'dung bailiff'. The prince's other *taeogs* paid food-rent to him, as their fellows did to his free tribesmen.

[1] Sir John Edward Lloyd, *A History of Wales...to the Edwardian Conquest* (1939), vol. I, p. 296, n. 65.

ANGLO-SAXON ENGLAND: TOWNS AND TRADE

In the five centuries after the original slow conquest of a country that Rome had never really urbanised, and in which what urban civilisation she had nursed into life was in decline before that conquest began,[1] the English and Anglo-Danes had gradually developed a town-life of a very un-Roman sort. Whether there was any continuity of town-life across the dark gulf of the generations of conquest has been much discussed. At some places there certainly was not. *Calleva* died and Silchester was born near its ruins. *Verulamium* died and in time St Albans rose near it. Whatever Rome had built at Cambridge became by 695 a 'waste chester' where the monks of Ely dug up a good stone coffin for their patron saint; though perhaps it had only become waste recently. That London and York, Bath and Gloucester, Chester and Lincoln, Dover and Brough on the Humber were ever completely deserted is unlikely; but even London probably became a village with its fields, and had to grow again into something like what economists think of as a town. And in 1086 the Archbishop had land in the fields of York.

The best approach to the town-life of those five centuries is backwards; for Domesday provides that very rare thing for the eleventh century, some figures which allow rough estimates of size, with a little information about particular town inhabitants; and there are some other scraps of evidence to fill in the Domesday outline. Most unfortunately there is no description in Domesday of Winchester or London, the ceremonial and the effective capitals; though an account of Winchester from a few years later survives. But there is a full account of York, that capital of the North where for a time a Viking had reigned, at which Harold Hardrada had struck before Harold Godwinson beat and killed him at Stamford Bridge in 1066. There is also a useful but much less full account of Gloucester, the western capital in which William sometimes 'wore his crown'.

York had seven 'shires' or wards. The return gives the number of houses they contained, inhabited or uninhabited. On this basis it is hard to suppose that the town population in 1086 can have been less than 5000: it was probably not less than 7000. Of the occupied inhabitants we hear only, besides

[1] See above, pp. 36–7.

the Archbishop and the Canons, of four judges, of 'a certain moneyer', one of at least ten who struck money for the crown in York, of Odo the catapult-man (*balistarius*) and of Landric the carpenter. No doubt Landric was a military carpenter who worked on the palisades of the early type of Norman castle, and Odo a siege expert. There were several mills: two new ones had been destroyed in the making of 'the King's pool', a fish-pond. The burgesses, or some of them, were cultivators. Many of the houses belonged to great men outside, who found a town-house convenient for buying, selling or letting. William's half-brother, the Count of Mortain, had fourteen such houses: he also had 'two stalls in the Shambles and the Church of Holy Cross': a butcher's stall and a church were both income-yielding property.

This is the outline sketch of an ecclesiastical, military and administrative centre, which must have had in it men of all the trades appropriate to the needs of its military, spiritual and judicial garrisons. Where money was struck other metals would be worked: we meet the butcher and must assume that earliest mechanical expert, the millwright. Of merchants we are not told; but two or three generations earlier York was said to be full of them, 'especially from the people of the Danes'. They left their mark at Copmanthorpe, 'merchants' settlement', downstream. It appears only as a village like the rest in Domesday, so we cannot tell whether they still used it. York, whose population had certainly fallen since 1066, had suffered terribly with all Yorkshire; not only by William's wasting but by that of Norse or Danish invaders. It was not William who had reduced the value of Bridlington (to the King) from £32 to 8s.: there is some forgotten tragedy in those figures. Probably trade was less active in 1086 than it had been when Canute reigned on both sides of the sea.

A remarkable thing about York is the astonishingly high proportion of the population of the great shire resident in it. The moors and dales, east, west and north, were very thinly peopled, and always had been. There were substantial villages in the open central country, especially just west of York. Elsewhere lonely moorland halls, Yockenthwaites or Goath-lands, with a handful of people about them, anticipated *Wuthering Heights*. Some of the best villages had escaped damage in the wars and wastings, but many had suffered and lay desolate. As a result, a generous estimate on the basis of

Domesday cannot make the whole population outside York much above 40,000, against York's 5000–7000.

For Gloucester Domesday Book gives us no total number of houses, as it does at York. (Returns of houses in Lincoln and Norwich suggest a population of some 6000 for each.) But we have another eleventh-century account of Gloucester, from which we may suppose a population of something like 3000. That only sixteen houses had been cleared away to build Gloucester Castle, and that only fourteen more were returned in Domesday Book as empty, suggests life on a smaller scale: at York the castle had emptied a whole ward, and house sites by the hundred were vacant. But Gloucester had an important group of moneyers and was in a position to pay substantial dues to the king. For an increase in these he had agreed to abandon some ancient dues that the Confessor had received— twelve 'sesters' of honey, thirty-six 'dickers' of iron, and a hundred rods of wrought iron to make nails for his ships.

The honey is evidently a token survival of an ancient food-rent or ritual offering. That the Conqueror could do without the two sorts of iron, and preferred cash, suggests that his agents knew where to buy nails; but perhaps earlier kings' agents had also known, and the ancient gift had survived through someone's inertia.

London, which had at least twenty moneyers in 1042 to York's ten, may well have had twice York's population. Its citizens had 'made' kings in the eleventh century, and the Conqueror dealt with them direct. There were Londoners known as borough-thanes who 'probably formed a recognized urban patriciate',[1] and there were London aldermen. The city had an elaborate series of courts, and an ancient 'peace-gild' to preserve order both within its walls and in the adjacent counties with which it had dealings. It had also what came to be called a 'knights-gild'. But as an eleventh-century knight was a *Knecht* or servant, only becoming a 'knight' when his master armed and horsed him, so making him a *chevalier* or *Ritter*, these may have been merely the thanes' juniors. (There were eleventh-century thanes' gilds in Cambridge and Exeter which contained both classes.) We do not know that London thanes or 'knights' were concerned with trade, but they may well have been. So far back as A.D. 686, when there were still kings in Kent, the Kentish king had a hall in London and

[1] Sir Frank M. Stenton, *Anglo-Saxon England* (1943), p. 531.

a reeve before whom cattle dealings by Kentish men were witnessed; and it is difficult to suppose that these London thanes and knights did not do some buying and selling, especially if they owned land outside the city, or acted as agents for earls or greater kings than a king of Kent.

‚Whoever did the trade of London, there was certainly plenty of it. The Kentish law of A.D. 686 points to that food-supply trade between town and country which Adam Smith called 'the great commerce of every civilized society'. Three hundred years after 686 London had also, as in Roman times, a well-developed and formally regulated long-distance trade, an even surer test of economic development. There were rules for wine and fish from Rouen, and there is reference to trade with Normandy in general. Flemings, men of Ponthieu on the lower Somme, men of 'France'—old France, the Île de France—men of Huy, Liège and Nivelles, to-day in eastern Belgium but then in Lower Lorraine, and 'men of the Emperor', from inner Germany, are also referred to. These last brought pepper, which must have come through Venice from the East, and across the Alps. That there were traders' quarters outside the city boundaries, the churches of St Clement Danes, by the Thames strand, and St Olave's (Olaf's) in Southwark attest. They served converted Danes and Norsemen, and may have been dedicated under the convert Canute.

The Domesday customs of the Cinque Ports show that they were active trading towns with their own shipping, whose cross-channel business William's conquest had greatly stimulated; but we learn nothing of their size. We do learn, by an accidental reference, that Dover had a gildhall—*gihalla burgensium*. So no doubt had some other towns, but Domesday Book does not happen to mention them.

Judged by the number of moneyers whose locally struck coins are known—a fair but imperfect test because of the accidents of discovery—the chief remaining towns of any economic importance in the eleventh century were Lincoln, Winchester, Chester, Canterbury, Oxford, Worcester and Thetford, still a bishop's seat in 1086. Thetford probably had more inhabitants then (4000–5000) than it had eight hundred years later. But this test by coin finds probably underrates the importance of Dover, Ipswich, Norwich and Bristol; though in general it agrees with what other evidence suggests. Lincoln, Chester with its Irish trade, and Oxford, are obviously important in Domesday. So are episcopal Canterbury, Worcester and Thetford. At Winchester, the ancient capital, money was perhaps struck in greater quantity than the town's economic importance warranted.

The list suggests how important official recognition had been in the rise of old English towns. To acquire that recognition a site naturally had to possess advantages, some of them economic—a ford, a bridge, a port, Roman walls, perhaps the ruins of a church, or the coffin of a saint like Durham or Bury St Edmund's. But it was its choice, at some date between A.D. 600 and 950, by a local or national king and his advisers, for the seat of a bishop or the quarters of a garrison, that was the turning point in its history. People came in whom the place's own fields might not be able to feed, and with that came the beginnings of the distinction between town and country. Navigable water helped, and most waters were navigable to the ships of early centuries, as Viking raiding voyages up both the Ouses and up the Seine show. There was Oxen-ford and there was Granta-bridge, the bridge, as we believe, that joined two early villages each of which had its own set of fields, fields which remained for more than a thousand years. Those fields were so much the dominant thing in the Cambridge of 1086 that almost all the townsmen's recorded grievances were farmers' grievances: Picot the sheriff had taken from them their common pasture, had forced them to do carting services, had forced them to lend him their plough-teams nine times instead of three times a year. Quarrels about ploughs or mills, rather than any commercial or 'industrial' grievance, were the most likely causes of friction in an average English town of the eleventh century. And, as has been seen, the eleventh-century gild of Cambridge, or its shire, was a gild of thanes, not of shopmen or merchants. If they had a gildhall it would be a place for drinkings, a place for gatherings to attend one another's funerals, or for sharing among themselves the expenses incurred when one of them had killed an outsider. These, and the heavy fine for killing a gild brother, are all in their rules written down about the year A.D. 1000.

Even these average agricultural and military towns had their markets, outside of which—if the law as laid down by Edward the Elder shortly after A.D. 900 was enforced—there was to be no buying and selling. No doubt the trade in such a place would be mainly of the simple town-and-country sort.

But we can assume intermittent visits of traders, chapmen, from a distance. According to Ine's law such people were supposed to do all their business before witnesses; and according to Alfred's law they were to bring before the King's representative, his reeve, at a public meeting, the men they were taking with them, by ship or cross-country caravan, to state their number and accept full liability for their conduct. A sound rule in a rough society, just the sort of rule that an African chieftain liked to enforce in recent times; but whether it was effectively enforced between Alfred's day and the Norman Conquest we do not know.

By another law often quoted—but was it as often obeyed?— these 'far-coming' men were obliged to shout or blow their horns if they wished not to be mistaken for robbers or enemies. The horn took the place of the caravan bells of another age and climate. On ship-board, the equivalent for honest traders may have been some kind of chanty. It certainly was in one recorded case. When the men on the 'Lorraine fleet', bringing Rhenish wine, came up the Thames, they raised their ensigns at 'the new weir' and, if they liked, sang their carol (*leur Kiriele*) all the way to London Bridge. The document quoted is of about A.D. 1130; but these traditional rituals have to grow up long before they are written down.

Merchants had moved in groups, by land or sea, from the beginning, if only for safety. So the 'far-coming' men of the Bronze Age must have travelled: it is not likely that flint-pedlars before them travelled alone. The flint-user in fiction who goes by himself to buy an iron knife is a moving figure, but not true to type.[1] You do not trade with strange tribes like that. If trade between town and country is 'the great commerce of every civilised society', this venturing long-distance trade everywhere preceded towns and helped to make possible civilisation, the ways of towns. The Anglo-Saxons had known it when they still feared and hated the real town. There was nothing urban about the Northmen, but they too were traders. To the men of all the Saxon centuries, the essential thing about the merchant, the chapman, was that he travelled. So he does in the early laws: so he does still in Aelfric's dialogue, of about A.D. 1000. Aelfric was no economist and his plan did not require perfect accuracy, but it gives the right impression: 'I go over seas', the merchant is made to say, 'and buy purple

[1] Rudyard Kipling, *Rewards and Fairies*: 'The Knife and the Naked Chalk.'

and silk, precious gems and gold, many-coloured garments
and dyes, wine and oil, ivory and brass, copper and tin, sulphur
and glass and suchlike things.' It is odd that Aelfric should
omit spices. He may be wrong about tin, though very likely
some was imported; for we have not certain proof of Cornish
workings in his day. About copper he is almost certainly right.
The rest of the list is correct: England has no sulphur and the
level of Anglo-Saxon glass-working was low. The most important items in the list for later history are the dyestuffs and the
wine. There were dyeing materials in Britain, but those most
prized were imported, and this affected the later development
of the cloth industry, as will appear.[1] Wine was the exception
to the rule that a primitive merchant normally handled things
of great value and small bulk. The wine required what in
modern language might be called a bulk luxury trade. First
made essential by the demands of the Church—which helps to
explain the Glastonbury vineyards—the Rouen and 'Lorraine'
imports show that wine had a more than ritual use in the
eleventh century, though it was not consumed so widely as it
came to be by the thirteenth. Both thanes and churls had other
drinks.

It was natural for Aelfric to overlook some 'vulgar' commodities that entered into trade. We have met the fish of the
men of Rouen. There would be some dried fish also, stockfish,
from Scandinavia; some pitch probably, perhaps some timber,
and to south-eastern ports probably some salt. But when
Englishmen went abroad, and by the eleventh century at latest
some did—not to mention the Anglo-Danes—they looked for
precious things. The other things we may suppose were carried
mainly in ships of the producing lands. What goods were
brought into Chester, by a trade mentioned incidentally in
Domesday, we are not told: we guess that they included hides
and slaves, from pastoral Ireland and the piratical Isle of Man.
We hear of a Bristol slave-market after the Norman Conquest.
The slave-trade Aelfric ignored.

The story of the *Angli* who were *angeli* illustrates the slave-
export trade of pagan England. No doubt the pagan
Scandinavian raiders of Christian England engaged in it.
After that the trade must have declined; but it is not certain
that it actually died; though we have no proof that it was
important even in early days. Certainly the agrarian slaves were

[1] See below, pp. 156–7.

too useful at home to be shipped abroad; it is of import only that we hear definitely in the eleventh century, though there was still some coastal raiding which may have meant export.

We know about English exports more often from rare continental references to them, or from archaeological evidence, than from any record on the English side. Before the Christian North and East were pillaged and ruined by the pagans in the ninth century, the monasteries had been homes of ecclesiastical art—embroidery, metal-work, manuscript-writing and illumination. The Anglo-Saxon missionaries to Germany helped to spread knowledge of these arts, as did the position of Alcuin at the court of Charlemagne. How far the undoubtedly deep mark that they made on continental artistic craftsmanship and penmanship was due to actual export, rather than to the influence of such migrants, is not clear: a certain amount of export, if only of the things the migrants carried with them, can, however, be taken for granted.

It was from Charlemagne's chancery that a letter which has survived was sent to Offa of Mercia, the greatest king in eighth-century England, in A.D. 796, begging that the *saga* exported from Offa's territory might be made of the old size. The usual translation is 'cloaks', suggesting military cloaks for Charlemagne's army. But did he equip his men? Perhaps 'cloths' or 'blankets' is just as likely. It is hard to suppose that we are not here dealing with some regular trade in which rough standards of length for the 'piece' were known to merchants, merchants who had confided a trade grievance to the Emperor's clerks. We seem to see darkly the earliest recorded export of English textiles—women's work from start to finish, there can be no doubt. Centuries later, Highland women who had spun and woven cloth sang as they dyed it with vegetable dyes of their own making. After 796 darkness falls over this textile industry —it was never well lighted; but a few scattered continental references suggest that the export may have continued; and Aelfric's reference to the imported, and therefore superior, dyestuffs suggests progress in technique which would help to account for the relatively high level of industrial organisation which is found in the twelfth century. The Frisians across the water, and after them the Flemings, had textile industries early developed; and the English, with better wool supplies, were well situated to develop their own.

Yet there is no doubt that the England of the tenth and eleventh centuries, like the England of the twelfth and thirteenth, was in the main an exporter of raw materials or foodstuffs. The total quantity would be small, as the ships were; but we either know, or can safely infer, some export to Scandinavia and Iceland of corn and meal and beer; some general export of the lead which the English certainly worked from the plentiful supplies that their neighbours lacked; possibly some export of tin. Wool and cheese, hides and skins and salt make up the list. When the King and the earl shared 'lastage' on each load shipped from Chester, there must have been some loads of salt for Irish consumption; for the Cheshire salt 'wyches' were the basis for a regulated trade, whose rules, like those about the levy of lastage, are in Domesday. The royal levy, it is to be noted, was on exports; ships coming 'with the peace and leave of the king' might 'sell undisturbed what things they had'; though no doubt the men of Chester would demand some market tolls.

ANGLO-SAXON ENGLAND: CRAFTS AND CRAFTSMEN

There had been craftsmen among all the invading tribes—smiths working in iron, in bronze, and in the precious metals; potters; shipwrights. No doubt every man was a handy rough carpenter, as every Russian peasant is, but the men who designed and directed work on the sea-going ships must have been in some degree specialists; the sagas contain memories of King Olaf's master shipbuilder. Tanning, like everything else preparatory to or connected with the making of clothes, would be done at home. Here again the Highlands of the eighteenth century furnish a parallel: leather for brogues was as much home-made there as the brogues themselves; but brooches and claymores were not.

Some of the smiths of the fifth, sixth and seventh centuries were wonderful craftsmen. Tribes had their patterns in brooches and other ornaments; so that archaeologists believe they can trace tribal boundaries by the occurrence of, it may be, Middle Anglian and East Anglian types in graves on either side of some suitable frontier. Most wonderful of all is 'the gorgeous barbaric jewellery of Kent'[1] which may date from A.D. 500, or even earlier, with its inlaid garnets and blue glass, its *cloisonné*

[1] R. H. Hodgkin, *A History of the Anglo-Saxons* (1939), vol. I, p. 91.

and metal filigree work. Great men had their gold-embroidered clothes; their buckles and brooches were gilt; their drinking-horns were mounted in silver-gilt or in gold. This is all from pagan times, because only pagans put treasures, weapons and jewels in the graves of their dead. They put their great women's treasures in also—beads and pins, needles and tweezers of bronze, even work-boxes of bronze, some highly ornamented. The workmanship we admire; some of it could not easily be bettered; but the workers escape us. Were any of them surviving Romano-Britons as has sometimes been supposed? Did the bronzesmith or goldsmith—and this seems most likely—move about from hall to hall, working for his keep and some reward? An expert specialist he must have been. No one else could have done such work.

The smith—swordsmith or common blacksmith—is less obscure. He had a wider range of customers, and so there were more of him. The greatest man would hardly keep his own bronze- or goldsmith; but it has been seen how a lord on the move might take 'his' smith with him.[1] At the end of the period, those eight smiths at Glastonbury[2] can hardly have all been kept at work as 'estate' smiths of the abbey; though they may have been. The six smiths reported in Domesday from the little hamlet of Hessle near Wragby in the West Riding must have been not merely specialists but a specialised group, a rudimentary industrial concentration, the solitary one revealed in 1086 in a bleak region that was to have plenty seven hundred years later. To such concentrations, and older ones, there is clear evidence from place-names in Yorkshire, Staffordshire, and elsewhere—Smeatons and Smethcots and Smethwicks, all of which, philologists affirm, have a plural as the basis of their first syllable: it was not Smith's *tun* but the *tun* of the smiths.

This is not in the least surprising. There was always a considerable output of iron goods of many sorts. Families would specialise to the trade, their members marry and transmit it. Very likely the 'half-naked' woman nail-maker, who rightly shocked nineteenth-century commissioners in the Black Country, was in the direct succession to a still more naked slave girl: there was always a good demand for nails. Also for axes, including the heavy battle-axes with which the housecarles fought at Hastings. Would these be the work of a blacksmith here and a blacksmith there? They may have been. But groups of armourers seem more probable, like the smiths who have given their name to a few villages.

Potters and soap-makers and salters are also to be traced in place-names. The last were certainly men who made salt—or had it made for them—at the 'wyches', and then travelled about selling it; for their name occurs oftenest at fords and bridges, and the like: Sawtry in Huntingdon is the salters' landing-place. What appears to be a shoemakers' village is found in Lincolnshire, Sutterby. At first it seems impossible; but as Aelfric's 'shoemaker' was a general leather-worker—he tells the boys what things he made—like an Indian *mochi*, we are justified in imagining a group of such people important enough to give that place its name.

A craftsman of any sort was originally called a wright. The word became specialised to the different sorts of workers in wood—shipwrights, wheelwrights, wainwrights; but you could still in the eleventh century call 'shoemakers' and masons wrights. Wood was, and long remained, the raw material for the simple vehicles and mechanisms of both country and town life—wood with perhaps some metal fittings. A four-wheeled waggon of about the year A.D. 800 that has been preserved in a Norwegian grave-mound is finely made of wood throughout, and probably represents the best workmanship of the day, for it belonged to a great man. It is certainly specialist wainwrights' and wheelwrights' work.

By far the most interesting of these wrights to the economist is the millwright, the earliest English harnesser of power and transmitter of it by the simple wooden machinery of the primitive water-mill. We meet him first by name shortly after the year A.D. 1000; but he had been at work long before. He appears at that date, with the plumber, as a possible workman on some big estate or group of estates; but it would be only a very important group that could keep such a specialist employed. The average millwright must have travelled like the salter, or had some district in which he and his mates undertook the building and upkeep of the mills and the mill-streams. He was both civil and mechanical engineer in embryo. As there are more than 5000 mills entered in Domesday, 537 in Norfolk, 436 in Lincoln, and 104 even in the wasted and backward county of York, work for a millwright's gang can be pictured in nearly every hundred or wapentake. After the

Norman Conquest, the mill appears as a manorial institution, its use obligatory on all the people of the mill-owning lord. How far back the beginnings of this obligation went is not known; but the mills are a source of revenue to their lords in Domesday. The early kings of Kent have been seen with grinding slaves,[1] which suggests that Augustine would not have come across many water-mills. Hand-mills, querns, had been the sole type in Roman Britain;[2] and they survived more or less everywhere, to become dangerous competitors with the manorial water-mill.

The spread of the water-mill from the zero[2] of A.D. 486 or 586 to the 5000 and more of A.D. 1086 is one of the greatest economic achievements of those five or six centuries; but it is completely unrecorded. Cattle and money and ploughs, smiths and reeves and crowds of murderers, are found in the early laws, but neither mills nor millwrights. These unknown men, in the half-civilised watery North, had done what Greece and Rome—with a sunnier climate, in places less abundant water, and everywhere more slaves—had never thought or never troubled to do in their great days.

Of the plumber, the lead-worker, who appears beside the millwright as a potential estate specialist, we know very little. Lead-mining went on, though perhaps not continuously; but we meet it in the ninth century in Derbyshire and Gloucestershire; and it appears in Domesday. Once mined and smelted, lead is easy to work, and any boy could turn out such things as the bob on a plumb-line. We hear in Bede of lead used for a church roof, '*ablata harundine*'—after removal of the thatch—and the writer of about A.D. 1000 who mentions the plumber would probably have a church estate in mind.

By the time that this 'plumber' is met there must have been a fair handful of masons with their plumb lines. The first invaders had no knowledge of stonework, but they were surrounded by the ruins of Rome. After the conversion of England, workers from Gaul coming in Augustine's train, or brought to the North by Benedict Biscop, used Roman brick or Roman stone for the first English churches, as can be seen in Wilfrid's crypt at Hexham, built in about A.D. 675. It is thought, however, that the work at Brixworth Church in Northamptonshire, 'perhaps the most imposing'[3] piece of seventh-century archi-

---

[1] See above, p. 42.   [2] But see above, p. 27, n. 4. [J.S.]
[3] Sir Alfred W. Clapham, *English Romanesque Architecture before the Conquest* (1930), p. 33.

tecture surviving north of the Alps, may have been done by native masons. Certainly by the eighth century a native school of stone-carvers had developed, whose craft is best shown in the so-called Anglian crosses of which many examples survive. After the dreary interlude of the Danish wars, stone building revived; and there seems no doubt that in the tenth, and more especially the eleventh century, there was an active 'school' of mason church-architects in England, of which we should know more if their work, on all the greater sites, had not been swept away or buried beneath that of their Norman successors. But the best of the surviving Saxon village churches, and the few in towns, like St Mary le Wigford at Lincoln or St Bene't at Cambridge, stand to show what the late Saxon 'stone-wright' could do. He had still seldom got beyond rubble walling, the stones sometimes roughly squared for the corners; but arches, windows and carving witness to a good, if simple, tradition. The buildings stand, but of the stone-wrights we know nothing, except that they appear to have worked exclusively for the Church.

ENGLAND UNDER THE NORMAN CONQUERORS

To the economist, the Norman Conquest is not so decisive an episode as it rightly seems to the general historian. It made no change in the economic resources of Britain or in its economic position in western Europe, and did not at once link it any more closely with other regions. The growing intimacy with the outer world that we notice after 1066 might have come in any event. Population was not appreciably reduced by the conquest, so far as we can tell, except in the poor northern territories that William wasted—there had been plenty of wastings before his, and were to be after it. To 'make' the New Forest William only cleared a few infertile villages; both he and his followers were too greedy and too business-like to reduce the human capital of the land by which they meant to live. True, the old ruling class vanished almost entirely—Thor and Sprot and Grim lost Harewood just as King Harold Godwinson lost his innumerable 'manors'. Some of the ruling class died at Hastings; some emigrated to serve as mercenaries at Constantinople; some may have been pushed down in the social scale to become tenants, or worse, where once they had been lords; a few came to terms with the conquerors. But in

their place appeared the immigrants—the *francigenae* of Domesday, 'Frenchmen' who might be Normans or Bretons, Flemings
or Lorrainers. The greatest landed proprietor of all, the Church,
was not dispossessed, though Archbishop Stigand and others
were; and a Lorrainer became Bishop of Hereford.

The land was cultivated as before, though the new ruling
class, lay and clerical, were sometimes innovators in what the
modern world calls estate management. But such innovations
take time to produce important economic effects. 'Already
before 1066...in the south and west, and sporadically even in
the northern Danelaw'—from the Fens to the Tees—we find
'the familiar form of social order by which the men of a village
maintained their lord's household by rent or labour in return
for...protection and justice....In the south and west, the
French...could ask for little more than...English custom
gave.'[1]

'Their lord': it is easy to slip unconsciously, when thinking
of eleventh-century, or for that matter twelfth- or thirteenth-
century England—of Scotland it is hard to think precisely on
these matters at all, for lack of evidence—it is easy to slip into
the assumption, one village one lord. For many villages all
over the country, especially in Wessex and on Church land, the
assumption can be made; but Domesday shows how untrue it
was generally in the eleventh century, either before or after the
Conquest; and twelfth- or thirteenth-century records will show
no change.[2] On the east side of England south of the Tees an
important village or parish with a single lord is a rare thing,
unless that lord is the distant king; and king's tenants, like
Czar's peasants in old Russia, were better off than other people's
tenants. From two to four or five 'lords', important people
interested in the village, is more usual. Churches were among
the greatest, as they were the oldest, landowners; Crowland
Abbey was as great an abbey as any, very anciently endowed.
Yet of the approximately fifty estates that it ultimately held in
east central England, only in two, besides Crowland itself, did
the 'manor' cover the whole village or parish. All the rest
were 'manors' not of, but in, such and such a place.

Maintenance of the lord's household by rent or labour had
taken most varied forms. In the far North there might be a
food-rent, as so usually in Celtic society. In Kent, always the

[1] Sir Frank M. Stenton, *The First Century of English Feudalism* (1932), p. 114.
[2] See below, pp. 89–90.

most 'modern' part of England, money-rents were very general at the Conquest, though a cash-rent might not be the tenant's only liability. From early times, as has been seen, a free churl might do work for his lord[1]—what work and how much would vary with local conditions and customs. Where a lord had demesne enough to employ slave ploughmen, and in the eleventh century he very often had, ploughing work by tenants who were not graded as *servi*, in the rather arbitrary classification of the Domesday inquiry, can hardly have been needed or normal. Help in harvest and carting work generally, what in Scotland came to be called 'carriages', would be more likely; but we do not know precisely how things worked out in different regions. Where the custom was to 'pay rent' in one or more days of work a week, the work must have been of a general kind; and when a lord was short of slaves he might naturally ask for ploughman's work in particular.

There had been no degradation in working for your lord. That ploughing might be reasonably demanded from the upper grades of tenants, even on the east side of England, an isolated reference from the Domesday of Holderness shows. It refers to a stretch of land about Burstwick, with many hamlets over which the lord of Burstwick had jurisdiction (*soke*). In eight of these, Drogo, the new lord, a man from near Béthune, 'had' five ploughs and six sokemen and sixteen '*villani*'; 'but they do not plough'—an entry which suggests that they might be expected to plough, especially as Drogo is not credited with any slaves, and someone must plough his land. We are left to guess who did: we note that the hamlets averaged not three tenants each.

The normal social grading in Domesday of men below what might be called the governing class is into freemen, sokemen, *villani, bordarii, cottarii* and *servi*. The freeman had occasionally been very free indeed; so free that he could even choose his own lord. The sokeman went for justice to some known lord's court, but was otherwise, we believe, economically independent; though he may have given his lord presents, or helped him in various ways. The next three classes were, it would appear, as a rule economically dependent—though the dependence might be merely that of rent-paying tenants in Kent. The *villani* are less free than the sokemen, and much less free than the freemen; but they are substantial peasants—decidedly not *servi*. It is

[1] See above, p. 45.

possible for men so described to take over and 'run' a whole 'manor' as at Willesden.[1] *Bordarius* was a term that died out in English, but survived in French as *bordier*. It had originally meant 'cottage man', and may have been applied in England to the men, or the heirs of men, for whom the lord had found a cottage, as in Ine's law.[2] But, taking England all over, the *bordarii* were the smaller men who yet had land and oxen, or an ox. 'Twenty-six *villani* and four *bordarii* having seven ploughs.' Seven ploughs means fifty-six oxen. That would allow for a yoke of oxen for each *villanus* and an ox for each *bordarius*. The *cottarii*, not found everywhere, are clearly cottagers with no land worth mentioning, except perhaps gardens as at Westminster,[3] and no oxen. The *servi* are at the bottom, most numerous in the Celtic South-West—21 per cent of the enumerated population in Cornwall against 9–10 per cent for the whole country—generally landless, but occasionally 'hutted'. None at all are reported from Lincolnshire or Yorkshire, big 'Danish' counties. As the thrall was a normal figure in Scandinavian society, it seems most likely that Danelaw thralls had also been 'hutted', and given land to live by; and so came to be entered by William's officials in the higher social grades.

Another class often planted out recently on the land were the knights, mostly foreigners, whom William's military system required his tenants-in-chief to provide for him. The knight type, as has been seen, was only rising, or recently risen, from that of the armed serving man—the *Knecht*.[4] Originally kept by his lord about the hall, when his position became permanent the knight was given land to live by like some of the slaves—but land with men on it. When the process began we do not know; but we do know that some of the Anglo-Danish kings' armed men—housecarles, bodyguards—had been maintained by grants of land before 1066. With the Conquest the arrangement spreads fast. On his great 'manor' of Clacton [on Sea] the Bishop of London has planted five knights, with two *villani*, forty-five *bordarii* and three *servi* under them. About Sherburn-in-Elmet—a big village with many outlying hamlets all grouped as one 'manor'—the knights of the Archbishop of York 'have' a tenantry of 135 households with thirty-four ploughs. We are not told how many knights the estate carried; but there was tenantry enough for ten or twelve.

---

[1] See above, p. 53.
[3] See above, p. 53.
[2] See above, p. 45.
[4] See above, p. 59.

There is no doubt that the first generation after the Norman Conquest saw, not only the almost complete disappearance of the old governing class, but a pressing-down in the social and economic scale of those below them. The sokemen of the Danelaw were many fewer in 1086 than in 1066: some may have fallen in battle or been dispossessed and replaced by 'Frenchmen', others called on to do services, and graded down. At Martham, north of Yarmouth, we find the Bishop of Norwich organising services from freemen systematically in A.D. 1101. Before A.D. 1086 at Caister, in the same county, Earl Ralph had 'made a manor' out of land held by eighty other freemen. 'Made a manor' in this case suggests the organisation of an estate on the full manorial pattern, with a large lord's demesne to be tilled in whole or in part by tenants' services. In the following century we can feel that some Bishop of Durham has done this in a group of villages near his episcopal seat. They are all organised on one pattern, of which Boldon is the model. Boldon gives its name to his survey: *The Boldon Book*, 1183. Farther afield on the Bishop's land are much more primitive conditions, food-rents, little or no demesne, services more casual and less organised.

Some have argued that in Domesday Book the word 'manor' has a technical meaning connected with taxation. Others have questioned the argument. For general economic purposes the word implies little more than our word 'estate'. Isolated halls, small hamlets, solid villages, parts of villages, whole tracts of country set with village and hamlet, centrally situated halls to which sokemen and others scattered over wide areas may owe allegiance and render some dues—all are classed as *maneria*, or in the alternative Latin word *mansiones*. *Manerium* was the Norman term for a substantial dwelling-house, for which the English equivalent was and is hall.

The sokemen dwindled, but a strong remnant of them remained in the northern Danelaw, and in time 'free and common socage' would become the lawyers' term for any tenure that was definitely free but not military like a knight's. *Servi* would slowly disappear, blending upwards, as it has been argued that they already had in places before 1066,[1] into the lower ranks of the not fully free landholding peasantry. And all these not wholly free peasants the lawyers would come to call villeins, lumping together men who did services of many

[1] See above, p. 50.

different types, attributing to them some of the degrading attributes of the *servus,* cutting them off sharply from the *liber homo,* and devising tests by which their attributed servility might be ascertained.[1] But all this is subsequent to A.D. 1100. However he was described, and whatever lawyers might begin to say, the average *villanus* or *bordarius* of A.D. 1100 had probably much the same amount of land, and certainly tilled it in much the same way, as the churl of A.D. 1000 or A.D. 900. Heavier services or harder terms of some sort he would certainly have in places. Above him was now a fully alien governing class, speaking a tongue that he did not understand, further from his dialect than old Danish or Norse had been. Yet his descendants would learn to call their oxen beeves and the flesh of their sheep mutton, even the man who killed them a butcher, though that French word, adopted south of the Tweed—the less Frenchified Lowland Scots said Flesher—originally meant a killer of goats.

[1] See below, pp. 94–102.

Book II

FROM A.D. 1100 TO A.D. 1500

Chapter IV

Agriculture and Rural Society

POPULATION AND SETTLEMENT

Among Domesday Book's gifts to the historian are figures which help him to estimate the size of the population, not exactly, but tolerably well. For no other country or region of A.D. 1100 is that possible. Domesday mentions, in round figures, 300,000 individuals south of the Tees and east of the Welsh marches. It omits some people—the Londoners for instance, the monks and nuns and other ecclesiastics, the outlaws and masterless men. The 300,000 hold land or occupy houses or are slaves—about 27,000 slaves. All are presumably adult men. Add as many adult women. Deduct some unmarried adults, probably few except perhaps among the slaves. At the average Domesday family we have to guess. Life was short: children would come and go fast. But the figures point towards a total of from 1,250,000 to 1,500,000. Add the undoubtedly thin populations of Wales, of England beyond the Tees, and of Scotland, and you get a much more hypothetical population in the whole island of from, say, 1,500,000 to 1,800,000.

Nothing so nearly accurate can be said about English population for many centuries; and for Scotland all is little better than guesswork before the eighteenth century. But there is plenty of non-statistical evidence of population growth or decline between 1100 and 1500. Growth was certainly rapid between about 1180 and about 1280. We can see it in new or extended villages and village fields, forest clearings, divisions of holdings to provide for new generations, an obviously active and growing demand for foodstuffs, rising food prices, a keen interest in agricultural development to meet it, growing towns, growing trade, great and successful building enterprises. After about 1280 there seems to have been a slackening, due to various causes including famine, before the catastrophe of the Great Pestilence; and this may have swept off so much as a third of the population. An opinion often expressed, which is perhaps near the truth, is that the population of England and Wales doubled between 1100 and 1300; fell sharply with the

Pestilence; and rose again to about its former maximum by 1500, when it was perhaps 2,500,000 or 3,000,000. But it is all a perhaps, and statisticians are wary about it. About Scotland they are rightly even warier; for they have no starting-point, and records far less abundant than the royal and manorial records of England. It has been supposed that Scotland's fifteenth-century population was nearing 500,000.

As at the Norman Conquest, so when Henry of Richmond won at Bosworth Field, the British was essentially a rural population and all the smaller towns were rustic, largely dependent on the produce of their town fields. The town bull is an important figure in the history of Coventry; the town commons and cow pastures were important everywhere. Poll-tax figures and a few other records of town population round about 1400 provide for some rough estimates, but many of the results are disputed. They suggest a possible 50,000 for London; little more than 10,000 for York; not above 10,000 for the three other greatest towns, Bristol, Coventry and Norwich; less than 5000 for the majority, and much less—1000 to 3000—for many towns reckoned important. The modern comparison, from the standpoint of size only, for representative fifteenth-century English or Welsh boroughs would be such county towns as Clackmannan, Appleby or Buckingham, with from some 1500 to 3000 inhabitants. Cambridge, with a double importance, had something over 3000. When the English were finally driven out of all France except Calais, it is doubtful whether 7 per cent, and fairly certain that not 10 per cent, of them were urban, and not too 'urban' at that.

As for Scotland, there is reason to think that sixteenth-century Edinburgh had about 9000 inhabitants, Glasgow about 4500, Aberdeen under 3000—and so down. The fifteenth-century figures would be less. And so to the village, the hamlet, the lonely hall; the oxen and the sheep; field and forest; villein and franklin; tenure by knight service or by free and common socage; the acres of the rye, the rising of the sun and the running of the deer. To harvest failures also and pestilence and famine; but in England less misery for the villager through foreign, civil, or private war than in any part of the continent.

Villages and hamlets were mostly where they had always been. There are a certain number of post-Domesday Newtons. There are also fresh names in -end or -green or -dene; a few perhaps in -thwaite. They are new groups of huts in forest or moorland clearings. Green is a common surname because there were so many Johns o' the green in a country still well wooded. A parish name had often covered at least two settlements in Domesday—Linton and '*alia Lintone*'—where a Saxon group had already hived off at some unknown date. The process of hiving off continued. The '*alia*' so-and-so might become Little so-and-so, or it might take the name of a Bishop or Abbot, or of some proprietor who came over with the Conqueror. In North Essex there are two Bumpsteads, Steeple and Helion, which last word is not Greek but Breton, Helléan in Morbihan where the Conqueror's Breton knight came from. But a Conqueror's knight seldom, if ever, started a new village. He came to take a going concern, not as a pioneer. If the site was waste when he got it, or was subsequently wasted, as many were in Yorkshire, Domesday regularly records the old valuation, the present lack of value, and the new holder. In course of time the owner or his heirs might get the land brought back into cultivation; we know that in Yorkshire they did, with some very interesting consequences.[1] But it was the old site and the old name; perhaps a few inhabitants had hung on, or drifted back, at the time of the wasting. Troubles in Stephen's time, and later, led to casual and local wastings, but not on a scale to leave important traces on the map: there are few if any certainly known deserted villages from these centuries. At least nineteen times out of twenty, the village was there in Domesday and is there to-day; and the one in twenty, or in thirty or more, that came into existence after Domesday is as a rule there to-day also.

The business of forest settlement, or of hiving off into a subsidiary village, may be said to have ceased with the slackening in the growth of population after about 1280. One might have expected the Great Pestilence of the next century, which here and there emptied whole villages, to have led to much abandonment of village sites. Abandonment following bad times or a shrinking population is met with fairly often on the continent; but there is very little evidence of it in Britain. Indeed, estate records which cover the years before and the years just after the Pestilence—those of the Bishop of Winchester, for example, or of the Abbot of Crowland—show an unexpected continuity of life and conduct. It looks as if

[1] See below, p. 82.

medieval man was so broken to plague, pestilence and famine, that even a heavy extra dose of one of these terrors did not greatly move him. If some tenant and his family are wiped out there is generally a landless man ready to take their holding. Men of the twentieth century have learnt to understand this animal courage or acquired apathy, and this readiness to step 'into his comrade's place the instant that he fell', in the battle with death.[1]

AGRICULTURAL TECHNIQUE AND COLONISATION

The actual technique of agriculture made little progress in these four centuries. No doubt the three-course rotation of crops—two-thirds of the land cropped and one-third fallow— that makes a maximum use of the arable, and was the base for the familiar three-field system, gained at the expense of two-course rotations and still more primitive methods; but we cannot trace the gain precisely. We have not enough manorial surveys or other material to enable us to say, for example, that many places where two-course rotation was practised in the eleventh or twelfth century had taken to three-course by the fourteenth. The extraordinary persistence of the two-course rotation—there was plenty of it all through these centuries and in those that followed, and it was by no means extinct even in 1800—suggests that a system once adopted was not easily changed. Some very strong force is needed, such as the later enclosure Acts of Parliament, to start any thorough reorganisation in the field system of a village. Where, as in most English villages, there was more than one lord—and might be half a dozen—change would be exceedingly difficult. Besides, the rotations were to a great extent determined by the nature of the soil—three-course on heavy and fertile lands, two-course on those that were light, relatively infertile, or stony. There were strings of two-field villages on the chalky northern slopes of the Berkshire Downs far into modern times.

What we can trace in the thirteenth century, when agriculture was booming and our records of it are becoming abundant, is a determination on the part of lords—especially those ecclesiastical lords whose muniments are our most

---

[1] Recent work suggests that there has been more abandonment of medieval village-sites than Sir John Clapham believed at the time when he wrote this chapter. But the subject awaits fuller investigation. [J.S.]

abundant source of knowledge—to make the very best out of their estates. At times they extend the demesne, the 'home farm' of compact blocks or scattered strips, by incorporating into it land which has fallen in by the death or removal of a tenant of some sort. They may stiffen up their tenants' services, to meet the needs of a demesne enlarged or more intensively worked. They are often seen eager to increase the area under wheat, for consumption in refectory or bishop's palace, or with an eye to its market price. It is now known that there was a vast deal more corn-marketing in the thirteenth century, and earlier, than used to be supposed. You may sell in growing towns, to infertile forest or moorland hamlets, to the king for his court or his wars—the army contractors of Edward I operated on a very large scale[1]—or, if you are conveniently placed, for export. Sometimes a big ecclesiastical corporation, not able to cover monastic consumption by its demesne crops or corn-rents, may itself become an important market buyer; Christ Church, Canterbury, was, as early as the first half of the thirteenth century.

More wheat growing only meant less of other winter-sown grain—less rye—not an overhauling of the general field system. But overhauling or modification of field systems was certainly going on, though it is not easy to trace, in the thirteenth and other centuries, but especially in the thirteenth. One evidence for it comes from the remarkable agricultural literature that thirteenth-century England produced, a literature unique in thirteenth-century Europe. As this literature discusses the relative advantages and disadvantages of the two- and the three-field systems, advocating the more 'progressive' and productive three-field, it is hard not to suppose that the change-over was in hand or at least in mind, among enterprising manorial lords, although the sad way in which agricultural practice has in most centuries failed to obey the advocates of agricultural reform is only too well known.

But it is reasonable to think that, where neglected land was being brought under cultivation and village fields extended, in regions where the soil and the lie of the land were favourable the three-field system was gaining ground. Occasionally we find that by the end of the thirteenth century a two-field has become a three-field village, by a shifting of boundaries which gave opportunity for varying the crop rotations. A most

[1] See below, p. 108.

interesting illustration of circumstances that might accompany the bringing of wasted or deserted land again under cultivation —and with the troubles of the eleventh and twelfth centuries and the subsequent growth of population there was plenty of room for such recovery—comes from the Vale of York, part wasted by the Conqueror as everyone knows. What the field system was when he wasted it no one knows; perhaps something rather primitive. By 1300 it was almost certainly three-field: the soil was all right. The more certain point, however, is that by 1300 more than half the villages have no demesne; and those that have demesne are largely those that the Conqueror did not waste—Church estates and others. In them, life has gone on in the old way, tenants working the demesne and the lords, resident or absentee, taking and perhaps consuming the produce. A set of wasted fields have neither produce nor inhabitants. The lord cannot live by them: demesne or food-rent tradition is broken. When he or his successors want to make them yield income, colonists must be found. With a growing population colonists are available. All over twelfth- and thirteenth-century Europe such colonists stand out for good conditions, and get them. Yorkshiremen would not be backward in demands. So, by 1300, they are found holding the land on pretty free terms, not obliged to work under a bailiff on a demesne farm; for there is no demesne farm. Their lord is getting rents of some sort, perhaps carting or other such service if he needs it, maybe in the north of the Vale—as was universal farther north still—fighting service when there is trouble with the Scots.

Another sort of recovery, not from man's waste but from God's, can be watched in the Fenland. Round the fen basin were villages with fully developed field systems of one sort or another, and cultivation in strips. To this day, in the more northerly Fens of the Trent, open fields and strips can be seen at Epworth on the Isle of Axholme; and the actual Isle of Ely, with other isles, had room for fully organised village fields. But all the time, in the true Fenland, on its boundaries and the edges of its islands, scraps of land were being reclaimed, dyked and drained, '*de marisco*'. These became detached holdings or bits of holdings that might not fit into any regular village system. Used in the first instance for all-the-year-round pasture —most of the Fens could only be grazed in summer, and not easily in a wet summer—they often became arable later. We read of cottages built along the raised dyke, as they can be seen to-day along the dyke beside Cowbit Wash; and we are led to speculate on the occasional creation on a small scale of what we know was often created during these centuries on a large scale in Holland and North Germany, the 'marsh colony' along the dyke, with holdings in single parallel strips running down to the fen, each house or hut on the base of its strip. But of anything quite so systematic in England we have not proof. There was, however, far more system and organisation in the life of the Fens than used to be supposed. Villages round about them had well recognised methods of 'intercommoning' in the fen for the summer. Villages A to F, let us say, all drove their cattle into a recognised section of common fen, when it dried out a little. The true fenmen were not the half-savage fishers and fowlers that they have sometimes been pictured. But the fish and fowl, with the cattle, dominated their economics; so that their agriculture, though making progress, tended to be both individualistic and subordinate. The isles were fertile enough, fertile as 'the garden of the Lord' monastic writers suggest, so exchange of fen products for bread-corn would be easy.

As in the Fens, a process of nibbling at waste heath, moorland and forest land was going on all over the country, but it is not so well recorded. Nibbling might occur on the edges of the elaborate fields of a big village: on the margin of those shown in one of our oldest surviving village-maps (of about A.D. 1600) there are groups of new strips and small enclosures marked 'late heath'. If we had medieval field-maps we should without doubt see plenty of this; perhaps sometimes a third great field gradually added to an early two. Or the nibbling might be about moorland hamlets of the North and West, where arable lay-out had been simple and where perhaps no crop rotation had been practised. (Centuries later, on the Welsh Marches, agricultural reformers were complaining that the farmers knew nothing but oats, oats, oats, in perpetual succession, the unvarying crop being no doubt helped with what manure there was.) Here again we can sometimes read the process on later maps or in later descriptions—a smallish field, the original one, named after the hamlet, and round it 'royds', cleared from the wood, or 'intakes' from the moor.

Thus more land was gained for the beasts or the plough; but when gained it was used much in the old ways, except for occasional improvements in the crop rotation. So much was it used in the old ways that some people have fancied that the arable land of England was getting worked out, through over-cropping and under-manuring, by 1500. It may have been, locally; but even of this there is no proof. Wherever we can test the facts we find no evidence of exhaustion. We can test them because the bailiffs of those great landlords whose records survive had, from an early date, the admirably businesslike habit of recording the amount of seed used and the yield of the crop. If the land were being worked out the ratio of yield to seed would get worse: in the rather numerous records that survive it never does. For this, perhaps one reason was the wretched crops raised, judged by modern standards. Of wheat, the yield averaged about four times the seed sown; a modern farmer would think eight times very poor.

One interesting novelty that the agricultural writers of the thirteenth century register is the use of the horse for ploughing. For some jobs—carting, packhorse work, harrowing perhaps— he may always have been used. Domesday England was full of horses of several grades, *equus in aula*, the lord's war horse at the hall; *equus*, just horse; *runcinus*, the nag. They cannot all have been used always for riding. But there is no evidence that they were used for the plough; and right through these centuries every picture of a plough shows oxen. But in some places, well known to travelled medieval Englishmen, the Paris region for instance, the plough-horse had superseded the plough-ox al-most completely by about 1450: it was perhaps known there at the time of our Norman Conquest. One thirteenth-century writer in England came down on the side of the ox. You can eat plough oxen when past work he says, but no one eats an old horse; you can only sell his hide. (The inferences about medi-eval diet and digestions are instructive.) But clearly the writer was familiar with *la charrue des chevaux*, for he discusses the cost of its upkeep, comparing it with that of the ox-plough, in strict businesslike fashion. One can imagine the literate monk-wardens of groups of Canterbury estates discussing with their bailiffs whether it would pay to change over to horses, and the bailiffs arguing for the ox. This debate between reformer and 'practical man' went on for centuries.

There was some progress in fruit growing and gardening, but dates of introduction or improvement are very difficult to establish. The Church was the main channel for new ideas; for novelties in fruit or vegetable growing all came through France from the Mediterranean. Yet, however it may have been in some monasteries, there is little doubt that the average medieval Englishman was a poor gardener, and the Scot a worse. It is no accident that in the best modern account of Scottish medieval economics the word 'garden' does not occur in the index. But the Scot had his kail, the Welshman his leeks, the Englishman his 'greens' of some sort. All knew beans and peas, which were generally grown not in gardens but in the fields. They knew cress, one of the few 'Nordic' vegetable names; but they probably picked it wild; the water-cress bed comes later. They knew onions even in Scotland, but we do not know how widely these were grown. By the fourteenth century a great development of gardening had set in in France, and this no doubt extended into England, but again we cannot say how widely or deeply; Frenchmen grew celery by 1500, but English gentlemen only learnt to grow it from Marshal Tallard, when Marlborough's prisoner after the battle of Blenheim.[1] We do at least know what vegetables were grown for a distinguished French prisoner in medieval England, King John of France in 1360—cabbage, onions, leeks, lettuce, spinach, beet, parsley and a few herbs. Roots of some kinds were grown by common people, of the turnip or carrot tribe: the 'nepe' in 'turnepe', though borrowed from Latin, is an Anglo-Saxon word.

Orchards were not for the average villager; but even in Scotland apples and pears of some sort might come into a town market in the sixteenth century; and in southern England, especially in Kent, there were plenty of orchards much earlier, and a regular marketing of fruit. But most of the fruit eaten on the land must have been wild—nuts and crabs, strawberries and raspberries, bilberries and blackberries in their seasons. Here was no room for progress. Medieval man collected his supplies from a country still half wild, much as prehistoric man had when it was wholly wild.

[1] John Evelyn, however, gave instructions for sowing celery in his *Kalendarium Hortense* (1664). [J.S.]

ENGLAND AND WALES: THE VARIETIES
OF AGRICULTURE

All over central England were to be found the substantial villages with their two or three great fields, subdivided into more or less rectangular furlongs, or 'shotts' or 'wongs', and they into the strips of parallel ridges whose mark is still on so much old pasture land that was never ploughed flat before it was laid down to grass. Such two- or three-field villages were normal but never universal. The boundaries of the area that they dominated may be roughly drawn on the east from Beachy Head, curving north-west, south and west of London, to about Wallingford on the Thames; then north-east to near Saffron Walden; so north and round the south and west of the Fens to the sea in South Lincolnshire above Boston. Thence along the coast into Durham. On the south the boundary is the Channel to about the eastern border of Devon; then north-west across Somerset; and so north-by-east in a sloping line to the southern end of the Derbyshire hills, with a westward bulge in Hereford and Shropshire; from Derbyshire north along the Pennine flanks to the Tees and across the Tees north-west to the coast near the level of Durham city.[1]

Within these bounds there was plenty of moor and woodland and forest in the medieval sense, that is, hunting ground with some wood and much waste. Such forest districts were not favourable to the true open-field village. It was the Weald of Sussex and Surrey and the forests of Middlesex and the Chilterns that had, so to speak, driven it so far west of London. Inside the bounds of 'open-field England' lie Selwood and Charnwood, Rockingham Forest, Cannock Chase, Sherwood and the North York moors, to mention only the chief forest names. What settlement there was in these areas was mostly in hamlets, as it always had been; their arable land was limited and laid out in some simple fashion, we can seldom know precisely what, but can guess at fields divided by a few 'mere-stones', or separate roughly fenced intakes from the moor or forest. We know that in Sherwood there was a little enclosed land, arable or pasture, about each forest village; that beyond this, sheep and cattle pastured with the King's deer;

---

[1] If the term 'open field' is widely interpreted, as it may quite properly be, much of East Anglia would be included, as in C. S. and C. S. Orwin, *The Open Fields* (1938), p. 65. For East Anglia see pp. 89–90 below.

but that the villagers as a group, or individuals, had the habit of enclosing bits of this grazing land, tilling these 'breaks' or 'brecks' for five or six years, and then letting them revert to grazing. It is a variant of the infield and outfield Scottish system of agriculture.[1] Our evidence for it comes from much later than 1500; but the eighteenth-century writer who called it 'an immemorial custom' was no doubt perfectly right. It has all the marks of primitive conditions; and we can safely imagine it reproduced elsewhere. Much of Nottinghamshire outside the forest was very 'typical' open-field country, and in it the village of Laxton near Southwell remains open to-day— a rather carefully preserved museum piece. The two systems existed side by side until modern enclosures swept both away, though not at Laxton.

Across the country, in the western bulge of the open-field area as here sketched, a similar contrast of types can be seen indistinctly on the lands of the Bishop of Hereford in the thirteenth century. His villages in the opener parts of the country look 'normal'—numerous tenants, demesne, services to till it, the two or three fields. But he has other little places in the Herefordshire woods and combes and twisted valleys, where there is no room for big fields and where his predecessors have not found it worth while to organise demesne agriculture. Tenants in such hamlets are few, and they owe hunting-services or carting-services or rents.

At the northern tip of the open-field region we see in *Boldon Book* (1183)[2] how the mostly alien Bishops of Durham have organised a group of villages all alike—'and they owe like the men of Boldon' demesne services and so on—for the supply of their establishment. The fields are not described, any more than fields are in Domesday; but something big and organised shows through the record of services; and it can hardly be supposed that these masterful ecclesiastics had not introduced the best twelfth-century practice, which was the three open fields. Up on the Durham moors they had very different estates, with an old Celtic flavour of cattle and food-rents.

Another adjustment to inherited conditions can be seen after Edward I's conquest in South Wales and the Marches. A lordship will have its 'Welshry' and its 'Englishry'. In the Welshry men live as they always did: there is not much agriculture; they are still pastoral; and they owe their lord tribute in money or in food. The Englishry is 'manorial': it has services and common fields of some sort. But the fields are not compact: the land does not often allow of that. They are many and of all sizes. The demesne for which the services are needed is also in many scattered bits. The rotation of crops is, however, three-course. Like the Bishops of Durham before them, the Marcher lords' agents use the best agricultural methods they know, adjusted to the country they have got.

Of South Wales it should be added that the Vale of Glamorgan was described as 'champion', that is open field of some sort, in Elizabeth's reign; and that South-West Pembroke, 'Little England beyond Wales', had with its non-Welsh place-names—Lambston, Haroldston—a general open-field system.

West Somerset, Devon and Cornwall; much of Shropshire, all Cheshire and Lancashire and North Wales; the far North, and so into Scotland, had not. There might be fields lying open which later were enclosed, but there was nothing systematic or general. Cornwall was all Cornish and its agriculture was rough and primitive even centuries later—bits of enclosure, temporary cultivation of the waste. Devon was very English; but that map black with little groups of houses, their names so often ending in -combe or -cott, is a poor one on which to hunt for village field systems; though in the opener parts of the county something of the sort may be found. Nor are they to be expected on Dartmoor or Exmoor or the Quantocks.

Cheshire, a poor country for corn, thinly peopled, with few big villages, many meres, high rough ground on its eastern side, and much forest, had to recover from the Conqueror's wasting of 1070, like parts of Yorkshire. But recovery began early; and right into the fourteenth century a gradual process of clearing —'assarting'—of forest and waste can be followed out. There is no trace of the midland field system: in its place there was something more primitive, near to the agriculture of the Scottish clachan, with these many scraps of land filched and enclosed from the forest.

Lancashire, like Cheshire, was thinly peopled and backward. Its gigantic parishes contained many little hamlet 'townships'. In its hills, life was mainly pastoral; and there grew up great cattle-ranches, 'vaccaries', in royal or baronial hands. The few tenants recorded in any one place, even late in the period, as well as the lie and use of the high ground, again suggest some small open fields of the Scottish sort, or little individually held fields, for what arable farming there was. Oats or rye would be the crops. It is not a wheat country. The 'intake' from the waste was easy and normal, as handfuls of people pushed up into what had originally been just hunting ground. We often hear of individual holdings of 'rodland', cleared land. Even in the open country between Manchester and Liverpool, and up to the Ribble, there are the barest traces of any large-scale organised agriculture. That is the home of Appleton 'township' and the little Appleton Field, which, it has been argued,[1] was all the arable there had been at Appleton in the beginning. As more fields were needed they were taken in and hedged. When hedging began we do not know; but it must have been before 1500; for four or five generations later, when Cromwell was planning his dash to make 'Darwen stream' run red 'with blood of Scots', the Lancashire hedges had to be considered seriously by tacticians.

The same process, enclosure with fence or bank or wall, had been going on from the beginnings of agriculture where small groups of settlers took in ground from moor or mountain slope or forest. That was why the west side of Britain was described by writers of the sixteenth century as enclosed country; they meant enclosed where used for agriculture; there was waste land enough. Tudor writers also treated as mainly 'enclosed' parts of Sussex, Surrey and Essex—forest enclosures these for the most part—sections of Suffolk and Norfolk, and Kent.

East Anglia and Kent stand apart from the rest of the country; Kent very much apart and that from the earliest times. From the sandy 'brecklands' of West Norfolk and Suffolk, which to-day Commissioners are turning into forest, villages round about took occasional 'brecks', as in Sherwood, long after 1500. This points to a primitive in- and outfield agriculture in earlier times. Elsewhere, on the better land, there was an arrangement less easy to describe, and in course of transformation from 1400 or earlier. Village, or rather parish, areas were large, manors small: one village, one manor was almost unknown. Arable land lay open, and the rotation of crops seems to have generally been three-course; but the field in the midland sense was not the important thing. The important thing was what was elsewhere its subdivision, the

[1] See above, pp. 50–1.

furlong, or *quarentina*.[1] There was no need for the tenant to have
half or a third of his land in each of two or three big fields. It
might be all in two or three adjacent furlongs. Indeed the
original holdings may have been either compact or made up
from groups of not widely separated strips. Legally, East
Anglian society was relatively free, in Domesday and later.
Free social conditions; the small manors that go with them;
a field system rather elastic because its unit, the furlong, is
small; all facilitated change; and as East Anglia was populous,
commercial and industrial, with an active market for land,
concentration of holdings in the fields, with perhaps actual
enclosure of what was concentrated, set in early. The records
do not yield quite a clear picture, but it is to something like
this that they point.

The failure of manor and village to coincide and the
existence of a market in land, leading to some concentration
of holdings, were not confined to East Anglia. In the North,
village and manor rarely coincided. In the Midlands, an
examination of many cases from the late thirteenth century
shows that the equation, manor = village, holds for less than one-
eighth of the villages examined in Cambridgeshire; for about
a quarter of those in Bedfordshire; for about half in Huntingdon,
Buckingham and Warwick; and for about two-thirds in Oxford.
This last may probably be taken as a maximum for any county,
and with the other facts quoted suggests that, for England as
a whole, the villages or parishes that were also manors were in
a minority in 1300; and so remained.

It is not only in East Anglia that a market in land and
changes in the map of village fields can be traced. Elsewhere,
change was no doubt slow, but it was continuous: at no stage
was medieval society really static. As soon as our documents
become abundant, that is in the thirteenth century, we note
a 'keen trade in land, buying and selling, leasing and exchanging, and the subdivision and consolidation of holdings'[2]
in the open-field villages of central England. The lord of a
manor, only exceptionally a whole village, may consolidate
his demesne by purchase or exchange of strips. He may let off
part of it, in strips or in a solid block. Free tenants can buy and
sell. The less free can get leave to exchange. The lord may

---

[1] This was also so in France, where there were open fields, but no two- or
three-field 'system': the unit was the *quarentina* (*quartier*).
[2] N. Neilson, in *The Cambridge Economic History of Europe*, vol. 1 (1941), p. 440.

acquire another manor in the village, whose strips—if it is a case of strips—may fit in with his; or whose demesne, already consolidated as it seems often to have been from very early times, lies conveniently near his own. Free men divide holdings among their children, as they legally may—less free men usually may not, but if they choose to get a living from the family holding for father, son and grandson, that is their affair.

As a result of all this, we can imagine from the documents and can see on the village maps when they begin to appear— but that is not before about 1600—irregularities that do not fit the neat diagrams of a village and its fields that have become familiar in text-books. There are blobs and blocks—a whole furlong perhaps in a single hand—and thick strips and thin strips. Except that every tenant who has to live by his holding must have about the same amount of land in each of the two or three fields, regularity may be greatly interfered with. There are, however, tenants, small folk, especially small free folk, who cannot so live, but yet have land—bits in the fields or perhaps bits enclosed, with or without leave, from waste ground outside the fields. There are the cottagers, who were there in Domesday times, and become more numerous as population grows faster than ploughed land. We shall return to them.[1] At this point our interest in them is that they make our imagined field maps more untidy.

Where there were no big set fields, untidiness was easier and greater—but we have fewer precise records to help us picture the result, as 'rodlands', and 'intakes', and 'assarts' increased about forest or moorland hamlets; or as bits of fen margin were dyked.

If East Anglia stands apart, Kent stands still more apart. So far as we can tell, Kentish fields had never looked much like those of other parts of England. It was a land of many hamlets and few big villages: the very word 'hamlet' occurs in the documents: *Wingham cum omnibus hamelettis suis* is a manorial headquarters with outlying dependencies. Kent's technical terms were different, before Domesday and after; its tenures were different; there were no hides in Kent in 1086. Kent kept its special form of inheritance, gavelkind, equal division among sons. The primitive standard holding seems to have been a compact *jugum*, yoke, 'often miles away from its neighbours or

[1] See below, p. 102.

from the central hall'.[1] And these 'yokes', when they can be traced, are apt to be roughly rectangular—which has led some historians to suspect Roman influence. They may be near one another, but they remain distinct, with the names of old owners—so-and-so's *jugum*. Division among heirs led to much cutting up of *jugera*; and by division and purchase a man might come to hold land in several of them. But they and their names are not forgotten. The manor is far from compact: the lord's fields are distinct scattered things, rather like the demesne fields of a South Welsh lordship. The hamlets of Wingham may be remote. The typical manor has still more remote detached woodland, a far-off dene in the Weald of Kent where another hamlet grows up—or detached and regularly divided 'doles' of grazing land in Romney Marsh.

Kentish cultivation and rotations were naturally various; but the three-course rotation was common. The land being fertile and well tilled, anything more primitive would not be expected. Indeed, on the demesnes of several Kentish manors in the fourteenth century, we learn that the fields can be cropped every year—'*possunt seminari quolibet anno*'—with what crops we are not told.

In Kent this repeated cropping was probably a mark of good management; in other places it might be a rather stupid primitive habit, the 'oats, oats, oats' of the Welsh Marches. Land not held under the village routine of the Midland open fields might be used well or ill, at its holder's discretion. Where, as in East Anglia, there was less compulsion than in the Midlands, variation would be easier. How far the routine remained binding in regular two- or three-field villages down to 1500 we do not know. We do know that in some places it had broken down by 1600, without any enclosure— just as it has broken down in the open fields of France and the still open fields of Epworth. The rotation might be two- or three-course, but it might go differently on different men's strips. And sometimes an extra crop might be got off a part of the fallow field.[2] When a section of the open fields had been consolidated, it might even be turned into grassland: we find such cases later. But, generally speaking, it seems that what was no doubt the primitive arrangement remained in force— the field all sown with winter corn, that sown with spring crops,

[1] J. E. A. Jolliffe, *Pre-feudal England; the Jutes* (1933), p. 7.
[2] See below, pp. 218–19.

that left fallow; though in two-field villages the proportion of
winter and spring sowings on the field cropped might well vary.
Any breakdown of routines that there may have been would
come late in these centuries, with the breakdown of manorial
control and the growing independence of all classes of tenants.

THE ENGLISH PEASANTRY IN THE TWELFTH AND THIRTEENTH CENTURIES

The Domesday classification of tenants had been simple and
arbitrary, in some places as arbitrary and inappropriate to local
conditions as the Domesday use of the word 'manor'. The
Domesday *villanus*, as has been seen,[1] is a fairly substantial
land-holding peasant, with two or three social grades below
him—'bordars' and 'cottars', not always easily distinguishable,
and slaves. There are *villani* in Kent as elsewhere. The sokemen
and freemen are above the *villani*, not necessarily more substantial, but enjoying certain privileges of property and person
which it is assumed that the *villani* lack. What happened
between 1100 and 1200 is obscure; but there is no reason to
think that there was much change in the holdings of individual
families in the different groups, though we can sometimes trace
—then and later—changes in the terms enforced by their lords
on which those holdings were held, increases of services
demanded and so on.

From Domesday onwards, there remained more freemen on
the east side of the country and in the North and North-West
than in the South and South-West. The northern part of the old
Danelaw—Lincolnshire, Nottinghamshire—was rich in freemen. It is there that we find quite humble peasants, freemen
and sokemen, in a position to give or bequeath land to
monasteries in the twelfth and thirteenth centuries. Nothing of
the sort is ever heard of in the more thoroughly 'feudalised'
territory of old Wessex—Hampshire, Berkshire, Wiltshire,
Dorset. These Danelaw freemen must have been very nearly in
the position of the modern freeholder, able to do what they
liked with their land, whereas the ordinary landholding freeman
of these centuries, though he had many privileges denied to his
humbler neighbours—though he could transmit his land to his
son or could subdivide it among his family and could throw it
up at will—was still his lord's man, a part of a manorial group

[1] See above, pp. 71–2.

though a privileged part, owing rent or service of some sort which the lord might lose if the freeman were able to transfer his land to the Church, but would retain if he merely bequeathed it or abandoned it. Twelfth- or thirteenth-century sokemen, we recall, were survivors of a class that had been much more numerous before the Conquest.[1] It is fairly clear from Domesday and some later records that many of them had been pushed down in the social scale between 1066 and 1200. Many said to have existed under Edward the Confessor have just dropped out by 1086—perhaps dead, perhaps degraded to a lower status. Degradation might continue. In 1275 some men who claim to be sokemen on the estates of the Abbot of Ramsey complain that a predecessor of his a century back had 'distrained their ancestors...to do ploughings and reapings...and other undue customs', as a result of which they were in danger of being confused with humbler, more servile, tenants.

What the Anglo-Norman lawyers did between 1100 and 1300 was to group all the rural populations, more simply and arbitrarily than Domesday had, under the headings of free or not free, *liber homo* and *villanus*. The term *servus* goes out of use, though the lawyers, having in the interval learnt some Roman law, now and then speak of *villani* as if they were *servi* in the Roman sense, and sometimes apply that term to them. The lawyers would be encouraged in this because the lower ranks of the classes that they lumped together as *villani* were certainly descended from men who were *servi* in Domesday. People did not forget their pedigrees in the twelfth century, and there would always be the oldest free inhabitant in the village who remembered very well, or had been told by his grandmother, that the ancestors of John Attewood, the shabby fellow whose hut was where his name tells, had been *servi*.

The most conclusive proof that the government of the thirteenth century did not regard *villani* as slaves comes from a writ of 1252 enforcing the Assize of Arms. Those who drafted the writ accepted the simple lawyer's division of society into freemen and *villani*, villeins; but they also mentioned the arms which the latter were to bear for the defence of the country. No true slave-owning society ever deliberately saw to it that the slaves should bear arms.

Again, lawyers said that villeins were, strictly speaking, the property of their lord. Their goods were his, goods which fell to

[1] See above, p. 73.

him at their death and had to be redeemed by a recognised payment, usually the 'best beast' on the holding. And yet, not only have we seen the *villani* of Willesden in Domesday making a bargain with the Canons of St Paul's to take over and run the demesne, at a time when *villanus* had not acquired its Anglo-Norman legal meaning,[1] but, two centuries later, when it had, it seems that the *villeins* of Brightwaltham in Berkshire—a part of England where freeholders were very rare—are being treated as a *communitas* which can hold land, can receive land, and can make a contract with its lord: it was about some woodland. 'Slaves' do not do that kind of thing.

Lawyers called all those below the line of freedom, not a very clearly drawn line as will appear, *villeins*. So did many of those who drafted the manorial surveys, court rolls, and other documents from which our knowledge comes. *Custumarii* is also a common word to describe these people, because the essence of a 'villein's' position was that he held his land not by any 'national' right or law—such a thing was not even conceived—but by the custom of the manor as interpreted in the lord's court. The term *nativi* is also applied to them, which seems to reflect conquering Norman arrogance. They are also called *bondi*, from the word which makes the second half of 'husband', and originally meant any cultivator or husbandman. The Scandinavian *bondi* had been, and remained, typical free cultivators; so it is not surprising that in the English North-East *bondi* might be free men. So for that matter might people called *villani*, sometimes.

The business of distinction between 'bond' and 'free' was very difficult, most difficult in the regions outside the Midland open-field belt. Within that belt, the lord or lords normally had his demesne, or their demesnes, mixed up to some extent with the holdings of their tenants. A favourite test of villein status was whether or not a man had to give so many days a week working for his lord, at the orders of his lord's agent. In open-field country with demesne, the work was wanted, was done in the fields where the tenant's own holding lay, was easily understood, and comparatively easily enforced. But if a lord had little demesne, or scattered bits of it, and if his tenants were also scattered, as they were in hamlet country and in all places where the 'manor' was a considerable tract of land, not a compact village or part of one, then week-work might

[1] See above, p. 53.

never have become customary, or might have been tried and proved a failure. One of the thirteenth-century agricultural writers warns his land-owning readers that 'customary tenants neglect their work'; they would; servile work is never willing. They would be all the more likely to neglect it if they were asked to trudge miles to do it on several days each week. It should be added that surviving records suggest that such experiments had seldom been tried.

Besides his week-work, the tenant in villeinage usually owed what was called boon-work, or some similar name in Latin, work done at his lord's request. That there was something voluntary about it, in theory and probably in origin, is proved by the usual obligation on the lord to feed his men when they do boon work. True, some of the 'boons' were 'hungry' boons; but our knowledge of how a medieval peasant fed comes largely from entries in manorial records of just what the lord had to supply. Whether the origin of the boon days was the lord's desire to get more work out of half-free people, as his demesne agriculture developed, we cannot say: the system goes very far back, both here and on the continent; but that is what it looks like. The explanation is the more probable because such work was never treated as legally degrading. Men fully free might participate in it, and regularly did. It was normally emergency work at busy seasons of the year—hay-cutting, harvesting, sheep-shearing, sheep-washing, and the like. How popular it may have been in England would depend on local customs about boon-day food and drink. It lies at the back of harvest-homes and similar idealised rural festivities. There are, however, in German economic history, authentic instances from later centuries of peasants who declined to be relieved of 'boon-days' because the traditional bill of fare was so generous that even a German peasant could eat his fill and carry something home.

As 'bond' and free might share in such work, the difficulty of differentiating between the classes was increased. It became hardest where the local agricultural conditions did not lend themselves to week-work. On some Cheshire manors, for example, the services that *nativi* owe are those of swine-herd or bee-keeper or parker. On others they owe certain days' ploughing in the course of the year, sometimes with their own oxen, sometimes with their lord's. Services of this kind, few and precise, could be arranged for in advance, and were never in themselves a sign of servitude. No regular week-work has been traced in Cheshire; but the men quoted were labelled *nativi* by other tests. They paid a stiff *merchet* when a daughter married off the manor, thus recognising that they and their brood (*sequela*), as the elegant legal term was, belonged to that manor. They also paid *leyrwite*, the fine for a daughter's misconduct, more or less on the same principle: the stock of the manor must breed true. Their goods fell to the lord at death, and had to be redeemed with a best beast by the heir, if there was an heir.

In Kent again there was no week-work. Kentish services consisted in specified jobs to be done or days' work to be put in during the year, especially carting. The forest denes and the marshland doles, remote from the headquarters of the manor, made carting work specially important in Kent, and the requirement of it was heavy.

Villeinage has to be distinguished from villein tenure. The former applied to the person, the latter to the land. It could be proved that you and your forbears had been *villani*, *nativi*, *bondi*. It could also be proved that a particular holding had 'always' been liable to the services and obligations of villeinage. But if a freeman took it that did not make him a *villanus*: he merely took over the obligation to play the villein game, so to speak, in respect of those particular acres. Similarly a proved *villanus* might take a bit of free land without thereby becoming a freeman. This situation, as revealed in the records of the thirteenth century, tended to blur the lines between freedom and villeinage, the economic line especially. And if the economic line was blurred, the legal line was far from clear: for its very basis was the varying customs of various manors. What was held to make a man a *villanus* in Sampford Courtenay, Devon; at Paddington, or at Hitchin? The King's courts were always worrying about this when asked to send out one or other of the writs bearing on the issue, the writ *de nativo habendo*, to the man who claimed the disputed body as his, and the writ *de libertate probanda* for the one who claimed freedom.

If you or your holding had any unquestionably free features, these might outweigh obligations which usually implied villeinage. Sometimes we get freemen doing week-work, usually regarded as a test of villeinage. The obligation to pay *merchet* was, as a rule, a safe test. So was the obligation to pay your lord *tallage*, a tax at his arbitrary will, to be *taillable à volonté* as the French said. Yet there is a case, or perhaps cases, in which a man who was obliged to make both payments was declared free, because—he could throw up his holding when he pleased, a very free course open to no true villein.

A true villein may not throw up his holding, but he or his son who sees no prospect on the manor may pay for leave to live away from it. There is no commoner type of entry in manor court rolls than this, from the rolls of Ramsey Abbey—'they [the jurors] say as they have said before that Simon Cadman dwells at Godmanchester, but pays two capons a year. And Henry Henry's son dwells at Stanton, but pays one fowl'. If Simon Cadman's son drifts out of Godmanchester, who will hunt down the capons presumably due from him?

The payments of *tallage* and *leyrwite* and *merchet* show that so far back as our full records go, and much further, as pre-Conquest records suggest, there was always money circulating in the manor. You might pay dues in capons, but you often paid in cash. There were all kinds of 'rents', not commercial rents but customary dues, whose details and origins are often obscure, paid in money as well as in kind. You may pay to secure occupation of a villein holding when the old occupying family has died out. The obligation to pay tallage at your lord's will may become fixed at a known customary figure in money. Some ancient customary food-rent, that oldest of obligations so common in Celtic society, may become payable in cash. Or, most common and best known of all, the lord or his agent may put a money value on your services owed—so much a day. This valuation of the services, which begins early, need not imply a bargain for permanent freedom of the tenant from his liability. The lord may find that he has more services due than he needs: cash he always needs or at least likes. He may take it this year, but find that he needs the labour next year. Yet, if he has gone on taking it for a long term of years, it may easily become part of the custom of the manor. And if he agrees with his expert literary adviser that 'customary tenants neglect their work', he may go over, more or less completely, to hired labour for his regular work, retaining some of those ploughing or harvest or carting services which need not label the worker as servile, though they may have a servile origin. By the close of the thirteenth century, lords everywhere are receiving more from their tenants by way of 'rents'—in money or in kind; from villeins or from freemen—than by way of services. The proportion, it has been estimated from sample groups of villages in various regions, varies from a maximum of 40 per cent services to a minimum of below 10 per cent; this last in Yorkshire and the North generally, where demesne agriculture had never been fully developed and regular services were not often organised. It is noticeable that, in this last group, a great number of the rents are paid in kind; the lords are not cultivating much demesne, but in the rougher society of the North, where corn-marketing is imperfectly developed, the lord still wants food for his establishment. Elsewhere, if he does not get the food by working his demesne with hired labour, he can often buy what he needs with his 'rents' and other cash receipts.

One important source of receipts was the fines levied in manorial courts. It is from the records of these courts that we get the most human insight into thirteenth-century village life, mainly amongst villeins; for it was over them that the lord's court had complete control. We also get evidence of the lord's takings in fines. Thus: 'from the whole [servile] township of Little Ogbourne [near Marlborough] for not coming to wash the lord's sheep, 6s. 8d.'; 'the following women have been violated and therefore must pay leyrwite' [in Norfolk]; 'Walter Hulle gives 13s. 4d. for licence to dwell [off the manor]...so long as he shall live...' [Ruislip, Middlesex: a stiff payment; perhaps Walter was going to London]; 'the wife of Gilbert Vicar's son [and someone else]...unlawfully struck Hugh of Stanbridge and dragged him by his hair out of his own proper house, to his damage 40s. and to his dishonour 20s.'. [Did Hugh get any of the fine?] People are fined for neglecting works due in autumn, for letting a daughter trespass in the corn, for not grinding at the lord's mill, for diverting a watercourse, for paying in bad money, for delay in doing their works. The court deals with minor criminal offences like the assault on Hugh, or like this one—'Alice wife of John Bert in evil manner took a sheet that was hanging on the hedge of William Roger's son and thereof made herself a shirt' (*unam camisiam*). And there is an almost routine fining of the ale-wives, in a great many manors, because they have broken the King's 'assize of beer'; we are not told how. Presumably they could sell their ale at prices to cover this recurrent fine, or they might have kept the assize.

The narrowness and haziness of the line between 'bond' and free in thirteenth-century England, apparent to the modern economist, was recognised by the lawyers of the day, as is shown by the endless cases about the side of the line on which a man was to be put. Once that man had been so put, the lawyer was clear; and his placing on the wrong side entailed some precise, and rather weighty, economic disabilities. But still he might be, and often was, a much more substantial person, economically, than many a man above him in legal status. A villein, we know, might hire another villein to work for him at a wage; there is no recorded rule that would prevent his hiring a freeman. This haziness of the dividing line was fully recognised in the social relations of the villagers. There was constant intermarriage across the line, and a whole series of law cases decided how the children of these 'mixed' marriages were to be graded. We even hear of a lord of the manor's son marrying a villein's daughter, as the squire's son in the ballad married the bailiff's daughter of Islington; but we hear of only one. It is in places where freemen and villeins are living, in fair numbers, side by side, that the haziness of the line of division is most obvious. But even in places where there was little or nothing but villeinage it is apparent. Such places include, for example, the Wessex manors of the Bishop of Winchester and the southern group of the manors belonging to the great Norman abbey of Bec—whose court rolls of 1246 are the oldest we have.

In an all-villein manor there will be a great number of fair-sized holdings—perhaps of twenty-four or thirty acres. The lord sees to it that they are not broken up, a policy both in his interest and in that of the tenants. It is the standard holding, the *virgate* as it is perhaps most often called, that owes the services and obligations and rents: the holding must not be atomised. How many people choose to live on it is their affair. If the right number of days' work is made up, it does not matter whether villein *père* or villein *fils*, or a man hired by villein *père*, reports for labour. Life is unhealthy and big adult families are few; but as population is growing under King Henry III, outlets for some villein sons will be required. They may work for hire on the manor, or they may pay for leave to work elsewhere. As has been seen, a capon or two a year or a hen might buy such leave. Runaway villeins are heard of: they are sometimes apprehended and brought into court. Perhaps they came from among the humbler grades or from those who had fallen into bad ways: it can hardly be supposed that the substantial villein's younger son would prefer the risks of the runaway to the price of an annual hen.

It was a Berkshire manor of villeins whose *communitas* made that contract with its lord about the woodlands[1] which, as Maitland wrote, would have shocked the Westminster lawyers, with their doctrine of the villein's lack of rights against his lord, and their knowledge of the servile law of Rome. For a man to make contracts with his own 'property' is most irregular. Little Ogbourne, a manor of Bec, was such another all-villein village, where the 'whole township', in 1247, was fined 6s. 8d. for not coming to wash the Abbey's Ogbourne sheep. (How did they get washed? Was the township fined and then obliged to wash? Or was hired labour called in? We are not told.) The fine was about the price of a quarter and a half of wheat or the equivalent of sixteen days' harvest-work pay, which seems very little when spread over perhaps as many villein households, perhaps more, who had neglected an obvious and important duty: Ogbourne is under the Marlborough Downs, where flocks were big and valuable. The Middlesex villein who paid 13s. 4d. to quit the manor was paying a fee for life, a capitalised yearly hen so to speak. Even so, these villeins of Ogbourne who only paid half that for their collective offence do not read like down-trodden serfs: they are not beaten for neglect, and it looks as if they could bargain about it.

How substantial a villein family might be, and how persistent, is shown by the story of a villein woman called Maud under King John. She was able to go to law for over ten years, not to prove that she was not a *neave* (*nativa*) but to prove that she was not the *neave* of a man who had ill-treated her. She said he had sold her to someone else. Maud must have been what Chaucer called an 'arch-wife'.

To see the freeman-villein dividing line at its haziest we must move eastward or northward from Wiltshire and Berkshire into country in which freemen were numerous; in which there was even here and there a village where everyone was free. Take the manor of Barham in Cambridgeshire in 1279. It is not in an abnormally free district, though it is ahead of its neighbours economically: there are fairs in the adjacent village of Linton and a little industrial life. But Barham was an open-field village of the regular midland type and was not

[1] See above, p. 95.

enclosed until the nineteenth century: it had inherited all the social and economic features of such a village, though modified by the presence of an unusual number of craftsmen. Among the free are several obvious cultivators, holding thirty-two acres each; another with twenty; another with sixteen. But cottagers predominate, their number being swelled by the smiths, potters, tanners and other craftsmen for whom free land has been cut up into bits. Smallest of all was the free holding of Melicia William's daughter, a cottage thirteen by sixteen feet. There are five customary tenants each holding thirty-two acres like the leading freemen, and owing 'works' and hens and eggs and carrying services. There are also three sixteen-acre customary men and nine eight-acre; and a very interesting group at the bottom of society who hold only an acre each but owe heavy works and services. The eight-acre men's services are also heavy. Service is not in any way proportionate to the size of the holding. Pressure increased as you went down the social-economic scale; and it can hardly be doubted that these men at the bottom were descendants of true *servi*, of whom there had been an unusually large number in the manor at the time of the Domesday inquest.

There are other customary tenants with small holdings—eight and five acres—besides these single-acre cottagers. Among them are Ida Carle and Matilda Freelond, both surnames suggesting a free pedigree. Perhaps they both had one, but were obliged to take 'customary' land for lack of anything better: any free land there was in the family would go to sons.

Such is the social and economic jumble as it has developed in this mixed manor. Most sizable holdings are held in villeinage; some are held freely. Holdings of all sizes are found in both classes, with, at the bottom, a few overdriven villein cottagers, but more free cottagers—some of whom however are 'in trade'. Leticia the ale-wife, for example, had a free messuage of a quarter of a rood: she also had *unam shoppam* in the adjacent street of Linton. There was a weaver also and a salter. But there were free cottagers enough outside trade to provide, with the small-holding villeins and other villeins' sons, any wage labour on the land that might be demanded. The fact that many free holdings were small, and that free land was more easily divided than customary land, renders it probable, almost demonstrable, that wage labour was largely recruited among freemen and their sons—at least on the east side of the country.

AGRICULTURE AND RURAL SOCIETY IN SCOTLAND

About Scottish agriculture during these centuries it is not possible to write precisely, and about Scottish tenures even there is grave uncertainty. Scotland has no Domesday Book, no surviving wealth of royal, ecclesiastical and manorial records comparable with that of England. Of Scottish agriculture there are no exact accounts before the eighteenth century; but then much of it bears that primitive stamp which no doubt had marked it from the beginning. The medieval Highlander was a cattle-man: he lifted his neighbour's cattle or sometimes traded his own cattle for corn. What agriculture he practised was subordinate, rough, and primitive. In the Lowlands, there must have been early forms of that in- and outfield agriculture, about little clachans—groups of cottage huts—that later accounts describe.[1] What there certainly was not, was the big village with its 'midland' open fields and demesne services.

As to tenures, the Scotto-Norman feudal lords of the twelfth and thirteenth centuries—Bruce, de Moreville, Comyn—established a very complete control over their lands and their tenants, but did not introduce any true close-knit manorial system. The country did not lend itself to that, any more than Cheshire or Lancashire did. From old Gaelic custom they could take over three obligations of the tenant—to fight for his lord, to feed him when he came that way, and to pay him a rent in food. From the food rents there survived into modern times those 'cain hens' that tenants paid their lords yearly.

There was certainly slavery or serfdom among all the primitive constituent elements of the Scottish people—Celtic, Anglian, Scandinavian. Traces of it are frequent in the few surviving twelfth- and thirteenth-century records, and occasionally later. There are buyings and sellings of people called *nativi* and *bondi*; but when the Prior of Coldingham in Berwickshire buys 'Turkil Hog and his sons and daughters' for three marks, it may not be the pure slave-market transaction that the words suggest: he may have been buying the holding of the Hog family, and them with it, just as an English lord might buy a manor and its villeins. Of a developed lawyers' doctrine of villeinage there is no trace in Scotland; nor do we meet the word 'manor'. When the laws speak of the people who till the

[1] See above, p. 48.

land they are 'vague and contradictory'.[1] They speak of *nativi* and *bondi* and *rustici*; also of *husbandmen, uplandismen* and *carles.* An Anglian *carl* had been a freeman and so had a Scandinavian *bonde.* A rustic or an uplandsman or native may be anything. You need an explanatory context, and that we have not got.

What emerges rather indistinctly in the fourteenth and fifteenth centuries is a population the mass of whom are regarded as freemen, but whether in Highland clan or Lowland lordship very much their lords' men. The land that they hold is very much his land: 'they were able', it has been said, 'to acquire no claim to it'.[2] Without exception, they were tenants or subtenants; and whether a Scots tenant's tenant was happier than an average English villein who shall say? He was certainly poorer. These tenants might owe food rents, or remnants of them. If the lord had accessible land of his own to be cultivated—the lords were great wanderers and clachans lay far apart—they might owe 'arriages', as later Scots law called them, ploughing and other agricultural services. They were very likely to owe 'carriages', carting services. The lord might have a mill which they ought to frequent. But similar liabilities might lie on freemen in England. What Scotland lacked, to her great advantage, was week-work that had to be commuted—she lacked this because of the lay-out of her land— and a theory of villeinage that had to be whittled away by judicial decision or royal action, as it was in England. What she retained, to her disadvantage, was the political and economic power of barons who were usually stronger than the crown, with—for example—a very absolute control over commons and waste land. However, they wanted men about them who would turn out to fight readily, and would fight well. Such men, whether along the Highland Line or the Border or in Afghanistan, must feel free. In all these matters, it may be added, conditions did not differ greatly on the English side of the Border, in Northumberland and Cumberland. Percy and Douglas were very much alike.

[1] Miss I. F. Grant, *The Social and Economic Development of Scotland before 1603* (1930), p. 75.
[2] *Ibid.* p. 79.

ENGLAND: AGRICULTURE FOR THE MARKET;
MONEY, WAGES AND PRICES BEFORE 1300

By the time of the three Edwards the government of England was more consciously interested in wool than in any other product of English agriculture. Wool entered into diplomacy; wool was a leading source of revenue; wool exported brought 'foreign exchange'—the right to receive money abroad that you could spend on a campaign or a royal meeting. Britain had always been good for sheep—temperate, moist, with open chalk or limestone downs and grasslands, and heather moors fit for grazing. Very early, the place of sheep on the arable had been recognised. 'Little Domesday Book', that covers the counties of East Anglia, contains many references to 'fold-soke', the obligation to fold your sheep on the lord's land. The practice, which must have been old, is based on a recognition of the manurial value of sheep droppings for corn crops.

Wool was exported before the Norman Conquest. A natural exchange was growing up with the young manufacturing cities of Flanders, a sodden land good for cattle and geese—the first polders enclosed from the sea were used as goose greens— not so good for sheep, mountain beasts originally, and very liable to rot on sodden land. The first generation of Anglo-Norman lords sometimes turned their greedy and calculating minds to sheep-farming, as the entries of Little Domesday show. Though an entry such as that for Forncett in Norfolk is rare—'then [i.e. before the Conquest] there was 1 sheep, now there are 80'—if we may argue from East Anglia to the rest of the country, for which sheep returns do not exist, the Conquest was followed at once by some increase in the flocks.

The greater lords, and the thinly settled districts, become very important in the history of the flocks; but there were sheep everywhere—in regions mainly arable and in those specially suited to grazing. Where hamlets predominated over villages and there was plenty of waste ground—as in Sherwood —the typical peasant's holding of ploughland tended to be small, because he had special opportunities for his sheep and cattle. In the regular organised two- or three-field village, the village flock was part of the corn-growing routine—though it had of course its independent value for meat and wool. In one region of Wiltshire, for which figures from 1225 have survived, more than half the tenants owned sheep. Among such villages, especially when they were near open downs as at Ogbourne, there grew up great landlords' flocks, based not on a single village but on a group of villages or manors. Separate flocks might be based on the various manors—breeding ewes on one, hoggets (yearlings) on another, wethers on a third; but the organisation of the whole mass of sheep was based on the estate, not on the manor; and the shepherds—most important men, and free—were, in modern language, estate employees. The accounts were kept for the whole estate—the Bishop of Winchester in 1259 on his great groups of manors mainly in Hampshire kept about 29,000 sheep, in a number of localised flocks. Half a century later, another Winchester religious authority, the Priory of St Swithin's, had 20,000. At the same time the Abbots of Crowland had a central headquarters, from which sheep were despatched to the various manors; at this headquarters a general account was kept and the wool was stored for sale.

It was in the thinly peopled hill districts, however, that care of the flocks was most completely divorced from manorial organisation, to become a matter for the estate authorities. When, from 1128 onwards, the Cistercian monks began to set up houses in Britain, they went west and north, partly because the best sites in the South—in Kent, say, or in Hampshire— were already in ecclesiastical hands, partly because they were by profession pioneers with a hankering after virgin sites, *novalia*. And so, about their houses—Tintern or Kirkstall, Rievaulx or Melrose—in regions that had never been close settled, and some of which the Conqueror had harried, their sheep-runs grew up, served from scattered granges with no systematic village connections.

Other monastic orders and lay lords did the same in the North, in the Welsh Marches—whence came the famous Herefordshire Ryelands sheep—and in other grazing districts. The nuns of the Holy Trinity at Caen—endowed with English land—had 1700 sheep on Minchinhampton Common before the first Cistercian house was founded. Greatest of all, and most completely outside manor or village routine, were some of the operations of the Duchy of Lancaster, which, early in the fourteenth century, owned immense estates all over England, from the South Downs to Lincolnshire, from Pickering to Pontefract. Many of these were in good sheep country. In Sussex and Lincolnshire the flocks were run on a village basis, under the lord's reeve; but in the North things were different. The extreme case was the Peak of Derbyshire where 'the stock-keeper [an estate official] had the disposal of huge pastures, a sort of ranch, on which he kept 5500 sheep'.[1] As a great part of the wool was sold for export, important producers and producing groups all over the country were brought early into indirect touch with the commercial and industrial capitalism of Flanders and Italy, the main buyers. The Duchy, the great lords, the great religious houses, were themselves agrarian capitalists—'rich men furnished with ability', not labouring with their hands, calculating carefully their gains, hiring wage-labour. There can have been few villages in the country whose inhabitants had not some notion, no doubt often vague, about the place of wool in national or international trade. The wool-buyer, native or alien, was known far and wide.

He might deal not only with the agent of an agrarian capitalist but also with a well-to-do peasant or group of peasants, 'villeins' very likely. No doubt the wool of the peasant's sheep went first to make the peasant's clothes, or for his wife to spin and sell as yarn: but peasant flocks, when we can trace them in the thirteenth century, were often so big that much of the wool must have gone to market: later they became still bigger. At Swyncombe near Wallingford in 1275 each of the ten villein tenants—there were also eleven cottagers—had only eight acres of arable, but with them free grazing for fifty sheep on the common pasture: there are good chalk downs above Swyncombe. With eight acres and fifty sheep a man's economic position is not too bad, whatever the lawyers say. Fifty years earlier, on the estates of three religious houses in South Wiltshire, well over half the tenants owned sheep —in one big village an average of nearly twenty each. Again and again on these estates the tenants' flock was much bigger than the lord's: it is good grazing country.

If the working peasant of the twelfth and thirteenth centuries —free or 'villein'—was more likely to sell wool than anything else, and if in out-of-the-way places he had little chance of selling anything, the general ability of such a man to make a few money payments was no new thing. There was no doubt a little buying and selling inside village society: the ale-wives were retailers and the price of beer a matter of public interest.

[1] E. E. Power, *The Wool Trade in English Medieval History* (1941), p. 28.

That lords sold the produce of their demesnes freely in the thirteenth century is now well established: we have evidence for it from the twelfth. To whom could they or peasants with little surpluses sell? Sometimes no doubt to men of a woodland or fenland or barren village near by. Where a town was near, to the townsmen. Though towns were small and had their own fields, there is no reason to think that they were often, if ever, quite self-sufficient. The bigger towns, the Londons, Norwiches, Yorks, certainly had a permanent demand strong enough to affect the life of neighbouring villages deeply. Then, as has been seen in the case of Christ Church Canterbury,[1] big monastic communities, and no doubt great noble households, might be substantial buyers. There was a certain amount of export demand locally for corn and cheese and beer and hides. And there was the King—a buyer for his households and on a larger scale for his campaigns, especially when he was campaigning in poor country. In 1277, for example, Edward I, campaigning in North Wales, sent corn buyers out into eight counties, and his army contractors also brought it for him from Ireland by sea. For land transport, religious houses in the eight counties were asked to lend their carts. Presumably the King's buyers would go to such agricultural capitalists first; they could most easily make bulk purchases on demesnes. To whom they went we are not told; but as some of the counties visited had not a very well-developed demesne agriculture, the surpluses of small men may well have been drawn upon.

There was a steady military and civil demand for hides and leather. As Tanner and Barker were surnames well before 1300, and that in small places, it is evident that when the fairly substantial peasant killed off an old plough-ox or one of his sheep, a money transaction would result; he would not do his own tanning, as the Highlander did centuries later, unless he lived in some very out-of-the-way place. Wages had long been paid in money or partly in money; and there were some wage-earners more or less everywhere. So, in these various ways, cash came into the pouches of even the humblest folk— to go out in court fines and customary rents, and to the ale-wife; to the priest on certain occasions; to buy a knife or a spade; and, if a man were ambitious and rising, as commutation for manorial services that no longer suited either him or his lord.

[1] See above, p. 81.

A word about this money that circulated with comparative freedom among villagers as well as townsmen, and was well known everywhere. The silver penny changed very little in its metal content from the Norman Conquest until after 1300. Its weight was rather uncertain even when new, for minting technique was primitive. It got clipped and worn in circulation. But when new it kept near to 22½ grains troy weight—that table in which the 'pennyweight' is 24 grains. For 250 years and more, we are dealing with a more or less uniform coin. In the reign of Edward I, for which facts are fairly plentiful, an unskilled country worker—a thatcher's mate, usually a woman—earned about one of these pennies a day; skilled men, carpenters and masons, might have 3*d*. or 4*d*. For reaping, binding and stooking an acre of wheat a man could get 5*d*. With his wife to bind, a good man might do this in a long harvest day.

About the 'purchasing power' of that penny—in 1300, or 1200, or 1100—it is wise to write cautiously. There were so many things that it could not buy—tea, sugar, tobacco, coffee, bitter beer. What it could buy was often not the same as its modern equivalent: a pound of beef from an old plough-ox would to-day rank only for dog's meat. Some things were very dear and some were very cheap. A whole day of unskilled labour would buy only about thirty strong iron nails ('boardnails' as opposed to 'lath nails'). Wood for fires could in most places be had for the taking. Wheat, the article about whose prices we know most, was not generally eaten pure by common men.

So changes in prices in relation to earnings cannot be made exact. Besides, the further back we go the fewer people do we find living by wages alone: under Edward I there were few; under King John or Henry I very few indeed. What mattered on the average was not the purchasing power of a wage but the yield of some wretched little holding—whether there was or was not famine, or a murrain among the cattle. Rising prices were good for the peasant who could take some surplus to market, bad for the man who had to buy; but the men who had to buy everything were a small minority.

Prices were far from stable, either over long periods or from year to year. And they were very local: you could have famine on one side of the country and plenty on another. Average prices were certainly rising from 1150 to 1300. Between the first half of the thirteenth and the first half of the fourteenth century, wheat rose by about 50 per cent; rye not quite so much; but all food prices rose. With 1*d*. the thatcher's mate of, say, 1290 could nearly buy a hen—price 1¼*d*. But what size and sort of hen? He or she could buy quite a lot of eggs—thirty or forty in the laying season. (About 1900 a countryman who was getting 2*s*. a day could also buy forty with his day's wage.) The thatcher's mate could also buy three or four pigeons and about 2 lb. of cheese. A fat pig cost about 3*s*., or six weeks' wages, which strikes one as dear. None of these facts should be pressed. We never know whether or not the day's pay had to keep a family. For a single worker, the terms are not too bad: the penny would purchase a fair supply of such things as were in the market.

CHANGES IN ENGLISH AGRICULTURE AFTER 1300

Between 1300 and 1500 there were important changes in rural life and society which must be discussed before anything more is said about money and prices. These changes the economist sees rather differently from the lawyer or the historian of liberty. Like the lawyer, he notes that in 1300 certainly the majority of countrymen were graded as villeins; by 1500 only a small minority were in any real sense servile. He is, however, more interested to note that, both as a cause and a result of this change, the 'classical' system of demesne agriculture, in which most, or much, of the work on the lord's land was done by tenants in villeinage, was by 1500 all but extinct; though such things as harvest services were more persistent. The 'classical' system had long been declining. Even in the thirteenth century, as has been seen, experts were advising lords that customary labour was unsatisfactory.[1] So far back as Domesday, we have met a case of the leasing of the whole demesne by clerical lords.[2] Later, we have met regions and estates in which there was no 'classical' demesne and no labour services to till it.[3] We have also seen, but as in a mirror darkly, some consolidation of demesne and of other holdings in open fields.[4]

A statistical enquiry covering the years 1332–42, before the Great Pestilence, found few services being rendered, beyond

[1] See above, p. 96.   [2] See above, p. 53.
[3] See, for example, pp. 82, 87 above.   [4] See above, pp. 90–1.

a certain amount of ploughing and some seasonal works, on any one of 212 manors in the North, North-West and the western Midlands. Many of these were outside the true open-field area, in regions where—as farther north in Scotland—the 'classical' system had never existed; in others the demesne had apparently been leased out. In the 'Englishry' of South Wales also, the few acres of demesne had usually been leased to the tenants by 1300: in the 'Welshry' there was no regular demesne. On the other hand, in England, south and south-east of a line running from Gloucester to Boston, on about one-sixth of more than 300 manors studied for the decade 1332–42, full services were still being rendered, and substantial services on nearly another one-third; but in Kent there were none, although so much of Kent was owned by the Church. 'Although', because in the country as a whole the clergy were conservative land-lords, and not infrequently controlled whole villages. The Bishop of Winchester, on his wide estates in Wessex, where village and manor often coincided, had no single manor in 1349 on which all labour services had been commuted for money payments. There had been commutation, plenty of it; but it was nowhere systematic or complete.

It is interesting to notice that by that time there had grown up, partly as a result of this decline in customary services, and partly, it may be assumed, as a result of the bringing of more land under cultivation, an important demand for migratory labour in harvest time. After the Pestilence the Statute of Labourers tried to keep labour on the land, where it was badly needed, by forbidding movement from place to place. But a significant exception was made. Harvesters might move to where they were wanted from the Scottish and Welsh Marches; from Craven (the Yorkshire Dales); from Lancashire; from Derby-shire and from Staffordshire. There was evidently surplus labour in these poor regions where three-field agriculture was little practised and where there had never been much demand for services on demesnes. It is equally evident that migration of harvesters was not a new thing and that important people in Parliament understood its economic value; otherwise it would never have got on to the Statute Book.

Commutation of his services no more made a man legally free than the rendering of services not counted degrading made him servile. The medieval English freeholder normally did something for his lord, or owed him some kind of rent; the medieval Scottish freeman normally did a great deal. But by 1500 English freeholders' occasional services had mostly faded out; though in Tudor times the lord could usually claim a small money-rent from the freeholder, sometimes a relief when his land was sold or passed at death, occasionally even a heriot from his heir. There had grown up also in the English North, where the full manorial system was so imperfectly developed, a tenure which came to be known later as customary freehold— customary because it had some of the features, and in its original form the occasional services, of villeinage; freehold, because no one doubted that these north-countrymen were free. The system closely resembled that which the end of the Middle Ages found established in Scotland, except that in Scotland, with a weak crown and weak royal courts, the Lowland lord had his men and land more effectively under control than Percy or Dacre or even Warwick the Kingmaker had farther south. In the Highlands, chieftains retained, down to the eighteenth century, the effective heritable jurisdiction over their clans that made their position so strong, economically as well as socially and politically.

Though the agricultural side of the manorial system was little developed north of Trent, at least one feature of the system survived to trouble even the nineteenth century—the monopoly of manorial water-mills, leased to millers who as might be expected were highly unpopular.

The mere absence of demesne and regular demesne services did not of itself put an end to villeinage as a legal status, though it tended to undermine it. In fourteenth-century Cheshire, for instance, where we hear of no week-work, the lords kept the villeins very much 'in their place', and saw to it that they carried out all their carting and other obligations with strict fidelity. So it might be elsewhere; yet week-work had been so regular a test of villeinage that where, having once been normal, it declined, the whole legal and economic system of which it had been part was weakened. It had already been much weakened by the distinction between villein tenure and villein status.[1] There was something odd and contradictory in a freeman holding land, as he constantly might, on terms which suggested that its holder was not free; that, for example, he might be turned out at will without compensation, and that his son owed a best beast if he wished to hold it after his father's death.

[1] See above, p. 97.

The system had been rendered workable because a medieval lord was seldom tempted to evict: his men were the most valuable part of his manor. They were supposed to hold at his will, but if they faithfully carried out all the custom of the manor for generations, they naturally felt that the land was theirs. At dates which we cannot fix some of them acquired copies of the manor rolls, in which the customs and their services were set out. Even in the fourteenth century we meet references to these copies; in the lawyers' French of 1368 a court finds '*que ledit J. tient...le terre del Prior per copy de court roll*', but '*a volunte le Prior*', at the Prior's will.[1] Then, fair-minded lawyers begin to ask—if a tenant has kept the rules, of which he has a statement, should not his tenure be safe and respected? From 1439 the Court of Chancery, the place in which new equitable decisions were made to meet new situations, began to say that it should. And from 1467 similar protection began to be offered by the more conservative Court of King's Bench. These did not make the copyholder, as he came to be called, a proprietor: there was more than one way of getting him out of his holding, as the Tudor age was to show,[2] and in early Tudor times copyholder was described as 'but a new-found term'. But it greatly strengthened his position.

It would be a mistake to think that by 1500 or even by 1550 all land that had been held by customary tenure, villein tenure, had become copyhold as a result of these decisions. The *custumarius sine copia* was common enough under Henry VIII. And although customary tenure tended more and more to be distinct from villein status, and villein status to fade away when it lost its economic meaning, there were men—perhaps not very many—in Tudor England who, in the eye of the law, were as servile as an Anglo-Norman lawyer had ever maintained that their ancestors were. St Mary had 215 families of bondmen on her Glastonbury lands in 1533.[3] In practice villein status under the Tudors seems generally to have meant that the villeins' lord or his agent could get money out of them by threatening to enforce his almost obsolete and obnoxious rights. The situation was repeated in France before the Revolution, when some of the few remaining legal serfs, *mainmortables*

---

[1] Sir William S. Holdsworth, *A History of English Law*, vol. III (1923), p. 206, n. 3.
[2] See below, pp. 204–5.   [3] See also below, p. 202.

as they were called, who might be priests or doctors, were subject to similar financial pressure.

When a lord ceased to cultivate his demesne with the aid of 'customary' services he might use wage-labour, or he might abandon cultivation altogether and let the demesne to a tenant or tenants. There was probably more letting done before 1300 than we know about. After 1300, and particularly after the Black Death, it became increasingly common. We sometimes hear, just after the Pestilence, of a letting to the 'whole homage', the tenants as a community. But that was rare and never became general. It was easier to lease the demesne in sections to a tenant or tenants. For a time the leasing of the stock with the land was a rather widespread way of meeting the tenant's lack of working capital; but it would seem that tenants as a class were gradually able to replace the original stock with beasts and implements of their own. Certainly the so-called stock-and-land lease had ceased to be a characteristic of English rural life by 1500, or rather later; though it survived here and there to suit special circumstances. As a result, the system known in America as share-tenancy, in Italy as *mezzadrìa*, in France as *métayage*, and in German lands as *Theilbau*, the system in which the lord provides with the land a share of the stock and the seed and so on, was never acclimatised here.

The frequent occurrence in modern English villages of something called 'the manor farm' illustrates the way the demesne was most often farmed out—intact; though by no means all manor farms go back to the years before 1500. A likely tenant was the headman of the manor, the reeve. The original reeves—we have met them in Anglo-Saxon England[1] —appear to have been servile or semi-servile men set over other servile folk. After the Conquest they were normally villeins; they could be nothing else in all-villein villages. Sometimes the lords nominated them, sometimes the men chose them. They might not be popular, but they tended to be strong and masterful, as Chaucer's reeve was. Where, as so often, there were several lords in a parish, the reeves, meeting to discuss local agricultural business, must have formed a powerful governing group, with their masters' authority behind them. But we have no records from such groups.

Above the reeve, a rich lord would have a bailiff to watch

---

[1] See above, pp. 45–6.

over a group of manors. Far above, a very rich lord—earl or bishop or great monastery—would have an estate council. But these are more constitutional than strictly economic matters.

By about 1300 at latest, the reeves had often become permanent or semi-permanent officials; and, as always in medieval society, permanency was apt to produce hereditary succession. A reeve of servile blood was in a strong position to shake off his servility: he could get rid of his services, take over free land, procure a copy of court roll. In time his origins would be forgotten. It was somewhat in this fashion that the Pepiz family of Cottenham, Cambridgeshire, the ancestors of Samuel Pepys, worked their way up from reeves into farmers of free or copyhold land. Such people, familiar with the village, its fields and its court rolls, and with a 'pull', would be among the first to bid for the demesne, or parts of it, when leasing began.

By the middle of the fourteenth century, the time of the Pestilence, the old freeholder class had gone two different ways. Division and subdivision of holdings had driven many of them to wage-labour, to the cities perhaps, or to some industrial occupation in village or market-town. A surprising number of industrial workers are found scattered over the villages before 1350. Not only carpenters, smiths, saddlers, thatchers, carters, as we should expect; but fullers, dyers, soapmakers, tanners, needlers, brasiers, and many more. From the small freeholders were recruited also foresters, minor retainers of all sorts, fighting men, knights' yeomen bearing 'mighty bows' as in Chaucer. On the other side were the freemen who had prospered and added field to field, the franklins.

Of the two types one is described and one at least suggested by Chaucer from experience gathered between about 1360 and 1380. There is the old franklin with his fine white beard and his sanguine complexion, who liked a sop-in-wine in the morning, in whose house it 'snowed of meat and drink'. Somehow the old fellow strikes one as more of a gentleman than Tennyson's northern farmer—early nineteenth-century representative of a corresponding social group. And there is the ploughman, the poor parson's brother, who had loaded up so many cartloads of muck, and could turn his hand to any agricultural jobbing work. He may have been technically free, or he may not. Not all fourteenth-century parsons' brothers were. But in economic practice he evidently was. We infer that he held a bit of land, from which he could not live, because one of his virtues was that he paid tithe not only of his 'swinke', the earnings of his toil—how many men did that?— but of his 'cattel', chattels, probably pigs or hens in his case.

Except as a surname, the term 'franklin' went out of regular use during Tudor times; though a writer under James I describes a 'franklin' who is very near to the gentry. 'Yeoman' took its place, how and why is not perfectly clear. Chaucer's yeoman was a knight's servant or retainer, as the yeomen of the guard were the retainers of King Henry VIII. Latimer's father, of whom he spoke in a sermon that has been quoted threadbare, was called by him a yeoman: by us he would be called a substantial farmer. Latimer boasted of his stock and his wife's hard work, but mentioned that he had no land of his own. He was a big tenant. By the sixteenth century the term 'yeoman' had come to be used to describe the substantial farming class who came just below the gentlemen and above the average smaller cultivators, the husbandmen. It had nothing to do with tenure: it was an economic and social not a legal term; though to a lawyer it probably suggested at least some freehold land. A yeoman might be a 'franklin'—a considerable freeholder. He might own some land and rent more. What he rented might be old demesne land, the property of a lord, knight or squire; or it might be copyhold land. There were places where all the yeomen were copyholders, holding their land on terms which to the lawyer were 'villein'; but the terms were very far from making villeins of these solid farmers. In late Tudor times anyone might occupy copyhold land: there were awkward liabilities attached to it, well understood by a businesslike tenant, but the tenure itself had lost all degrading associations as a tenure. It survived until the other day, with curious symbolic remnants of its origin still clinging to it.

THE GREAT PESTILENCE AND THE PASSING OF MEDIEVAL AGRICULTURE IN ENGLAND

The Great Pestilence certainly marks a watershed in social and economic history, but its significance and the steepness of the slopes to and from the watershed, so to speak, may easily be exaggerated. Immensely destructive of life as it was, it was only one, though no doubt the greatest, of those destructions to which the Middle Ages were hardened—by disease, by famine, by the sword. It was perhaps because southern England saw so little of the sword that the Pestilence seemed so terrible. A Scots raid down towards Tyneside often did as much killing in relation to local population as the plague did nearly everywhere; the plague did not burn crops or houses but the Scots (and in reverse the English) did. Our most exact 'vital statistics' of deaths from the Pestilence come from ecclesiastical records—institutions to benefices—and from the King's *post mortem* inquisitions into the affairs of his tenants-in-chief. Chroniclers' and traditional figures are worthless. It looks as if 40 per cent of the parish clergy died—but then the clergy, who appear to have stuck well to their parishes, ran special risks. Yet the high rate among the King's tenants, people who could run away as Boccaccio's people did in the *Decameron*, is significant. Possibly the traditional figure of a third of the population dead may be correct: many scholars have accepted it. But modern experience of plagues suggests a fair number of spots which would remain immune, and affect the total. Perhaps 20 or 25 per cent may be nearer the mark than 33·3. It is to be remembered that upwards of 5 per cent per annum would be nothing uncommon for the Middle Ages; it is not so long since the percentage was over 2·5 in England, and it is still often above 3·5 in India. It shot up above 6 in the influenza epidemic of 1918 for the whole vast Indian subcontinent; and to 20 or more in places.

We hear of depopulated but not of deserted villages.[1] When villages can be studied in groups, what surprises us is the continuity of their life. On the vast estates of the Bishop of Winchester in Wessex there is 'no sign of chaos, of complete depopulation';[2] and following the Pestilence there is 'no revolution either in agriculture or in tenure.'[3] Across the country, on the East Midland and Fenland manors of Crowland, it is just the same: the estate accounts run on and, what is most important, there seems always to be someone ready to take over a vacant holding.

There had already been, as has been shown,[4] a considerable decline in villeins' regular labour services long before 1349. That the Plague should check this decline for a time was

---

[1] But see above, p. 80 n. 1.
[2] A. E. Levett, *The Black Death on the Estates of the See of Winchester* (1916), p. 72.
[3] *Ibid.* p. 142.   [4] See above, pp. 98–9, 110–11.

inevitable. Labour was certainly short. Unpaid labour would be most attractive to the lord or his agent. The valuation of services in money—already an ancient practice—did not mean formal abandonment of them.[1] Originally the lord had taken service or money as suited him. If it had been money for a generation, however, a demand for service would seem outrageous. Cases of this are known: a lord is found arguing that he had taken money 'of his grace', and now wanted service. A Kentish lord claims that his tenants still owe him the abandoned 'boon' of shearing his sheep. Kent was a free county and the indignation can be imagined: Wat Tyler's rising started not far away, though this was not its immediate cause. Such precise records of 'putting back the clock' are few; but no evidence is needed to prove that to keep the clock stopped was in the lord's interest. The evidence suggests that, for twenty or thirty years, in manors where works had been the rule in 1349, they were retained. On a group of 126 south-eastern manors between 1350 and 1380—mostly ecclesiastical and apt to be conservative—more than a third retained either complete works or considerable reliance on them.

The abundance of unoccupied holdings gave their chance to the younger sons, small holders and cottagers from whom wage-labour had been recruited. Such people were in demand both as wage-earners and as tenants. Besides, King Edward III had been putting less silver into the pennies. As labourers they asked for more pennies. Government, by Ordinance and Statute, tried to fix wages at the pre-pestilence level. Hardly a Parliament between 1350 and 1380 omitted to legislate about this; and a whole system of Justices of Labourers was designed to enforce the law. It was meant to apply not only to country labourers but to 'goldsmiths, saddlers, taylors and other work-men'. It failed all along the line. The thatcher's mate who had earned about 1*d.* a day under Edward I[2] still got no more than the 1*d.* in 1347. The Plague brought a sharp rise, to over 2*d.* in 1350. That was a boom wage, while social conditions were somewhat dislocated—and legislation followed. The law, or the better articulated social order, had some effect—but the wage never again fell below 1½*d.*; and it settled down, after a time, at about what had been the boom level of 1350. Day wages as a whole, unskilled and skilled, did much the same;

[1] See above, p. 98.   [2] See above, p. 109.

generally speaking they doubled. Skilled men did not do quite so well as the unskilled; that seems to be the rule when a wage rise is due to broad external causes; it is what has happened in England during the last thirty years.

Meanwhile, once the immediate effects of the Pestilence had been got over, food prices on the average rose very little. There were vast fluctuations from year to year and from place to place, as there always had been. But the averages are remarkably stable for a century and more after 1350.[1] Comparing the half-century 1300–49 with that of 1400–49, wheat comes out almost exactly the same; rye is a little down; the price of oxen is a little up. When, however, we come to a list of things into whose prices more labour enters—tiles, nails, canvas, and many more—we find, as we might have expected, a rise comparable with that in the wages paid to the workman. If the prices on this list for the years 1300–49 be called 100, the corresponding figure for 1400–49 works out at 174. (The change in wages, it will be remembered, would be roughly represented by 100:200). That is why historians have often written in picturesque terms of the happy position of 'labour' in the fifteenth century. It was a century of war, foreign and civil, but it was a century in which a man's wages, if he could hold on to them, would buy him plenty of the available foodstuffs. And that there was a margin for buying better clothes—these were not cheap—the shocked accents of Parliament, legislating against popular 'luxury' in clothing, plainly suggest.

Thirty years after the Pestilence had come what used to be called the Peasants' Revolt, sometimes the Villeins' Rising, of 1381. The traditional and symbolic name not of Peter Ploughman but of Wat Tiler should have been enough to discredit either term as an adequate description; though, as the vast majority of Englishmen were peasants of one sort or another, 'peasants' no doubt describes the composition of the rebel bands not too badly. There were all sorts of economic grievances and economic ambitions at work, rural and urban. As everyone knows, the immediate cause of the Rising was a socially unjust, not merely a heavy, tax;[2] and one of its most active centres was Wat Tiler's very free county of Kent. That there was discontent among villeins, or holders of villein land, over the slow movement of the manorial clock there is no doubt.

---

[1] Contrast the period before 1350; above, pp. 109–10. See also p. 173 below.   [2] See below, p. 176.

There was much burning by the rebels of the rolls and records to which lords might appeal. The Rising was of the East and South, regions where heavy services had survived—but it included Kent where they had not. John Ball's preaching, revolutionary literature, and the couplet about Adam and Eve —it was not a new one—appealed not merely to villeins or free peasants but to all who delved or span, in town or in country, and who watched meanwhile the parti-coloured cavalcades of the gentry, the jewelled elegance of Chaucer's prioress, or the gross abundance of his huntin' monk.

Parliament, it is true, heard of some villeins who had apparently employed a lawyer—employing of lawyers, we recall, was no new thing among villeins;[1] and many villeins of 1381 were men of substance—to turn up Domesday Book and see what it said about villeinage. If he did his job, he would not have found much beyond the word *villani*; not villein blood, nor week-work, nor merchet, nor best beast; and if he reported, his clients may have been encouraged in a sort of villeins' strike. We do not know. But we know that the programme put forward in the rebels' name was meant to appeal to peasants of all sorts; and that those whom rebels most often murdered were men who had been active in the enforcement of the Statutes of Labourers, which affected freemen or the free activities of men of servile blood.

King Richard's broken promises show that the legal aboli- tion of villeinage appealed to an important section of the rebels. But there were grievances about rents and leases which were essentially those of freemen. With the rising cost of living—if not for basic foodstuffs, certainly for luxuries, manufactures and services—landowners had tried to raise the rents and shorten the leases. Grievances about game laws were common to freeman and villein, and so might be the complaints of filching of the commons which occur locally. The country once up, all sorts of grudges were worked off—of East Anglians against immigrant competing Flemings; of Cambridge towns- men against the gown; of one faction in a town against another; of a large section of the populace in town and country against those held responsible for poll-taxes and general misgovernment.

Like so many social upheavals, the Rising came when the people were anything but sunk in misery. Old grievances were

¹ See above, p. 101.

going, but not so fast as they wished; with increasing comfort, they felt themselves strong enough to resist uncomfortable novelties. Froissart, it has been said, 'is broadly right, in spite of his class prejudice, in attributing the revolt to "the ease and riches that the common people were of"'.[1]

Fortunately its repression did not affect the economic forces that were working in their favour. There was increased reluctance to perform 'works', an increased number of men who took the risks of running away from the manor without leave. This was easy, partly because there was a demand for rough labour and for horse-men in the towns, mainly because lords or big tenants who were short-handed—and the course of wages shows that they still were—would not make inquiry into a good ditcher's pedigree. Some people before this had wailed at the absence of what to-day might be called class solidarity among employers; but the grasping litigious squires and rising yeomen of the fifteenth century were very tough individualists. They hired men as they needed them. Early in the century, on one lagging conservative manor of the Isle of Ely, regular services were finally commuted; on another, deep in Hampshire, the demesne was leased to the reeve; and the thatcher's mate was getting 3*d*. By about the time of Agincourt, the 'classical' demesne farming and the services that went with it were most certainly moribund; though it was not until 1443 that the Duchy of Lancaster farmed out all its Wiltshire and Dorset demesnes. The men who took copyhold cases to the courts in 1439 and 1467 were more probably tenants in villeinage than demonstrable villeins.

It is significant that a few years after the crushed rising of 1381, in 1389–90, Parliament abandoned the attempt to keep wages down, instructing the Justices or town authorities to regulate them 'according to the dearth of victuals'—the cost of living, as we should say. As a result of this, there have survived a wage-scale for Coventry of 1420 and one for Norfolk of 1431: at Coventry, 4*d*. or 5*d*. is the normal skilled wage, 3*d*. the unskilled. It is true that in 1445 Parliament reverted to the policy of a maximum wage; but by that time wages were well set at a higher level and, for another generation and more, necessaries remained cheap.

Although tenants for holdings made vacant by the Pestilence were often found with what seems rather surprising ease, some

[1] Anthony Steel, *Richard II* (1941), p. 61.

difficulties naturally arose. It might not always be easy to secure a new tenant on the old 'customary' villein terms. We hear of the reeve, or some other farmer of the demesne, agreeing to add such a holding to his farm, but on leasehold terms. The recorded cases are few but the arrangement is natural. It has often been thought that vacant land may have been used for sheep-grazing. It may. But in an open-field region it would not be easy to graze holdings made up of scattered strips, when the adjacent strips were being tilled—and we have little evidence of any systematic enclosing of the open fields at this time. No doubt sheep need less labour; and it is quite likely that, for example, the farmer of an already consolidated demesne would find that his stock of sheep could be increased with advantage. But 'it is difficult to find signs of that wholesale substitution of pasture for arable farming which, according to textbooks, happened after the Black Death'.[1] On the contrary, the evidence makes it as nearly as possible proven that in the century following the Pestilence the wool output of the country as a whole declined. Certainly the exports of wool, or of cloth reckoned as wool, declined. The big organised sheep-runs[2] were vanishing, cut up and leased out to tenants on the Peak and Yorkshire and Lincolnshire manors of the Duchy of Lancaster by 1400. By the fifteenth century the typical sheep-owner was not a Duke or Bishop or Abbot, but a farmer, large or small, with perhaps an occasional small agricultural 'squire'. Rather uncertain calculations, based on the export figures and the taxation figures for home-consumed cloth, suggest that the national clip of wool at the end of the reign of Edward IV was well below the level of the years about 1300. There are neither figures nor other evidence even to suggest the contrary. It has been an experience of agrarian reform in Europe since 1918, with the break up of great estates, that the transfer of any branch of agricultural production from well-organised ranches or big farms to smaller units may be socially most wise, but may not lead, does not at once lead, to increased production. And this was precisely the transfer that was taking place gradually in English sheep farming between 1300 and 1500. Peasant flocks, small men's flocks, and farmers' flocks, there had always been: as Tudor times approached there was little else.

[1] E. E. Power, *The Wool Trade in English Medieval History* (1941), p. 35.
[2] See above, pp. 106–7.

As the word 'enclosure' occurs among the grievances of 1381, it is well to remember that this overworked word has at least three distinct meanings. There is the enclosing, the in-taking, from moor and heath, forest and fen, that had been going on from the beginning; this went on fast while population was growing between 1100 and 1300, more slowly or not at all while it was falling or recovering from a fall between 1300 and 1500. Such enclosure generally meant rough walling in stone country, dyking in fen country, fencing of some sort in forest country to keep out wild beasts. But it might lead, as has been seen, simply to an extension of open field at the expense of waste heath.[1] Then there is enclosing of those commons that were regularly used for pasture in well-settled districts. It was a law, or strong tradition, of the thirteenth century that a lord of a manor might enclose land from these, if he did not encroach on the grazing rights of freemen. In villages in parts of the country where there were no freemen the restriction would not apply; but it was to a lord's interest to leave enough common for village needs, so long as the true open-field system remained intact, as it generally did until long after 1500 in the regions where such villages were most common. Grievances about enclosure of commons, before and just after that date, are apt to come either from wild or forest areas, where old-fashioned rough grazing was being interfered with, or from near towns where grazing rights were valuable and the old system was breaking down.

It is to be remembered that everywhere and at all times, so far as we know, grazing rights on the regular commons went with holdings in the fields, and were proportioned to them. A cottager with a scrap of land might have grazing for a cow; by charity and custom, but not by right, humble landless folk might be allowed to run a few geese or dig a bit of turf.

In the open fields themselves, holdings had at times been partially consolidated by exchange or purchase of strips.[2] That might lead to actual enclosure. Of this there is little direct evidence before 1500. The regions which Tudor writers call enclosed are those in which enclosure was ancient or primitive. After 1500, such evidence is sometimes found, but we cannot tell how old the enclosure referred to was. For example, near Leeds in 1612 we meet a bit of land called Little Garth, 'jacentem in le Middle Field de Knowstrop'. Middle Field

[1] See above, p. 83.   [2] See above, pp. 90–1.

implies the three-field system and a garth or yard is an enclosed area. When had Little Garth been enclosed from 'le Middle Field'? It is near a town. Near Coventry, as early as 1423, 'parcels' in the fields were being made into gardens—'honestly made' it was pleaded before the Mayor.

The enclosure that later agricultural reformers advocated, and social reformers often deplored, was not such piecemeal work but the large-scale partitioning and fencing of commons and the rearrangement and fencing of open-field land, accompanied sometimes by a change in the use of the land from corn growing to pasture farming. Complaints about this begin only a few years before 1500; and it is unlikely that it affected any appreciable part of the country until after that date. How much it affected then is for discussion later.[1]

[1] See below, pp. 194–200.

Chapter V

Trade and Industry; Public Policy and Economic Doctrine

MERCHANTS, GILDS AND CRAFTSMEN

Medieval townsmen, except in the largest towns, were often farmers. Even so late as 1690, men of Cambridge can be seen working in their corn fields in David Loggan's prints. In the villages there were always a few craftsmen, sometimes a fair number, men who might also hold a bit of land but lived mainly by their trade. Mining, salt-making and smelting were necessarily country trades. And, long before the medieval centuries were over, and earlier than has often been supposed, much of the cloth which by 1500 was England's great article of export, was a product of the smaller country towns and the villages. But even so, all the industrial and commercial population of England, in towns and villages combined, would certainly not be above 20 per cent of the total population by 1500, and may have been a good deal less.

One minority of this minority, and a small one at that, was in some ways its most important section—the merchants. The word merchant, *mercator*, might be used in a very wide sense, as it still was in early modern Scotland, to describe any trader, great or small, including sometimes the 'merchants who carry their goods on their backs, called hawkers'. Yet all through these centuries can be seen, rather faintly at first but afterwards very clearly, the true merchant type—the man who may go overseas, like Aelfric's merchant,[1] taking miscellaneous cargoes out and bringing others in; who, whether he goes overseas or not, is ready to trade wherever he sees a chance of gain and in any commodity that will give him a profit; whose main chance of profit—always a mystery and a sinful mystery to the medieval mind—lies in the different values that men living far apart may attach to articles of commerce. St Jerome had taught that if one party to a bargain does not lose the other cannot gain; yet a savage who gets beads for gold may be convinced that he has had the best of the bargain.

[1] See above, pp. 62-3.

One early source of profit for merchants was trading or administrative work for the King—supplying his court, getting his money struck, assessing or farming his taxes, serving as contractor for his armies. Men who did such work must always have become fairly well-to-do through their own trade before they could take it up. A high proportion of them were always citizens of London. How or where they got their start we can usually only guess. Some may have been descended from the class known before the Norman Conquest as 'borough thanes',[1] and may have inherited property in the City. Certainly the leading Londoners of the late twelfth and the thirteenth centuries were urban landowners; but very likely they made money first and then bought urban land, just as they made money and then acquired rural manors. In later centuries, when we know more about them, we generally find that the leading Londoners are immigrants, as their names show— Henry le Waleys (Welshman) *c.* 1280; John of Northampton (*c.* 1380); Richard Whittington (*c.* 1420)—fortune seekers. Henry Fitzailwin, the first Mayor of London, who died in 1212, held a great deal of land in the home counties. It is not certain that he was ever a merchant. There was something very knightly about some of these early mayors: Fitzailwin's Cambridge contemporary—Harvey, the son of Eustace, the son of Dunning—had an armed knight on his seal. But most of the aldermen and mayors of thirteenth-century London certainly were merchants of one kind or another, indeed of several kinds. They were 'woolmongers, vintners, skinners and grocers by turns or...all...at once'.[2] Specialisation became commoner after 1300, as single branches of trade— wine perhaps or wool—grew important enough to fill an active man's life; but no more in the fourteenth century than to-day would a man with the flair for buying and selling confine himself to one 'line'. It became an established part of the custom of London, when her gilds and companies were fully organised, that a man who was free of one company might practise the trade of another—a fishmonger might deal in wool, or a vintner in leather. In 1383 a London armourer was imprisoned for selling wine in Fleet Street, imprisoned not because he was an armourer but because he sold at 8*d.* instead of 6*d.* This was a crystallisation of the 'by turns or all at once'

[1] See above, p. 59.
[2] George Unwin, *The Gilds and Companies of London* (1925), p. 58.

practice inherited from the thirteenth century, and from the earlier miscellaneous business of men who 'fared over seas'. And as membership of a London company was—and is— hereditary, it is not surprising to find that by the end of the period—under the early Tudors—a high proportion of the Drapers' Company of London were not drapers at all.

The opportunities which an able thirteenth-century merchant might seize can be illustrated from the career of William of Doncaster, citizen of Chester, in the reign of Edward I. He had agents who bought wine in Gascony, for sale to the public or to the crown. He sent wool over to Ipswich for the Flanders market. He traded with Ireland, apparently in corn. He once did 'a big deal in horseshoes and nails with the King';[1] and he was convicted of circulating bad money. He farmed Welsh lead-mines and sold lead. As a result of all this, and in spite of his conviction, he became a collector of the duty on wine in Chester and the North Welsh ports, and 'searcher of money' in the same places: he would know bad money when he saw it. He invested part of his fortune in land, as all successful traders did for centuries: it was the certain and permanent investment.

Chester was an important place, base-town for Edward's Welsh wars. William was the head of its small group of leading men. Not far below him came another capitalist who however is not called a merchant—Richard the Engineer, overseer of the royal castle buildings at Carnarvon, Beaumaris and Harlech, and lessee from the crown of the valuable mills beside the river Dee. If more were known of personal histories in other towns, no doubt similar small groups would be found. We do know that the first recorded Mayor of Winchester (1207) was a wine merchant. In London, of which much is known, the group was naturally considerable. So it had been since the twelfth century, and certainly earlier. Lanfranc made London Englishmen knights in Kent. The Bishop of Winchester in 1141 addressed great men of the City as noblemen or princes (*proceres*)—it is true in a political speech. Whether their importance was based on trade, whether they were descended from men who through trade had become 'thanes', we do not know; but it is hard to believe that a prominent Londoner under Henry II was not in some sense a merchant, even if part of his income came from urban property and another part from doing jobs for the crown. There were goldsmiths in England

[1] H. J. Hewitt, *Medieval Cheshire* (1929), p. 130.

important enough to be named in Domesday: the goldsmiths had a gild of their own in London by 1180. The London weavers had one before 1130, a gild whose wealth shows that, like the goldsmiths', it was not just one of craftsmen but included traders. The fishmongers were a great London power for centuries: they also were traders, their leaders obviously men of substance.

Men from these small, strong, economic groups, the *potentiores*—traders, crown agents, urban and perhaps rural landowners—formed the governing bodies of the towns of the twelfth and thirteenth centuries; and, in spite of constitutional changes in some places, they held their position in those of the fourteenth and fifteenth. British towns were neither democracies in origin, nor did they, like some continental towns, go through regular democratic revolutions; though from time to time 'the commonalty' made its voice heard in a noisy sort of town meeting, or by riot; and though in the fourteenth and fifteenth centuries a Common Council may appear. But common councils 'did no more than broaden the basis of civic oligarchy'.[1]

We have noted the Dover gildhall of 1066 and have guessed that there may have been similar halls elsewhere.[2] There was a 'knights hall' in Winchester before 1100; a Chapmen's Hall before 1129, and a *gilda mercatorum* before 1158. But no rules of strictly town gilds have survived from before 1100. No doubt such gilds, where they existed, covered conviviality, religion, mutual help in quarrels, and defence of local commercial interests. When, after 1100, towns began to obtain royal charters, they usually bargained for a *gilda mercatoria*, mercantile or merchants' gild. Some, like Winchester, had something of the kind before their charter. In the thirteenth century, most English and at least six Scottish towns had this clause in their charters, or are noted as having a *gilda mercatoria*. Some organised special bodies, regular merchant gilds, to supervise matters of trade. In Scotland the merchant gild or Gildry, wherever it existed, became in course of time 'a separate but constituent part'[3] of the town administration; but in many English towns there is no evidence of this. 'The

[1] James Tait, 'The Common Council of the Borough' in *Eng. Hist. Rev.* vol. XLVI (1931), p. 2.
[2] See above, p. 60.
[3] Charles Gross, *The Gild Merchant* (1890), vol. I, p. 225.

merchant gild' is granted, but we cannot prove that 'it' was organised. 'It' certainly became simply a function of the governing body, and may have been this from the start. The object was the same, whether there was a separate gild or not—protection of the monopoly of trading and controlling trade that all towns aimed at when they bought charters from the Crown.

In England the town monopoly was limited by the town boundaries; but in Scotland the Royal Burghs were given monopolies over whole, and large, districts. 'I firmly forbid', King Alexander II says in his charter to Aberdeen of 1214, 'any foreign [that is non-Aberdonian] merchants within the sheriffdom [shire] of Aberdeen from buying or selling anything except in my burgh of Aberdeen'. That is typical; and some burghs which were not royal but ecclesiastical, like Glasgow, secured almost equally sweeping monopolies; though we do not hear of a Gildry in Glasgow before the reign of James Sixth and First. These Scottish burghs came near to realising the old ideal of Saxon kings—that no one should trade outside a town.[1]

If a town was old enough or strong enough to manage its monopolising without a formal grant of gild, it did so. Neither London, nor Norwich, nor any of the Cinque Ports, ever asked for a merchant gild, so far as we know.

The habit of forming gilds was widespread and very deep rooted. Groups who had something in common, groups of neighbours, groups of men of the same class or the same trade, groups who felt special reverence for a particular saint, often formed fraternities or gilds which were partly religious, partly social, and might also be partly economic. You could belong to more than one such society—to a first perhaps for trade, to a second for religion. Among Chaucer's pilgrims were 'an haberdasher and a carpenter, a webbe [weaver], a dyer, and a tapicer' [tapestry worker] all clothed in the livery of one 'solemn and great fraternity'. There was a London trade gild in Chaucer's day for each of those men; but each had this other interest, presumably religious—a man may be a Chartered Accountant and also a member of the Society of Friends. Before town governments got shape and power, with their twelfth- and thirteenth-century charters, some trade groups paid for licences and monopolistic privileges from the crown. They included the London bakers and weavers, with weavers,

[1] See further on Scottish town monopolies, pp. 147-50 below.

fullers and leather-workers in a few other towns. Other groups
formed gilds in London without leave, or behaved in some way
irregularly—and were fined for it by Henry II in 1180 as
'adulterine', illegitimate. Of eighteen so fined only four
have trade names—goldsmiths, pepperers, clothworkers and
butchers. The goldsmiths were very rich and were fined £30.
(They never paid; nor did the others.) The pepperers were
fined £10. 13s. 4d.; the clothworkers and butchers only 13s. 4d.
each. We see a gap between the merchant class and the working
tradesmen. Five of the other gilds, three rich and two poor, are
called 'gilds of bridge', and it is thought that they were social-
religious societies pledged to help in the rebuilding of London
Bridge, begun—in stone—four years earlier. There is the gild of
St Lazarus, presumably charitable: Lazarus never became the
patron saint of a trade as St Dunstan was of the goldsmiths.
We have a 'gild of strangers'; a local gild, of Haliwell (? Holy-
well); and six more, two of rich men and four of poor, described only by the names of their aldermen. One of the rich
men's gilds was rated at £20: its alderman, a certain Goscelin,
is met with later as a repairer of Holborn Bridge.

The royally licensed weavers' gilds of the twelfth century
have been much discussed. About the year 1200 London
and four other towns contemplated putting pressure on them,
first, to forswear their craft privileges if they wished to become
freemen of the borough, and, second, to sell only to townsmen.
This has been turned by some modern writers into a fight
between 'capital' and 'labour'. That it evidently was not: the
weavers were not poor and had paid the King well for their
privileges. Downtrodden working weavers are not likely to
break local rules and sell outside the town. The struggle
probably was one between English townsmen and alien immigrants or their sons; for there is good reason to think, as the
original records suggest, that groups of professional Flemish
master-weavers had bought privileges from King Henry I. We
hear of no male weavers in England before 1100, though there
may have been some. What is quite certain is that this was a
fight by the governing groups in the towns, no doubt also the
richest groups, for control of local economic life. They were
getting their charters from the crown and becoming independent of the king's man, the sheriff. They did not propose
to tolerate bodies with older privileges, especially if those
bodies were not right English.

A few years later, after a fire, we find the Mayor and Aldermen of London regulating building wages. In 1256 Henry III's charter to Norwich ordains that there shall be 'no gild to the detriment of the city', no gild that is of which the city fathers do not approve. Between 1288 and 1293 the city is fining fullers, saddlers, tanners and cobblers for starting gilds without permission. In 1299 a group of smiths, not yet a recognised gild or mistery, are brought before the Mayor of London for making 'a parliament and a confederacy'; agreeing to back one another up and to work only with those of their confederacy; collecting subscriptions to pay for candles to the Virgin; drafting a charter; taking oaths, and refusing to work at night. They defended themselves. They said they did not work at night because of the stink of sea coal—*propter putridinem carbonis marine*—and generally made out so good a case that they went quit. Had the Mayor and his Court thought that their action was to the detriment of the City things would no doubt have gone differently. We note that next year the Mayor is inspecting the ordinances of the Weavers, who are now well in hand.

This is not a case of employers controlling wage-labour: the smith was a small independent worker, as he remained, if the weaver was in some danger of becoming an out-worker for a bigger man. But it is control by these big men, the *potentiores* —the merchant class. Even in London, few of the handicrafts had acquired fully recognised gilds before 1300, though they might have fraternities and candles for the Virgin. A list of twenty-five groups of masters (misteries) authorised to choose their own officers in 1328 'consists almost entirely of the mercantile crafts [grocers, vintners, fishmongers] and of the wealthy manufacturing crafts'[1] [goldsmiths, cordwainers, i.e. fine leather workers or superior shoemakers]; though it does contain a handful of humbler groups such as cutlers, hosiers and painters.

At that time, so far as we know, specialised gilds, what are generally called craft gilds, were rare outside London. In many towns they always remained rare; partly because the towns were too small to carry specialised industrial or trading groups, partly for local reasons at which, for lack of evidence, we can only guess. All that we know is that 'craft' gilds have no important place in the records of this group of towns.

[1] George Unwin, *The Gilds and Companies of London* (1925), p. 87.

Important as the gild is in social and religious history—there were innumerable social-religious gilds in villages before 1500—its importance in the strictly economic life of the towns is easily overrated. A great town could regulate trade and secure privileges for its freemen without having a Merchant Gild. Similarly, many of the economic ends at which a 'craft' gild might aim were attainable without a full gild organisation. A gild liked to keep out of the town, or to tax, competing goods. It might try to limit its numbers in the interest of those already in the trade. It might seize and destroy badly made goods. All these things the town authority might do, in one way or another. A gild might also try, rather secretly, to control prices in its own, as opposed to the public, interest; there is plenty of evidence that people not in regular gilds also did this, just as mere labourers 'conspired' for higher wages. Such attempts the town authority might resent in either case. The members of that authority, the Mayor and 'the twelve' or 'the twenty-four' as it often was, kept an eye on all these matters, gild or no gild, partly in the general consumer's interest, partly no doubt in that of their class or group. At the very end of this period, in 1484, the bakers of Coventry leave the city riotously, in protest against a newly fixed rate of pay for baking—but they submit and are fined.

The economic life of a town where gilds were many did not differ much from that in which they were few—York from Norwich, for example.[1] In technical processes, gild or no gild made no difference—except that in course of time some gildsmen stuck too faithfully to old-fashioned routines. Gild members were always a minority of the population, even in highly organised towns. London of the fourteenth and fifteenth centuries abounded in companies and gilds: at one time it had over a hundred. Their members were freemen of the City. Yet shortly after 1500, not much more than a quarter of the London population belonged to citizen's families. The rest were genuine proletarians, carriers and drivers and haulers and diggers and beggars and citizens' *servientes* who had never been apprenticed. To practise clothworking well an apprenticeship was certainly necessary, but you could roll the bales about without years of training. It was into these low jobs that runaway villeins' sons had been able to go and shake off their villeinage. The towns, and under Richard II the law,

[1] For gilds in York and Norwich, see below, p. 143.

tried to keep them out, but not with much success. Yet a law of Henry IV which said that an apprentices's father must be worth 20*s.* probably did something to keep them down.

Apprenticeship of some sort goes back to the flint-chippers: fathers must have taught their sons how to chip, and if short of sons then other lads. It is only a curious not an important fact that the first English apprenticeship referred to in writing is that of St William of Norwich, to a skinner in the twelfth century. By 1271, one of Europe's oldest sets of 'craft gild' regulations, that of the London cordwainers, shows apprenticeship well developed—with an entry fee so high that only sons from the governing group can have hoped to get in. The earliest surviving apprentice's indenture is from 1291, to a Norwich spicer—the governing mercantile group again.

As trades slowly acquired full gild organisation, apprenticeship was regulated by ordinance and its duration was often fixed. This ordering process went on slowly and unequally. London settled down to a normal seven years' apprenticeship: some other places and trades imitated London; but there were great variations in practice. Coventry, a town of highly organised gilds, only decreed seven years for all, 'frohensfurth', in 1494. Everywhere things were so arranged that a craftsman's son had the best chance of entering his father's trade.

The man who came to be known as a journeyman was not originally an ex-apprentice: in the Latin of official documents he was a *serviens*. In the small-scale operations of ordinary towns and average trades he cannot have been much wanted. With his lad, and perhaps his 'black-thumbed maid', a cobbler could manage. But, in bigger towns and some trades more prosperous, masters began gradually to employ men who, as a Norwich record of 1310 put it, got 'a penny a day for a penny of work'—day-work men, *journée* men. They were not part of the master's households, as apprentices were. A century later (1408) the rules of the London Bladesmiths contain the clause —'no one of the said trade shall teach his journeyman... secrets...as he would his apprentice'. A century and a half later still, in Edinburgh—Scotland of the sixteenth century was often very like England of the fourteenth or thirteenth—it was stated, perhaps not quite fairly, that 'the great multitude of journeymen [day-men] or taskmen [job-men] of the crafts' were 'nothing else but idle, vagabond persons, bound to no master'.[1] That was the trouble, in Norwich of 1310 and Edinburgh of 1583—no one was responsible for them. But beside them there began to appear, in some trades and in the bigger towns—by 1400 or earlier—groups of ex-apprentices who could not find a place among the masters. Some gilds began to require a spell of service as a journeyman—the word was losing its original meaning—before admission as a master. But this rule came late and was never general.

Apprenticeship was just as necessary outside as inside a gild, if skill was essential. Some very important trades were carried on mainly outside gilds, though they might have their fraternities or other informal organisations. Some were outside because the trade, like mining or quarrying, was inevitably carried on beyond any town boundaries: in England all gild authority was limited by these. Consider shipbuilding. It was an important Thames industry and there were shipwrights, freemen of London, settled in Wapping outside the City. But the main centre, also outside, was at Rotherhithe across the river. The Rotherhithe men were given an ambitious organisation by the crown under King James I; not before.[2] Shipwrights were strong folk, and must always have been; few trades can have called for a more serious apprenticeship. All round the coast, in regular ports and seaside villages, ships might be built. We see their builders, graded, with graded pay, in a late fifteenth-century wage statute—the 'maister Ship Carpynter taking the charge of the werke, havyng men undre hym'; the Hewer; the 'able Clyncher'; the mere Holder; with 'maister Calker' and 'meane Calker'. The Master Carpenter evidently took on a job, perhaps a contract, from a merchant or other prospective ship-owner, who may or may not have found the timber. No doubt these men had their strict customs and perhaps their fraternities like other skilled men; but because most shipyards were not within the boundaries of towns, we seldom hear of a shipwrights' gild.

The building trades, probably the biggest group in London or any other important town, are specially interesting. As private houses were rarely built of stone or brick, most of the digging and lifting work for a timber-frame house must have been done by unskilled 'proletarian' labour—labour whose

---

[1] Miss I. F. Grant, *The Social and Economic Development of Scotland before 1603* (1930), p. 439.

[2] See below, pp. 258–9.

pay the London authorities were regulating before Magna Carta. Organisation among the skilled building workers only comes to light late. There are traces of some organisation in London in 1306; in 1356 the City is imposing rules on the masons, after a quarrel between stone-hewers and stone-layers. In 1376, among the 'misteries' that sent men to the Common Council of London were 'Joignours', Masons and 'Peyntours': plumbing was not yet part of ordinary house-building. These same trades, except the masons but with the carpenters and plasterers, appear on a list of companies or gilds in 1422. The tilers do not appear; although there is evidence of a tilers' mistery in London six years earlier. The omission may or may not be significant. Tiles had been nominally essential on all London houses since the great fire in John's reign; but tilers, even in the fifteenth century, were still sometimes treated as labourers, not allowed to organise themselves; their gilds were precarious. At Coventry, however, we hear of gilds of masons, tilers and wrights (carpenters) about 1450.

Although the first mention in surviving records can never date the origin of a gild, it is evident that these building-trade gilds were important nowhere before about 1350 or later. They were genuine craftsmen's societies; for though there were a few great carpenters like William Hurlee, carpenter to King Edward III and consultant carpenter to Ely Cathedral Chapter, the average 'wright' was a workman; and if he sometimes took a modest building contract—from that day to this, contractors have generally sprung from among the carpenters—the ordinary medieval arrangement was for the prospective house owner to arrange with the various groups of craftsmen himself.

The relative insignificance of masons' gilds is easily explained. Only a town in which churches or public buildings were constantly going up or undergoing repair could carry an important body of resident masons. Such places were few. It has been estimated that towns of this class—York, Norwich, Oxford—may each have had about a dozen resident masons in the fourteenth century. Coventry had seven about 1450. The mason was a migrant—moving as cathedral building or castle building or city-wall building drew him. Cathedral authorities might keep a few masons permanently for repair and tombstone work; they might carry out a fairly important enterprise, say the building of a lantern tower, so leisurely that not very many men would be employed at one time; though some migrants would have to be called in. For a big undertaking, a new or remodelled cathedral, there would have to be many, even if work was again leisurely, as it generally was.

Only the King was in a position to have work done against time—and to get it so done all his authority had to be deployed. How the Conqueror built the Tower of London we do not know; but we know a great deal about how Edward I built his Welsh castles and how Edward III built Windsor. It is a very interesting page in the history of what one might call royal capitalism or, from another angle, state socialism. As financial security, Edward had his power to tax—like the Soviet government. To recruit labour he had his power to order—like the British Parliament in time of war. He spread his net wide. There were not many masons in Wales, though it is a stone country where 'dry stone' walls for fields or houses were well known. To get his masons Edward I ordered the sheriffs of many English counties to impress them and send them into Wales: in 1282 the sheriff of Somerset was ordered to send fifteen good ones, and the sheriff of Rutland twenty with a foreman. In 1360 Edward III ordered 320 masons to be sent to Windsor from twelve different shires, including Northampton, Leicester and Warwick. These wide sweeps were required because masons were mostly countrymen, and few counties could supply many. The best counties for recruitment were naturally stony ones like Rutland, Northampton and Somerset —since many, perhaps most, masons started their careers in stone-quarries.

The scale of some of these royal enterprises might be gigantic, as the summons of masons to Windsor suggests. Employment figures varied with the urgency of the work and the state of the royal finances. If taxes gave out the King might have to borrow—Edward I from Italians, Edward III latterly from his own subjects. When the pace was hot, employment figures might be very high indeed. Once, early in the reign of Edward II, there were 400 masons and 1230 carpenters, boatmen, carters and labourers on the works of Beaumaris Castle.

These numbers called for directing ability like that of Richard the Engineer. More technical ability was found among the pick of the masons. In the late thirteenth century, Walter of Hereford, mason, was master of the works at Vale Royal Abbey in Cheshire and at Carnarvon Castle. In the mid-fourteenth the great William Yevele—master-mason, stone-dealer and contractor—made a fortune and bought a manor. Adam 'the marbler', who paved old St Paul's, looks like a contractor. There had been employers and contractors among the masons even in the thirteenth century: Thomas of Weldon (where there are famous quarries) was one of these. With the technical experts appear clerics who may really have been architects, and educated clerks of the works like Chaucer. It is all very businesslike and modern.

As Thomas of Weldon proves, masons often got their surnames from quarry areas. They were so few and so scattered that formal organisation for apprenticeship is hardly to be expected, and it is rarely to be traced even in the fifteenth century. No doubt fathers taught sons as flint-chippers had. This would serve to keep up the relatively small supply of masons that the country carried. A mason's true corporate life began in the lodges run up on great building sites. There must have been ancient customary rules for conduct in these lodges, but none has survived from earlier than 1352. A lodge would be a handy place for comparing the King's or the Bishop's wages with those current in Rutland or Somerset. We know exactly what the King paid, but not how the rates were arrived at, though we have Wyclif's evidence that 'men of sutel craft, as fre masons and othere...conspiren togidere that no man of here craft schal take lesse on a day than thei setten'. Statistically, their money wages moved rather closely with skilled wages in general, increasing by about 50 per cent between 1300 and 1400, after that remaining fairly stable until after 1500.

A 'fre mason' in Wyclif's day was the man who worked with 'sutel craft' in fine-grained freestone—which you could carve into capitals and mouldings. The mere splitter of intractable whin-stone, or sawer of blocks for the 'sutel' man, was not a free mason, though he had the same chances for conspiring about wages. For the building of plain walls, as in the Welsh castles, the masons were divided into hewers and layers. Except here and there, no very 'sutel craft' was required; and the North Welsh stone is not very 'free'.

CAPITALISTS IN MEDIEVAL ENGLAND

The King, an agrarian capitalist with his royal manors, was also ultimately responsible for these national 'capitalistic' building operations—capitalistic because of the accumulated resources that they required and the masses of wage-labour assembled to complete them. Other great men, lay or ecclesiastical, and corporate bodies, reproduced this royal character on a smaller scale. All over Europe it was the same. The largest shipbuilding establishment of Dante's day (*c.* 1300), and it was very large, was that in the arsenal of the republic of Venice. From Gascon manors in the 'claret' country men acting for the King of England shipped wine in bulk to the London market. Sometimes the agrarian capitalist was interested in corn and other markets, as has been seen.[1] And sometimes he was interested in productive industry: a good deal is known about the Bishop of Durham's iron forges and about the fulling-mills which manorial lords began to have built in the twelfth century.[2] On Alston Moor silver-lead was mined, on behalf of or by concession from the King. In Cornwall and part of Devon also the crown was rather a 'mine owning' than an agrarian capitalist. Cornish manors were not rich. The tin-workings were. The King taxed them in various ways and, especially in the thirteenth century, often made use of his right to buy up all the tin—at the King's price —as a commercial proposition. He usually leased his rights to someone, a prince of the blood, a courtier or one of his Italian creditors. The tinners and the merchants resisted; but under John, Henry III, and the Edwards without much success. Pre-emption is last heard of (before its revival in the sixteenth century) in 1367 when the Black Prince, as Duke of Cornwall, bought up the tin at 20*s.* a hundredweight and graciously permitted the merchants to have it at 26*s.* 8*d.* All this is, however, more a blackmailing than a productive operation. Neither the King nor his agents organised or directed tin-mining. Still less did they find capital for it. They simply milked tinners with a low price and merchants with a high one; or, when pre-emption was not being exercised, they taxed tin just as they taxed wool or wine or any other commodity that would bear taxation. But in the stannaries the crown had

---

[1] See above, pp. 105–8.
[2] See below, pp. 154–6.

a specially strong position, a traditional and legal claim to the tin which it had not to the wool or the wine.

Agrarian capitalists, from the King down to the smallest lord of a manor, who held the most important 'means of production', land, rarely undertook directly productive enterprises outside agriculture, in spite of the Bishop's forges and the fulling-mills. Beaumaris Castle called for a 'capitalistic' building organisation; but it produced, not anything for market, only fear in the Welsh and a measure of peace. The most active non-agrarian private capitalists of the twelfth and thirteenth centuries were commercial, not industrial—Jews, Italians, the rising native merchants. Of the Jews as money-lenders we know a great deal, but not much about where they originally got the money that they lent: it was probably from continental trade. There is no certain evidence of Jews in England before 1066; but about the year 900 they had been trading all the way from 'France' to China, and they may have crossed the Channel in the next 150 years. However, they certainly followed the Norman conquerors, as 'Court-Jews', to use a much later German name. Their great day in England was the twelfth century, and for that we have few commercial records. So we meet the Jew as money-lender not as merchant. It was Aaron of Lincoln who financed the building of nine Cistercian monasteries, and boasted of the home he had made for St Alban. There were Jewries in more than a dozen English towns. The Jews lent to great men and small; and the King squeezed their profits out of the Jews, whom he regarded as his private property. He had a special court for trying cases in which Jews were concerned, where they could swear a binding oath on the Law. It was not for their convenience but for his.

After a time some of them began to touch the land—but not with spade or plough. Now and then they got it as security for a loan, or bought it. More often they bought a rent-charge, a contract to pay so much from the rents of certain lands or houses in return for a sum down. This was the only form of regular investment, except buying land, known to and approved by everybody at the time. Monasteries often bought rent-charges, and the Church never declared this form of investment to be usury. The Jews were naturally unpopular. There were pogroms, and any ill-treatment of them by the King was welcomed: it was his protection of them that was disliked. They were the most hated of those foreigners whom the

English nationalists of Simon de Montfort's day abused. Pressure was put on them after 1265: their rent-charges were declared invalid: they were forbidden to hold land. When Edward I drove them out of England he was doing a popular thing, and his people backed him brutally. He could afford to do it because he had other financiers available; and the Jews were no longer the great capitalists that they had been in the twelfth century: the Jewish goose was now too hungry and too much worried to lay many golden eggs.

The Italians are much more important than the Jews. We know far more about their operations; they were more closely associated with English economic life; and they set many precedents in commercial practice and commercial law for all northern Europe. Whether any of them were here in the eleventh century is uncertain. Some were in the twelfth. Richard I found the merchants of Piacenza financially useful. So did John after him. But the great days of the Italians in England were the thirteenth and early fourteenth centuries, and the greatest firms that operated in England were Florentine. From 1252, when Florence first struck her golden florin, *fiorino d'oro*, to about 1340, her monetary and financial leadership in the West was hardly disputed.

The great firms of Florence—Bardi, Peruzzi, Frescobaldi, Pulci, Acciaiuoli—were merchants and financiers of the widest scope. An agent of the Bardi, Francesco Pegolotti, who was resident in England from 1317 to 1321, knew and wrote about every article that entered into trade from England to Armenia —all about English herrings, all about Cyprus sugar. The *societates*, companies, of these firms took money on deposit from members of the family and others, and traded with it. They collected the Pope's revenues—it was to do that that some of them first came to England, when the Pope had secured his financial stranglehold on the country after Henry II's defeat over Becket's murder, and John's surrender. They lent money to princes. They sold to them technical knowledge of minting. They accepted various concessions of royal rights— over the stannaries for instance—as security for the interest due. A Frescobaldi once sat on Edward II's Council. Besides, the firms did some ordinary money-lending, which made them as unpopular as the Jews had been. And in the late thirteenth century they were the greatest buyers and exporters of English wool.

For the convenience of travellers—clergy, pilgrims, merchants—they issued 'letters of payment' which could be cashed abroad. In 1300 the Pulci drew such a letter in London for £17. The man who got it was a dishonest parson who had stolen the £17 that he paid to the Pulci. In court, the Italian explained his *bona fides*, and said that he had warned his Paris house not to pay, and to instruct his other branches not to pay. (All these big firms had many branches, sometimes on infidel soil.) He could not promise that one of these might not cash the letter before learning that, in the language of to-day, it was stopped. Language and legal technicalities apart, this money-remitting business is curiously modern. Only Italians carried it on at this time, so far as the records tell us.

It was a rule of the Wool Gild (the *Arte della Lana*) of Florence in Dante's day, a gild whose members made the finest cloth, that only English wool should be used. Hence Italian interest in it. Agents of the Italian firms, often English middle-men, paid special attention to the monastic wool clips; but a middleman could also buy in markets where an alien might not have been popular. We know something of the export trade by individual firms under Edward I. The Italians dominated it and did the biggest deals. But natives were also important. In 1273, when for political reasons wool was only shipped by licence, natives handled about 35 per cent of the licensed trade. Some exporters broke the King's order and smuggled wool out from Lincolnshire, Yorkshire, even London. We meet up-country merchants from Dunstable, Ludlow, Shrewsbury and other places. Of these, some acted both as agents for the Italians and as independent exporters.

As his subjects got richer, the King had less need of the foreign financiers. Edward I never fought a campaign without their help. The change-over came under Edward III. Whether, when he repudiated his debts to Italian firms, he felt assured that he could raise enough money elsewhere we do not know. The repudiation was a great blow to Italian finance, though not the sole cause of the ruin of the firms of Bardi and Peruzzi. They had done bad business elsewhere, with other princes. This lending to princes was risky—as lending to governments, kingly or republican or totalitarian, has very often proved.

Watching the resources of his subjects, King Edward had in hand, by 1350, a list of 169 rich men who might be asked to lend when required. Three years earlier he had for the first time conducted a campaign entirely on English money: it was the campaign that led to the capture of Calais. He got his money partly by borrowing, partly by taxing the wool exported, or seizing it. He was constantly dealing with merchants, with an 'estate' of merchants, or rather of wool-merchants; and he had difficulties with the rising power of Parliament—because in Parliament big men and small men all knew that if a merchant had to pay a heavy tax he would offer the grower a lower price. The end of the struggle was a fairly moderate permanent export tax, and the concentration of the bulk of the export trade in the hands of the Merchants of the Staple, a semi-official body through which the crown could watch, tax, and direct the trade; and use it to put 'diplomatic' pressure on wool-consuming communities abroad.

A staple was a depot, a place where something is likely to heap up: in its French form, *étape*, it still means a military depot or dump. There were natural staples and made staples. The three Edwards found it convenient, financially and diplomatically, to be able to say—the staple for wool shall be here or there, at Dordrecht, at Bruges, in England, at Calais. It was the small Englishman who liked to have it in England, the small Englishman and the Italian: one could freely sell there, the other freely buy. So long as the Italians mattered, their interests helped those of the small men. But before 1360 the English paid as much in customs duty as all the alien exporters. Three years later Calais was first chosen; and at Calais the Merchants, now a Company, finally settled down for over a century and a half. They were recruited originally from the biggest wool-shippers in all the English ports; but in the fifteenth century the main body was a group of London-Calais men.[1]

The Calais Staple never controlled all the wool trade. Nor did it get hold of other export trades—tin and lead for example —that the crown tried to force through it. But it was always important; not least because this permanent establishment of Englishmen across the sea affected commercial practice. Men began to use the Italian 'letter of payment': it was easy to make such a letter payable in Calais where English wool-merchants were owed money. 'Debentures' of the Merchants of the Staple, that is sealed promises to pay, circulated in Calais and at the wool fairs. If you were a mercer, wishing to

[1] See further on the wool trade, pp. 164–5 below.

import miscellaneous French wares, you could buy from a merchant of the Staple a wool-bill payable abroad. So the risky transport of cash was economised; and so, by 1500, the letter of payment, the origin of the bill of exchange, was already regularised; and it already contained words still familiar to business men and lawyers, such as 'for value received'.

ENGLISH GILDS IN THE LATER MIDDLE AGES

The growth of gilds no more caused the growth of trade or handicraft than the foundation of the Merchants of the Staple, which occurred when the wool-export trade was at its height, caused that peak of exports. But both gild formation and our knowledge of the gilds are at their maximum between about 1350 and 1450; the gild is an interesting part of medieval economic life; and sometimes gild history reveals the economic realities behind it. We have a list of no less than 111 crafts 'exercised in London' under Henry V, all of which seem to have had some fraternity or 'mistery' organisation, though not all had received from the City authorities formal powers of self-government. We cannot always be sure of their position. Another list has been compiled of 130 occupations, 'crafts exercised' in Norwich before 1300—but these were not misteries with rules. The governors of Norwich seem always to have been shy of recognising new regular misteries or gilds: there were only sixteen all told in 1440, though by 1448 ten more had been recognised. About that time, Winchester had twenty recognised misteries and Coventry twenty-three. The trade or craft went on much the same, mistery or no mistery. At York and Bristol there were many misteries: York had forty-one whose rules the Mayor had approved; including ten separate ones connected with the iron-working trades, and seven of these with an average membership of only eleven. At Southampton and Nottingham misteries were negligible, at Southampton because the town was run by a strong, closed, Merchant Gild— of real merchants, who kept the craftsmen in their place. Cambridge had its artisans and small traders, with their *shoppae*, in abundance under Edward I; but there is hardly a trace of a trade gild in its records. The first known at Durham appears only in 1447. And how should there be such specialised organisation in a town like Liverpool—it was one of a large class—

where in 1378 there were five fishmongers, four drapers, four bootmakers, two tailors and a tanner?

When making a law about industry[1] and entrusting its application to the wardens and masters of gilds, so late as 1463, Parliament, we notice, made provision for its observance in cities or towns, not only where the crafts in question were 'used', but 'where no such wardens nor masters be'. They knew that there were gild towns and no-gild trades and towns.

The story of the London Gilds, or Companies as most of them became, does reflect real changes in commercial and industrial organisation. The traders' gilds—Fishmongers, Mercers, Vintners—and the handicraft gilds that worked for the luxury market and threw up rich men—Goldsmiths, Cordwainers—were the oldest and had always taken the lead. Towards the end of the fourteenth century they begin to seek, and to acquire, charters which make them—in the words of one of these—'sound, perpetual and corporate fraternities', with power to hold land 'in mortmain'; that is, to deprive the King of the valuable rights that came to him on the death of a tenant-in-chief; for they did not die. The first such charters were granted to the Goldsmiths, the Mercers and the Saddlers in 1394–5. The Livery Company, as such an organisation came to be called, was at once a fraternity with important social and religious activities, a court to judge among its members, a body of chartered traders with a monopoly area of their trade, and a mistery (French, *maîtrise*) to determine how the trading in textile fabrics and articles for clothing (mercery) or the making of some class of goods (saddlery) should be carried on. This last function led to the confusion of 'mistery' with 'mystery': how saddles were made by the mister saddlers was a trade secret, a mystery not to be revealed. As in all organised gilds, the Livery Company's officials had the right to search out bad work or dishonest dealings. As a perpetual fraternity it became a body corporate with a common seal.

It is to be recalled that, from the beginning, there was no obligation for a Mercer to confine himself to 'mercery'[2]— though most Mercers handled textile goods, often as export merchants. Nor was there a sharp division between wholesale and retail trading; though the great men of the Companies were usually wholesalers.

'For nearly half a century incorporation remained an

[1] For which see below, p. 178. [2] See above, pp. 126–7.

exceptional privilege, even amongst the wealthy fraternities whose members constituted the ruling class of citizens'.[1] The very ancient and powerful Fishmongers only became incorporate in 1433, the Cordwainers only in 1439. Incorporation was expensive and only societies of rich men, or societies that contained rich groups, could afford the expense.

A dozen humble-sounding 'crafts' were, however, incorporated under Edward IV, including the Barbers, Ironmongers, Carpenters and Cooks; but ironmongers may be, and later often were, iron merchants; carpenters may be builders; cooks may be substantial innkeepers; not many years later the Barbers became, by an amalgamation, the Barber-Surgeons, and no doubt they were rising towards 'surgery' when they got their charter in 1462. By 1530 about thirty 'crafts', great and smaller, were incorporated; there must have been a few well-to-do men in the smallest of them.

These and other second-grade Companies did not, however, become the equals of those to which the richest citizens belonged. After 1500 there finally emerged, in the constitutional organisation of London, the Twelve Great Companies who dominated City politics. At their head were the Companies of traders—Mercers, Grocers, Drapers, Fishmongers, Haberdashers, Ironmongers, Vintners. With these were the Companies, originally of craftsmen, which had long contained wealthy groups—Goldsmiths, Skinners, Salters. The other two Great Companies are specially interesting. They illustrate the late development of the Great Twelve and some economic developments also. Both took their final form after 1500. In 1503 the old and strong fraternity of Tailors and Linen Armourers was reincorporated as the Company of the Merchant Tailors. In 1528 the Fullers and the Shearmen, both already incorporated, came together as the Clothworkers. The name chosen for the Merchant Tailors is a reminder that its leading men did not ply needle and thread—though they may have done so as prentices. The men who paid for the Clothworkers' charter would not be those who sweated as working fullers, or those who handled the great shears which cut the nap of the cloth, but people who employed such men. Both Companies in the sixteenth century were rich and splendid.

Changes of name, and the amalgamation of the Fullers and the Shearmen, have no special economic significance: they

[1] George Unwin, *The Gilds and Companies of London* (1925), p. 160.

seem to have been mainly the result of ambition. Trading tailors did not change their economic status when they became Merchant Tailors; rather they changed their status and then claimed the merchant's rank. The Fullers and Shearmen had found that their wealthier members were 'being drawn away... by the superior attractions of the Drapers' Company'.[1] As Cloth-workers incorporate they could stand up to those proud Drapers, some of whom evidently were already clothworking employers.

Other London amalgamations, however, have true economic significance. We see, or we feel, a richer trading group getting on top of a handicraft group. Take the Leathersellers. What they sold was made by Pursers, Pouchmakers, Glovers and Whittawyers. They tried, during the fifteenth century, to get a hand in the 'search' of these trades, to see that the goods were well made. Between 1498 and 1517 the Leathersellers' absorption of Glovers, Pursers and Pouchmakers was formally sanctioned by the Mayor. There is no need to suppose that all glovers or pursers lost economic independence and became wage-earners; but many did tend to become jobbing workers for the leathersellers, just as to-day a tailor working at home may take work from one or more shopkeeping tailors. The Whittawyers drop out. Their job was to treat horse, deer and sheep hides with alum and oil, and they were nearer to the Curriers and Skinners than to the Leathersellers. In fact, long before 1500, they were jobbing for the Skinners just as the Glovers were for the Leathersellers.

Another constitutional development, but this time inside London Companies, also has economic significance—the evolution of a 'yeomanry'. In trade, as in the army or in agriculture, a yeoman was a second-rank person of some importance, below a knight, below a gentleman, below a full member of a gild. When the term is first used in the City (1390–1400) it refers to a serving man or journeyman,[2] second adult in a small workshop. These yeomen are often on strike. They are organis-ing their own fraternities, illegally as the masters say. They begin to wear a 'livery' of their own, some trade-union badge. They even have feasts, 'small drinkings' one supposes. Some-times they are met by an offer of a subordinate place in the 'mistery', as the Blacksmiths' yeomen were in 1434. So things stand in London up to about 1450.

[1] George Unwin, *The Gilds and Companies of London* (1925), p. 168.
[2] For whom see above, pp. 133–4.

But during the next half-century we can see quite clearly in many large London industries—goldsmiths, tailors, clothworkers, and so on—how some yeomen who have served an apprenticeship start business on their own account, when not yet admitted masters, generally in the suburbs where the writ of the Companies does not run and no one can 'search' them. The Leathersellers in 1482 put the case very clearly—ex-apprentices 'will not serve masters but take upon them every one...a shop, having no goods nor ware of their own to put therein...but are fain...to take other men's goods to occupy themselves'.[1] (They must have got the goods, as the saying is, on tick.) By about 1500, the fraternity organisations among such men appear to have generally become recognised as subordinate sections of the main Company—its second rank. In a Company like the Goldsmiths it is composed of working masters as opposed to those great trading, money-changing, and perhaps money-lending goldsmiths from among whom eventually the bankers sprang. These yeomen are below those full members of a Company who already before 1500 had come to be known as the Livery, those who could wear the Company's full dress, with the hood; but they are no longer journeymen or anything of that sort. By Elizabethan times there may be big men among them, men for whom at the moment there is no vacancy in the Livery. With growing wealth, economic and social subdivision has increased—here the subordinate grade differentiates out inside a Company; there a mistery, composed mainly of jobbing workmen, is absorbed into one whose members are real if modest capitalists, like the Leathersellers.

GILDS, MERCHANTS AND CRAFTSMEN IN LATE MEDIEVAL SCOTLAND

In the burghs of Scotland there begins in the fifteenth century a struggle between the handicraftsmen and the merchants of that Gildry which in nearly all of them was 'a constituent part of the town administration'.[2] This struggle goes on for generations. It has no parallel in England, where lower grades of workers and inferior fraternities or gilds, with a few brief exceptions, were curiously docile to town authority. The Scots merchants had been very jealous of their monopolistic position

[1] George Unwin, *The Gilds and Companies of London* (1925), p. 226.
[2] See above, p. 128.

from the start. In the thirteenth-century Berwick statutes, which were probably the model for other places, no one but a Merchant Gild brother, or a visiting foreign merchant, might buy hides, wool or woolfells to resell them. A butcher might not buy them—he could of course buy ox or sheep— unless he abjured his poleaxe and promised to kill no more. Now wool and hides were medieval Scotland's chief exports. Her main import, wine, was also imported or bought from foreign importers, and retailed, by the merchants only. Among themselves, Gild brethren shared bargains in these and other things in what seems a friendly co-operative way; but it was only among themselves. A rule grew up generally that not merely butchers, but all craftsmen, must abjure their crafts before they could be admitted to the Gildry.

Some of these late-medieval trade-monopolising Scottish merchants must have been substantial men. Although in the earlier centuries Scottish monasteries had been the chief traders, doing their own wool exporting, by the fifteenth century the lay merchants did a considerable export trade; and a Scottish 'staple', a main overseas depot for taxable exports, is found flitting about Flanders and Zeeland. (In the sixteenth century it settled down at Veere in Walcheren.) Yet if some merchants were substantial, many cannot have been; and outside the thinly spread burghs there were pedlar-merchants, 'having no certain dwelling-place in the sheriffdom [of Aberdeen], but being vagabond in the country'.[1] This class remained familiar in Scotland; on the continent familiar into the seventeenth century; and in northern England, as 'Scotchmen', familiar into the nineteenth.

The beginnings of the struggle between crafts and Gildry are not important in the general economic history of Britain; for they neither sprang from, nor brought about, any considerable economic changes. They mark only a natural semi-political resentment against an old and strict monopoly. The craftsmen wanted more trading liberty and a greater say in town control and town affairs, including their own; something more than their existing right to buy the raw materials of their craft and sell their stuff at their own stalls. They were not rising capitalists. As a class they were very small men indeed, and so remained far into succeeding centuries. Some Edinburgh

---

[1] Quoted by Miss I. F. Grant, *The Social and Economic Development of Scotland before 1603* (1930), p. 146.

figures from 1558 and some Glasgow figures from 1604 prove this. In 1558 certain Edinburgh crafts were offering men for military service. The offer included nearly as many masters as servants—275 against 283, not counting twenty-five 'servants in merchants' houses'. It is not unfair to masters to assume that had the men been, say, two to their one, the offer would have been at least two to one. Evidently the average master, like the working plumber of to-day, had a mate and nothing more. Not all had that. When one thinks of the London goldsmiths of Elizabeth's reign and their hall and their splendour, the offer from the goldsmiths of Edinburgh has a very humble showing—fourteen masters and six servants: half of the masters must have worked alone. So, judging by the figures, did most of the tailors. There is no figure for merchants, but the twenty-five 'servants in merchants' houses' do not suggest many, or any large establishments.

From Glasgow in 1604 we have merely the numbers of the different crafts. Tailors are the most numerous, as they were in Edinburgh. Glasgow had only thirty weavers and only twenty-seven 'Hammer-men', that is blacksmiths and any other metal-workers there may have been. There were eleven masons—and in a stone country—five dyers, two surgeons, and not a single goldsmith. Now, 150 years earlier, Coventry had counted fifty-seven weavers, thirty-seven 'deysters' (dyers), and nearly 100 metal-workers of various sorts.

If things stood so in Edinburgh and Glasgow under Mary or James VI, they cannot have been more highly developed in Aberdeen, Cupar or Ayr: they must have been less developed in all these towns under the succession of King Jameses of the fifteenth century. And outside these little scattered, vigorous, contentious and monopolising towns lay the open country with its 'upland men' and '*rustici*' in their clachans, and pastoral raiding Highlanders in their glens. Some think that no clachan ever grew into a true village, with a fair sprinkling of village craftsmen, as in England, because the towns were so successful in asserting their monopoly both of trade and of craftsmanship. No one might make any dyed cloth or even set up a tavern in Aberdeen outside the burgh—except that a lord or a knight might have one tavern at his place. Hence, no doubt, the qualities of the later Scottish inn as described by Dr Johnson, and the private distilling of 'usquebaugh'. The situation was much the same in the wide rural area which every privileged

Scottish town dominated. German towns had similar *Bann-meilen*, radii of control. In Scotland it was a very long mile indeed.

THE INTERNATIONAL FAIRS OF ENGLAND

The Scottish pedlar-merchant was a humble survivor of the early merchant type who regularly moved about with his goods. As trade became more fully organised, communications better, and commercial correspondence possible, this constant movement declined—especially movement over very great distances. The merchant never became quite sedentary: travel was always needed for the opening up of new trade routes; but on the well-established routes it was less necessary than it had once been. There were agents and correspondents in Bordeaux or Cadiz or Danzig: a member of an English wool-exporting firm might be domiciled semi-permanently at Calais: foreigners bringing imports to Britain could dispose of them to merchants at the ports, instead of going with them up-country, as they often did in earlier times. By the fifteenth century, it was a popular grievance that some foreigners rode about in England buying wool: let the wool go from stage to stage along the proper channels, English channels: there are merchants of various sorts who understand the handling of it; in few foreign countries may we ride about buying or selling. So the grievance ran.[1] A group of German merchants, men from the Hanse towns, had bought for themselves various trading privileges from the crown in the thirteenth century; and, as these Hansards became a political and naval power in the fourteenth, they were able to retain their privileges by treaty in the fifteenth. But they did not then travel about the country. They sat close in their walled 'factory' by the Thames, the Steelyard, on part of whose site Cannon Street station now stands; and if they retailed Rhenish wine it was a grievance. The London vintners would see to distribution and sale.[2]

At some remote date, places and times at which the old-style travelling merchants, native or foreign, could get into touch with the local consumer or buy from the local producer had, so to speak, selected themselves. The places were likely to be at seaports or near high points on navigable rivers. The merchants would not be looked for except in the travelling and trading season; there might not be much to sell to them until after

[1] See below, pp. 177–8. [2] See below, pp. 165–6.

sheep-shearing and harvest. So it is that these fairs, occasional gatherings for large-scale trading as opposed to the markets for week-to-week exchanges, generally fell in the high summer or early autumn. They must have existed, though no doubt at first informally, long before the Norman Conquest; but there is only a single reference to them in Domesday. We begin to learn about them when national records begin to become abundant, in the twelfth century. There are charters; but a charter would not often create a trading place, though it might encourage and improve one. In the reign of King John the greatest fairs, so far as we know, those of international importance, were at Bristol, St Ives (Hunts), Boston and Stamford. In the thirteenth century Winchester came to the front; and either in that century or earlier a great number of local fairs were approved, we need not say created, by charter. Many of these did only a local cattle-selling business, plus a little trading in manufactured and other goods not available locally. It is interesting to notice that three of the most famous international fairs, at the time of Magna Carta, lay about that Fenland entry into the heart of England which had been so useful to early invaders. Stamford was particularly well placed —close to the Fenland waterways and on the hard stone ground that carried the North Road and supplied the material for the town's splendid churches. Many centuries later the north-bound summer motorist might find his way impeded by the stalls of Stamford Fair, no longer international.

We know what a late thirteenth-century international fair was like from the records of St Ives (1270–1324). It belonged to the Abbots of Ramsey in the Fen. Its charter dated from Henry I; but likely enough piratical vikings coming up the Ouse had traded and robbed on what, before St Ive's bones were discovered about the year 1000, was called Slepe, the slippery shore.

The fair was so important before 1270 that Henry III's tailor went there to buy fine imported Flemish cloth for the King; but its importance was already waning under Edward II. We know it at its height and from the records of the Fair Court, where every sort of case came up for decision—from the finding of harlots in the house of William Redknave to great international disputes about wool that involved the Countess of Flanders, who had not traded in it however but seized it. In that court we meet in 1270 Reginald and Arnulph, 'Easterlings', that is Hansards, Gerard of Cologne and Gottschalk of 'Almaine'. It was Gottschalk (who though of 'Almaine' had been admitted a burgess of Lynn) who sued the men of Ghent, Douai, Ypres, Lille and Poperinghe, subjects of the Countess of Flanders, because her bailiffs had impounded his wool. Men from all these places were present, or were represented in court. In 1287 we meet men of Brabant: it was before their booths that Henry of Bytham threw another man 'into a certain well', a case of common assault. Four years later, when weights and measures are being inspected, Hugh of Spain has a true quart pot but a false pottle (half-gallon pot). Robert the Scot, Honorius of Stamford, who sounds like a German, and John Liesegang, who certainly was one, for he came *cum vino reneys* (Rhine wine), all had good measures. There are English people from a distance—Robert of Bury St Edmunds and Amy of Plumstead, whose clothes that she had pawned were, she said, unjustly detained; and others from near by, like John of Eltisley whom Roger Barber agreed to cure of baldness: John paid a large sum (9*d.*) in advance and Roger put him twice 'in plaster' before absconding with it. In 1300 we meet again buyers for the King's wardrobe. In 1312 comes the most international gathering of all—men of Bruges, Ypres, Ghent and other Flemish places; men of Louvain and Dinant; men of Caen; the *societas* of the Bardi, the London *societas* (was it another Italian company?) and everyone else. All complain of a rowdy group who 'came and carolled to the terror of the fair'. Certain sorts of singing, probably accompanied by dancing, might be treated as breaches of the peace.

There are many cases in commercial law about selling in secret places, using false measures, buying up goods on their way to market to resell them. That was 'forestalling': William Wythe is convicted of 'forestalling small hams'. But the main interest is the motley assemblage of traders. No one would expect to-day, or would have expected under Henry VIII, to meet a Spaniard or an Italian banker or a man from Caen at St Ives. To-day its fair goes on, as a cattle-fair, and over it the statue of Oliver Cromwell presides. It seems that the rise of Sturbridge Fair on the Cam first tapped its trade; but the early history of Sturbridge is obscure. In the fifteenth century, moreover, we should not expect to meet many miscellaneous aliens at an English inland fair. Successors to William Liesegang and Hugh of Spain would not be likely to go up-country with their wines. The days of the Italian bankers were over. Flemish cloth had lost ground in England, as the native industry had grown; and in any case Flemings would not normally have travelled with it then beyond Orwell, Aldeburgh or Lynn.

The fairs remained an important feature in the economic life of the country until the eighteenth century; but they ceased to be international gatherings. If foreign goods came to a fair English traders brought or sent them.

ENGLISH INDUSTRY: TECHNICAL PROGRESS AND THE POWER OF CAPITAL

The development of the English cloth industry is a famous story, about which something fresh is always being learnt both on the technical and on the economic side. Technical progress there was in every medieval industry, slow no doubt but steady. In many trades it was mainly progress in that manual skill and artistic tradition which, with good fortune and ability, could be handed on by apprenticeship from generation to generation. The silver vessels 'great and small' in the fifty-two goldsmiths' shops on the Strand, richer in 1500 than 'all the shops in Milan, Rome, Venice and Florence put together' as a Venetian thought, were made by men whose technique would not differ much from that of those who served Otho the goldsmith of Domesday. The amazing and progressive skill of masons and architects was not influenced or aided by anything essentially new on the technical side: the windlass is the only mechanical aid that is mentioned in the records; and there is no reason to think that it was a new one. The masons' acquired knowledge of weights and stresses must have been based on trial and error: their towers as we know sometimes fell down. The noble art of the bell-founder developed slowly in the hands of many local and some almost national experts: John of Gloucester and at least six of his men crossed England to cast bells for Ely in 1345–6. From the art of casting bells developed that of casting bronze and even iron cannon, without any important change in the process. The prosperous manufacture and the considerable export of English pewter, that enabled the London Pewterers to pay for a charter of incorporation in 1468, was based not on any new technique but on England's ample supplies of the main raw materials—tin, copper and lead. In mining for these, as in mining for coal, some modest technical progress was made: but the greatest feat was the cutting of adits or 'avidods' to let out subterranean water; and that was only applicable when the pit was in a slope and the 'avidod' could be driven in to drain the sump from a point well below the pit's mouth. We first hear of 'avidods' in the thirteenth century, but such an obvious device may well be older. Pumps or 'baling engines' in mines are mentioned just before 1500; but they were certainly not much used.

The cloth-making trade was the first to take over the use of water-power from corn-milling; and we now know that it did this early and on a large scale with important economic and social consequences, a genuine 'industrial revolution'.[1] Fulling was the process for which water-power was used. In fulling the rough cloth is cleaned, thickened and felted in water and some soapy material—originally fullers' earth. Its surface can then be raised with teazle-heads and cropped or sheared to make a nap—but in those processes there was no important change, any more than there was in spinning or weaving. (We hear of spinning-wheels from the late fourteenth century and can see pictures of them from the fifteenth; but they had not become general: women span on the distaff as they always had.) The fulling of heavy cloth had been done, time out of mind, by stamping with the bare feet of 'walkers'. Light materials, for caps and such, were fulled by hand.

Who first thought of stamping the cloth by water-driven hammers, or where, we do not know. We hear of a fulling-mill in Normandy in the eleventh century; there is no reason to suppose it the first. There were fulling-mills in Italy in the twelfth—and so there were in England, where water-driven corn-mills were far more widespread than in Italy. The four earliest mills yet known here are of the reign of Henry II; they stood at Stanley-on-the-Marden in Wiltshire, at Kirkby-on-Bain in Lincolnshire, and on lands belonging to the Knights of the Temple in Yorkshire and the Cotswolds—and perhaps another Wiltshire mill (but its date is doubtful) at or near Malmesbury. Yet another fulling-mill was standing at Minster Lovell in Oxfordshire by 1197. Some of these were certainly not brand new when we first hear of them, and the scantiness of

[1] E. M. Carus-Wilson, 'An Industrial Revolution of the Thirteenth Century', *Econ. Hist. Rev.*, vol. XI (1941), pp. 39–60, reprinted in her *Medieval Merchant Venturers* (1954), pp. 183–210.

twelfth-century records makes it most unlikely that they were the only fulling-mills then at work. After 1200 references multiply and, though they only become numerous from the reign of Edward I, between 150 and 160 have been collected from years before 1327. There must have been many more mills than these: for we know little about estates that were not either royal or ecclesiastical. On those that we know the fulling-mill, like the corn-mill, became manorial and a source of revenue to the lord.[1]

The mills that have been traced before 1327 are mainly found where there was plenty of natural water-power, as a modern engineer might expect. There are few yet known in East Anglia and the South-East. There are only two in the London district—at Stratford-le-Bow and Enfield. They increase as you go west—the upper Thames valley, the Kennet valley, the Cotswolds, the Welsh Marches. There are ten in Devon and eleven in Cornwall. In the Midlands they are spread thin; but there are eleven in the West Riding and no less than nineteen in the Lake District—including one at Grasmere and one in Grizedale, of all out-of-the-way sites.

Only a handful of the mills were in or near places that were of any importance as towns in the thirteenth century—Carlisle, Wakefield, Monmouth, Winchester, Stratford, and a few more. Plenty are in places well known later as centres of the rural, or semi-rural, cloth-making industry, or of other textile industries later still, but at that time insignificant villages or rural townlets—Kendal, Manchester, Bradford, Leeds, Kidderminster, Crediton, Taunton, Minchinhampton, Witney. This process of cloth-making at least is establishing itself in the country.

Now in the country women had always spun the wool and in early days had woven it too—as they still do in Himalayan villages and other places up and down the earth. No doubt the more remote fulling-mills worked at first for local consumption on the rough local cloth—the 'household' cloth as it was called later. The finer, better known, cloths of the twelfth and early thirteenth centuries, cloths some of which were exported, were

---

[1] Some thirty further examples of fulling-mills in existence before 1327 have come to light since Professor Carus-Wilson's article was first published (E. M. Carus-Wilson, *Medieval Merchant Venturers*, p. 210 n.). Sixteen of these have been collected and listed by Mr Reginald Lennard in the *Econ. Hist. Rev.*, Second Series, vol. III (1951), pp. 342–3; they include the twelfth-century mills at Kirkby-on-Bain and Minster Lovell, and the mill at or near Malmesbury. I have revised the figures originally given by Sir John Clapham in this paragraph accordingly. [J.S.]

woven by men in or about towns where early fulling-mills have
seldom been found—York, Lincoln, Stamford, Oxford, Colchester and others. In several of these towns, as we know, both
weavers and fullers had gilds. Winchester is an exception: it
had a gild of fullers, and by 1209 the Bishop owned fulling-mills
in several of the surrounding villages.

Some weavers' and fullers' gilds in the towns had been
strong enough to annoy the town authorities in the twelfth
century.[1] The towns brought them to heel, being aided in this,
as may fairly be assumed, by the weakening position of the old
urban wool industry as rural competition developed. The early
London fullers had certainly stamped their cloth. At what date
they began to send out to the mills at Stratford and Enfield—
first mentioned in 1298 or later—we can only guess.

It is not at all surprising that, in the thirteenth and fourteenth centuries, we hear of urban textile gilds that are im-
poverished, whose numbers are falling. York is quite explicit
about the reason, in 1304—'divers men in divers places in the
country' are making their sort of cloth, and so the weavers
cannot pay the King what they should. Weavers and fullers
move out from such towns, or are not replaced as they die.
And by the fifteenth century the cloths that people know about
are named, not from the old town industries, but from newly
risen towns or districts where the water flows strongly to the
mills—'Kendal greens', 'Cotswolds', 'Stroudwaters'.[2]

The transfer of fulling, and changes contemporary with it,
added to the power of capital in the national wool industry.
When first towns fought the early weavers' gilds, they fought in
the interests of merchants: weavers were not to sell outside the
town: if there was any such 'export', the mercantile group
was to get the profit of it. The position of the merchants was
strengthened, in connection with the making of the best sorts
of cloth, because it was they, or their correspondents at the ports,
who handled the best imported dyeing materials—as they had
in Aelfric's time.[3] Blue woad, as every schoolboy used to know,
will grow in England; but it was imported, from Bordeaux and
elsewhere, on a very large scale. So perhaps was madder, and
weld, which yields a yellow dye. So was alum, the 'mordant'

---

[1] See above, p. 130.
[2] Besides the new fulling-mills, the prospect of cheap labour and freedom
from the restrictions of the town gilds probably helped to attract clothmaking
to the country. [J.S.]   [3] See above, pp. 62–3.

that makes the dyes hold. So above all was 'grain', a grain of dried insects akin to the cochineal insect, which dyed the scarlet cloth that denoted eminence, in aldermen, doctors of law, fighting men—as it still does. Sir Thopas, in Chaucer's mock ballad, had a complexion 'like scarlet in grayn'.

The sort of thing that happened is illustrated from the old London trade of the 'burellers', which disappears by name from about 1350. Originally they seem to have been dealers in a rough cloth called 'borel'. Then they get cloth made. Then they buy woad and other dyestuffs and have it dyed and finished. They are employing the weavers who, after a long struggle with the City, are well tamed by 1300. In 1335 the burellers are asserting proudly that 'they are not weavers but freemen of the City and as such are entitled to carry on any trade or mistery'. By this time, as the reference suggests, the weavers' charter was 'practically abrogated'.[1] The weaver is a small jobbing master and the 'bureller' type—found later among the drapers or the clothworkers—is what came to be known as a clothier.

But the true clothier, clothmaker or director of clothmaking, never became an important figure in London. Cloth was not much woven there after about 1350. London weavers, towards 1500 and later, are found working on linen or silk. The rising London capitalists are the leading fullers and shearmen who finally get their charter as the Clothworkers Company in 1528.[2] And they are 'working'—that is getting raised, sheared and pressed, perhaps also dyed—cloth that comes up 'white' in great quantities from country clothiers who have had it made near those water-mills where the laborious process of fulling had ceased to be done by bare feet. The working fuller, to his great advantage, had become a machine-minder, a sort of transition which in the modern world is often rather ridiculously lamented—as if it were not better to mind a sweet-running if noisy power-loom than to warp one's breast-bone by ten or twelve hours a day over a hand-loom.

What happened in the early days around the country fulling-mills we must guess. Some weavers from towns may have moved out to settle near them. Locally, there can be no doubt that weaving became more professional and more of a man's job. Most of the water-power districts were also good sheep districts—rough wools in Cumberland, finer ones on the Welsh

---

[1] Frances Consitt, *The London Weavers' Company*, vol. 1 (1933), p. 28.
[2] See above, pp. 145–6.

Marches, the Cotswolds, and the downs above the Kennet and the Thames. Two types of clothier developed during the fourteenth and fifteenth centuries. First, the small man who bought or grew his wool; had it spun by his family and his neighbours; wove the yarn; had the cloth fulled at the manorial mill; and sold it locally or to a buyer from one of the towns, especially London. Second, the capitalist clothier who bought wool in bulk and gave it out to be spun, or bought yarn from spinsters for the market who can be traced quite early; gave it out to jobbing weavers; and had it fulled at a manorial mill of which he had the lease or, when he could get it, the ownership.

The rise of these men was not all of a pattern. Some were immigrant Flemings, the encouragement of whom by the Edwards, especially by Edward III, was important in the history of the industry, but not so important as was once supposed: English cloth-making was neither undeveloped nor decadent in the thirteenth century, even if King Henry III did send his agents to buy foreign stuff at the fair of St Ives. Some clothiers may have been wool merchants who decided to have their wool worked up into cloth; more, probably, men of the bureller or draper type, originally dealers who knew all about the qualities and markets for cloth; some no doubt just small working clothiers who had prospered and concentrated on buying raw materials, supervising the manufacture, and selling the cloth. In the fifteenth century the big clothiers multiplied, their importance varying from district to district—few in the North, most in the South-West. In spite of a relative lack of easily harnessed water-power, but aided by the Flemish immigration, they became important in East Anglia.[1]

The introduction of water-power into other industries came later and slower than into the cloth manufacture, and the facts are less well known. Bellows had always been used at the little furnaces in which iron was smelted. They were worked by hand or by foot. No water-driven bellows have been traced in the iron industry before 1400; but during the fifteenth century water-power was utilised in many parts of the country. Iron-making was more remote, more detached from everyday life, less under manorial control, than cloth-making; so that it is far from certain that the earliest record which happens to have survived refers to the earliest use of this or any process. That is

[1] See further on the distribution of the cloth industry in the late fourteenth century, pp. 190–1 below.

specially true of the other main application of water-power to iron-making, the use of water-driven hammers, 'tilt-hammers' for forging 'blooms' of wrought iron. Originally done by hand with a sledge hammer, forging was certainly done by 'great waterhamors' in Ashdown Forest just before 1500. As the process is merely an application of the principle of the fulling-mill, but with bigger and far heavier mechanism—there is no need to beat wool as you must hammer iron—and as there were fulling-mills almost everywhere before 1400, and in many places before 1300, it is most unlikely that it had never been tried until 1496, the date of the Ashdown record. Moreover, although iron-working was less 'manorial' in its organisation than fulling, it should be remembered that iron was worked on such great estates as those of the Bishop of Durham, where the relatively heavy expenditure necessary for setting up a tilt-hammer would present no difficulty.

That both bellows and hammers for iron-making were some-times driven by water much earlier than the records yet examined have proved, is suggested by a reference to water-driven bellows used in smelting lead ore in Devonshire so early as 1295. There is no reason to suppose that they were new.

After 1500 water-power was applied, either on the continent or in England, to a wide range of grinding operations, to wire-drawing, wood-sawing, and metal-rolling; but as the wire mill was a Nuremberg novelty late in the fifteenth century, and as some of the other applications of power look like novelties when first referred to, we are not entitled to assume that any of them had been tried in Britain before 1500.

As for the windmill, it had been known since the end of the twelfth century. At Bury St Edmund's, as Jocelin of Brakelond records, Herbert the Dean, *Herbertus decanus, levavit molendinum ad ventum*, and had a quarrel with the Abbot about it. The windmill remained a very rough and imperfect affair, used so far as is known only for different sorts of grinding. Its application to pumping, as in the Fens, comes later.[1]

Of shipbuilding, that vital industry for an island, we know much less than we could wish, on the technical as on the economic side. The beautiful and seaworthy viking ship, long and narrow, with oars and sail, had long gone out of use—perhaps because it was not much of a cargo-carrier and, on a knightly military expedition, would have made a poor horse-

[1] See below, p. 197.

boat. The 'galley with oars' was in use for fighting in the twelfth century, but vanished from northern seas later, surviving only in the Mediterranean. For cargo, the typical carrier from the Conquest to the fifteenth century was the 'cog', a very broad-beamed, blunt-nosed tub, with a square sail on its single mast. It could not sail into the wind and liked best to run before it, at a very few knots. It was steered by a modified oar on its 'starboard' side. Carrying capacity was measured—very loosely—by tuns, a witness to the importance of the wine trade: a tun was a big cask that contained some 250 gallons. It could hold water or beer, but beer export could never compare with the import of wine. Indeed beer was mostly shipped for the crew.

Down to 1300 a thirty-tun ship seems to have been about normal; so that when a King was entitled to a 'prise' of one tun of wine before and one abaft the mast, as he was in the twelfth century, he got a tax in kind of about 6½ per cent. Now and then bigger ships are heard of, up to 100 tuns or even more; but they are rare.

With the fourteenth century a *magna navis* of 200, even of 240, tuns may occur. Two masts were sometimes stepped, and the stern rudder with its tiller came in. How generally the rudder was adopted in that century is unknown; but as a drawing of Noah's ark from about 1350 shows an excellent one, with two pintles, it was evidently known for big ships that stood high out of the water. One would hardly draw the ark with a novel gadget attached. (A French fourteenth-century MS. shows a horse coming out of a big port low down at the stern, like a tank from a landing craft; but that may have been only an artist's bright notion.) To turn a fourteenth-century cargo-boat into a 'man-of-war', you built on it a forecastle—an actual timber castle—perhaps an aft-castle, and certainly a top-castle, or top, on the mast.

The fifteenth is the revolutionary century, but most of the changes were borrowed from Mediterranean practice and most of our evidence for them is late. Forecastle and aft-castle, or poop, became structural—first naturally in ships of war. Ordinary cargo boats grew bigger. About 1400 the average wine cargo into Bristol was eighty-eight tuns; by 1500, 200 tuns was not unusual. Nine ships in the Spanish trade, near that date, averaged 142. And some of these bigger ships were built with rather sharper bows and rather finer lines.

But the real revolution on the big ships was in rig. Two, three, masts appear, even in one drawing four. There is a rudimentary bowsprit, which in the pictures may cock up to carry a little square sail below it—as it still did in Pepys's ships—but not a jib above. The main-mast, and the fore-mast if there was one, carried the old square sail, eventually with a topsail over it; and on the mizzen was a lateen sail such as had been used for centuries in the Mediterranean. Even without the jib, this rig, when the yards were properly handled, enabled a ship to sail fairly close to the wind and to tack with reasonable success. Who first introduced these new things, and when, we are left to imagine. If private medieval shipbuilders kept specifications and accounts, none have survived. King Henry V had a fine fleet. His *Jesus of the Tower* is credited with 1000 tons, his *Holigost of the Tower* with 760, and seven other ships with from 400 to 600; but 'there is very little information as to the conditions under which' these great ships were built.[1] We know about crews and provisioning, and guns, and the cost of building forecastles and aftcastles. We know that blocks were used; and a few more technical facts are known. But about designing and building we are very ignorant. We cannot trust the pictures on manuscripts or medals implicitly. It is only with late fifteenth-century drawings that we get on to fairly firm ground.

Of Scottish shipbuilding as an industry we know even less than of English. There are a few sixteenth-century figures of shipping movements, a few records of foreign ships in Scottish trade; and the interesting fact that when the *Great Saint Michael* was to be built for the King of Scots, just after 1500, the master-builder was a Frenchman. For the rest, we must picture small 'cogs' in the overseas trade of Scotland and all sorts of rough fishing boats among its firths and sea-lochs and islands.

FOREIGN TRADE: WINE AND WOOL

There is some temptation to exaggerate the importance of English overseas trade because we have the facts, or many of them. From about 1300, in some cases earlier, customs accounts, port books and other sources tell a great deal. No one knows the bulk or value of the goods handled at the fair of St Ives, say, in the year 1290; but how many sacks of wool were shipped

[1] M. Oppenheim, *A History of the Administration of the Royal Navy* (1896), p. 13.

overseas in that year, and from what ports we do know. Yet it is not easy to exaggerate the importance of the export of wool in the earlier centuries, of the growing export of cloth in the later, or of the import of wine throughout. These affected all sorts of out-of-the-way districts and people. William of Doncaster, under Edward I, will collect wool somewhere in the North-West and ship it through an eastern port.[1] He is only one of many collectors and exporters. A great nineteenth-century economic historian, who knew the Middle Ages well, used to say that it was easier to get wine in an English village inn in the thirteenth century than it was in his own day: his evidence came from entries in the travelling expenses of academic clerics from Oxford.

The wine fleets we have met already—the fleet from the Rhine into the Thames of the twelfth century[2] and the fleet into Bristol of the late fifteenth.[3] More and more, during the three centuries of English rule in Gascony and after the loss of Normandy, the trade centred on Bordeaux; though the Rhenish and Spanish and eventually the Mediterranean wines also came in. It was natural for Chaucer to picture his bibulous and piratical shipman—who, for all Chaucer knew, might have come from Dartmouth—tapping surreptitiously the merchants' casks 'from Burdeux-ward'. So completely was the 'claret' country given up to wine-growing for export that it had to import grain, fertile though it was. At first the initial carriage to some main British port was mostly in the hands of seamen from Bayonne; but by 1308 ships of a score of English towns, from Chester round to Ipswich, had a hand in it, though the Bayonne ships still predominated. By 1372 Froissart speaks—but was he exact in figures?—of 200 English, Welsh and Scottish ships loading with wine at Bordeaux. He does not give tunnage, but probably by that time the average would be well over fifty, seeing that at Bristol rather later it was eighty-eight.

The Welsh ships are interesting. There was a great wine trade up the Irish sea, either from the continental ports direct, or after transhipment in some English West Country or South Welsh harbour: about transhipment we are not informed. Ships from 'Aquitaine', the Bayonne ships, were well known at Chester by the year 1200. After that date 'probably every port

---

[1] See above, p. 127.   [2] See above, p. 62.
[3] See above, p. 160.

in the Irish Sea engaged in some measure in the wine trade'.[1]
When in 1282 Edward I was providing for his Welsh war he
could order from Ireland 600 tuns of wine, 20 average thirteenth-century cargoes, as an ordinary commissariat operation.
There seems to have been no doubt that this large supply would
be available.

The Scots' ships of 1372 are interesting also. We know of
big Scottish wine-fleets in the sixteenth century—four-score
ships in 1596 it is said, mostly Scots—but about earlier centuries we are ill-informed. Froissart's casual reference suggests
that the Scot acquired his traditional taste for claret when the
claret country still owed allegiance to the 'auld enemy'. And
if, as is said, even the 'rascal multitude' of Edinburgh drank
a good deal of wine in the sixteenth century, there is no reason
to think that the habit was new.

English Kings, who owned vineyards in the claret country
for centuries, naturally favoured the export trade from Bordeaux. They both taxed their subjects' wines in transit and
exported their own by proxy. Royal regulations in the thirteenth century tried to preserve for the King's wines the first
of the London market in the shipping season. The loss of
Bordeaux in 1453 was a blow to the trade. From that time
forward the place was often enemy territory and its produce
might always be subject to extra customs duty. It is not altogether an accident that we begin to hear more in literature
of 'malmsey'—a Mediterranean wine—and 'sack'—from
Spain or the Canaries—as time runs on towards Shakespeare.
But, with their French alliance, the Scots retained their old
trading connection and tastes.

The luxury wines of the Middle Ages, not only in Britain,
were the strong sweet vintages that came first from the eastern
Mediterranean, 'Syrian' wines, wines of Cyprus, of Crete, of
Greece. They took their trade name in the North from Monem-
vasia in the Morea—*malvoisie*, malmsey. These, with some of
the choicer Italian and Sicilian vintages, went regularly westward through the straits, though in necessarily rather limited
consignments, after the sailing of Venetian fleets to Bruges
became annual events from 1317. Later the Venetians called
on their way up-channel at Southampton. Sweet wines from
Spain—Malaga, Tarragona—had long come in native shipping.
English customs officials made a distinction between these

[1] H. J. Hewitt, *Medieval Cheshire* (1929), p. 131.

sweet southern wines and the others. In 1443–4, when the trade was well established, a year's imports into Southampton totalled 345 tuns of the sweet and 896 of the ordinary wines, presumably from Bordeaux—not yet lost. All the rarer wine, it is interesting to find recorded, was brought in by aliens, but four-fifths of the other by Englishmen. The medieval English wine-shipper was well established at Bordeaux, but had never won a firm stance within what were known as the Straits, not of Gibraltar, but of 'Marok'.

Thirteenth- and fourteenth-century Englishmen were proud of their great wool export. They had almost a monopoly of a prized raw material. They said that the Flemings, well ahead of them industrially and commercially, were just England's weavers. Their Kings knew the diplomatic uses of a block or a diversion of the outward flow of wool; but had to learn that you could not block too freely or direct too often—just as you could not tax too heavily—without getting across the rising power of Parliament, in which great magnates and those who spoke for smaller men were united in wanting the flow to be regular and the price good. The export, as has been seen, was somewhere about its peak at the end of the thirteenth century.[1] After that, and after Edward III's various experiments with wool as a source of income and power, the export fell away almost precisely as the manufacture of cloth developed—the country, for various reasons, seems not to have increased its flocks to meet a double demand; and the demand of some of the old buyers, Flanders and Florence notably, was not so insistent in the fifteenth century as it had been in the thirteenth.

However that may be, in every port for which we have separate statistics, the export of wool at the end of the fifteenth century (annual average for 1472–82) was less, in most very much less, than it had been two hundred years earlier. From Hull and Boston the decline was immense. Apparently, as Tudor times approached, the North was using nearly all its own wool. (On the average in 1282–90 more wool had gone out from Boston than from London.) The export from Southampton was down by nearly two-thirds. From London alone the late fifteenth-century export figure was comparable with that of the late thirteenth—comparable but about a third less. This concentration of the surviving trade into London was a result mainly of the monopolistic Staple policy: the Staplers of

---

[1] See above, p. 122.

1472–82 were a London-Calais group and they handled most of the wool that was still shipped. They sent it all in English ships, as might have been expected—English or Calais ships, which is the same thing. Under Edward I a fair proportion of the wool shipped from London, and at Boston and Hull seven bales out of every eight, had been loaded into foreign ships—Hansard, Flemish, and French.

FOREIGN TRADE: ENGLISH CLOTH EXPORTS;
OTHER EXPORTS AND IMPORTS

The history of the export of cloth is naturally the reverse of that of the export of wool. We know little about its details before 1350; for our knowledge comes from customs accounts and until 1347 Englishmen could export customs-free, whereas foreigners were taxed both when importing and exporting. About the foreigners' trade we know something from the year 1303. As would be expected, at that date—the story of St Ives fair shows it[1]—their main business was import of that fine Flemish cloth in which kings dressed. But it is a remarkable proof of the growth of the English industry in the previous century that these aliens found it worth their while to take some English cloth out from most of the ports, and from some of them—particularly Boston—great quantities.

When we get figures of exports by Englishmen round about 1350, we find that they do nearly all the business from two of the great shipping centres—Bristol for the Cotswold broadcloths and Yarmouth for the lighter East Anglian 'worsteds'. The foreign shipper was still dominant in London, and in one or two minor places; but in most he was no longer important. Before the end of the fifteenth century, even in London, more shipping was done by natives than by foreigners, in spite of the great strength and the privileged position of the Hanse merchants in their Steelyard; but everywhere else except at Southampton, where the visits of the Venetian galleys gave facilities to the foreign shipper, the natives dominated the trade.

The power of the Hansards was political and naval as much as economic. They kept fleets at sea, fought battles, and made treaties with kings. Late in the fifteenth century, by helping Edward IV to regain the throne, they bought the favourable

[1] See above, p. 151.

treaties of 1473–5 which were much resented—and eventually abrogated—by Tudor Englishmen. They paid the 'old' custom on wool and other things, and the 'new' of 1303 which fell on their cloth. Under a bargain made with the crown in 1317 they claimed to be free of any future additional customs; and it seems that they often were; though in the course of almost perpetual politico-economic squabbles with the English crown they were at intervals obliged to pay all. They won a strong position from Edward IV; under the early Tudors the position was this: on miscellaneous imports reckoned by the pound they paid less poundage than Englishmen, but not less tunnage on the wine; however they had the right, heartily disliked in England, to sell off their wine retail at a sort of 'jug and bottle' section of the Steelyard. On cloth exported (by that time England's great export) they also paid less than the Englishmen, far less than any other foreigners. And though, in the early fifteenth century, there were groups of English merchants established in their towns so far east as Danzig, they had to sell and buy without any special privileges. In the later fifteenth century, English merchants lost even this limited share in the Baltic trade.

These few facts show how hard it is to discuss the economics of medieval customs—what lines of trade or manufacture they encouraged, what they discouraged. Like taxes in modern war-time, they were changed in relation to their revenue-yielding capacity and their utility in international affairs. It is hard to guess the precise consequences of an export duty on cloth levied in three separate grades. At least there is no reason to think that it checked the growth of the industry in England; though no doubt, if it had been intolerably high, some of the widely scattered, and to us mostly unknown, foreign consumers might have been forced to dress in linen—which was to be had everywhere—or in leather.

Englishmen who shipped cloth abroad, going with it or sending their agents to see to its sale in continental towns, were usually known as 'merchants adventuring', and their organised groups as Merchant Adventurers. 'Adventuring' had been the merchants' business from the beginning; and the term came to be applied, after the thirteenth century, to those men who retained the old character, as opposed to the Staplers carrying on their steady, single-commodity trade on a beat prescribed by government—after about 1350 the short beat from London to Calais. As cloth became England's great export, merchants 'adventured' predominantly in cloth; but it would be a mistake to think of the adventurers, at any stage of their evolution, as all, or mere, cloth-merchants. The bigger they were, the wider were their interests: this, as we know, was not a new thing among merchants,[1] though we only see it clearly among adventurers at the end of the period. Round about 1500 a big man might be both a Stapler and an Adventurer, extending his cloth export as the exports of wool shrank. He might also be in the wine trade. And he might, as a Mercer —often his original position—import silks, and arras, and 'mercery' generally from the continent.

There were groups, or organised societies, of these adventurers in various towns—the Gild of St George at Hull, the Mercers and Merchant Adventurers of York, the Merchant Adventurers of Newcastle-on-Tyne; but the greatest, and by 1500 the dominant group, was that of the London Adventurers who came to call themselves the Merchant Adventurers of England. They were much mixed up—as their records are— with the ancient Company of the London Mercers. But they were by no means all Mercers: they included Grocers, Drapers, Skinners and Haberdashers, with occasional Tailors and Fishmongers. It is never to be forgotten that the custom of London made capital and enterprise fluid between Company and Company, at least at the top: it was the cobbler who stuck to his last, and the small Mercer who merely retailed his silks and his ribbons over the counter.

The Hansards, with their control of the northern continental markets, and privileges won from the English crown, had kept down 'adventuring' in cloth from the northern ports of England in the fourteenth and fifteenth centuries. But the Londoners fought them; concentrated their business on the Netherlands, when Antwerp, rising into its short-lived commercial splendour, became an excellent market; and under Edward IV not only shipped more broadcloth from London than all foreigners, including the Hansards, put together, but approximately as much as all the other ports of England. The London which the Tudors acquired and ruled, and whose amazing growth in the Tudor century their various policies stimulated, was a very rich place when the first 'Welshman' came with his crown off a thorn-bush from Bosworth Field.

[1] See above, p. 126.

That wool, 'woolfells', and hides were the great items in English trade outwards until cloth overhauled wool, needs no more mention. They remained, with herrings, the chief items in Scottish export trade throughout. In England, lead and tin were such important sources of revenue for the crown that attempts were made to canalise the trade in them to staples, as the profitable wool trade was canalised, to simplify control. Other crude exports were dried or salted herrings and pilchards and—in small quantities—Purbeck stone and Derbyshire alabaster. The tin and the alabaster were also exported in the manufactured state—a few worked alabaster monuments from Nottingham, and latterly quantities of pewter ware, mainly from London, foreigners having acquired a taste for 'garnishes' of 'good flat English pewter'.[1] Many other things were sent abroad from time to time; for the voyage to France or the Low Countries was easier than many of the coasting voyages, which helped to make England a commercial, a buying and selling country earlier and more completely than many of her neighbours, who lacked her long indented coastline and the nearness of most of her important towns to estuaries or the sea. That Winchester was not near either helps to explain why it lost its Anglo-Saxon position as a capital.

Among the goods carried coastwise and occasionally exported were timber, especially oak from the Sussex Weald, oak-bark for tanning, and—far more important—coal. The range of the coastwise coal trade is illustrated by the occasional arrival of cargoes of coal from the North at Southampton, and the export of coal from Southampton noted now and then from so early as 1309. There was short coastwise movement of Forest of Dean and Bristol coal along the shores of the Bristol Channel; but the great trade was from Newcastle, the trade which brought to London that sea-coal, the 'putridity' of which was the excuse given by the London smiths for not working at night in 1299.[2] (Coal was used in smiths' work, centuries before it was used as coke in smelting.) Evidently it had been coming in coastwise, and had been used mainly, perhaps entirely, for industrial purposes in the thirteenth century at latest, though it is only from the fourteenth century that we know much about the trade.

[1] William Harrison, *Description of England*, quoted by L. F. Salzman, *English Industries of the Middle Ages* (1923), p. 141.
[2] See above, p. 131.

And if London smiths, and some other artisans, could use Newcastle coal, so could all those in towns on or near the east coast and even beyond the straits—though it seems that the Tyne colliers seldom went below Dover. How much coal had got into domestic use before 1500 is uncertain; but not very much. Its use generally goes with the chimney, and the ordinary medieval house had no chimney. Astonished Italians' accounts of these stones that would burn, used in the bleak North, suggest little use in London. That use, and chimneys, came in rapidly under the Tudors; but in Shakespeare's time fastidious people still sniffed at coal as a domestic fuel, though Mistress Quickly kept a 'sea-coal fire' in her Dolphin Chamber.

The coastwise trade in coal led easily to its export in the political sense. It was as easy to make the Netherlands ports as to make the Thames; and fourteenth-century customs accounts show that Newcastle coal was well known in them, from Amsterdam to Dunkirk. Beyond Cape Gris Nez we cannot trace it. In the Baltic we can, just. It was an easy return cargo for a foreign ship, and might go as ballast. These beginnings of a great trade are interesting; but probably one fair-sized modern tramp would take on a single voyage all the coal shipped abroad from fourteenth-century Newcastle in a year.

England's export trade was more miscellaneous than the dominance first of wool and then of cloth might suggest. Most things can be found now and then, and corn fairly often—butter and eggs, horseshoes and daggers, leather bottles and boots, with some foreign commodities re-exported. But the variety is not comparable with that of the imports. They included all the 'precious things' from abroad that prosperous people coveted, as they had in Aelfric's time[1]—only the list of the late Middle Ages was very much longer. Some raw materials and some foods were on the list—pitch and hemp and spars, with other kinds of timber, and occasionally whole ships, from the Baltic; from the Baltic also some fine Swedish iron; and from Sweden or Solingen in 'the Ruhr' steel in bundles of 'gads', short rods. Bow-staves of Spanish yew came in bigger bundles, with Spanish wool, reckoned not so good as the best English but useful for blending. (Bow-staves from some great distance also came through Danzig, with the Baltic timber.) A little cotton came from the Levant, but its sole certainly known use was for the candle-wicks of Candlewick

[1] See above, p. 63.

Street (Cannon Street) London, and some other places. The commoner and the rarer dyestuffs always came, with the alum that they required. Caen stone went out of use after the loss of Normandy, and local stones, such as that 'millstone grit' which has given its name to a geological formation, gradually drove out the millstones that at one time had been imported from the neighbourhood of Paris.

Cordovan leather, a half-manufactured article like the steel, came in regularly. The import trade from Ireland of hides, furs, some oakwood and some corn—among other things—is best treated as part of the coastwise trade, with the wine transhipment from Ireland, or from Bristol, to Welsh and northern English ports. Of the wine trade generally, and of its importance, there is no need to say more.

With the growth of population and the recurrence of famine or semi-famine conditions, corn of various kinds was sometimes brought from remote places—from Danzig for instance—but this was not a regular food trade like those in Scandinavian stock fish ('poor John'), and in Biscay salt to ports which were far from Droitwich or Northwich. Apart from these things, and the wine, average Englishmen and Scots had little acquaintance with imported food or drink; though now and then vegetable seed and vegetables occur in the imports, especially the onion.

But the governing class in Church and State, the merchants, and all who could afford them paid outrageous prices for imported table luxuries, especially in the prospering—if unwholesome—fourteenth and the rich—if turbulent—fifteenth century. There were the spices which, long before, had made trade for the London gild of Pepperers. These came by various routes but most often latterly by long sea in Genoese 'carracks', Catalan vessels, or, from 1317, in Venetian galleys —until the Portuguese diverted the whole trade; but the first Portuguese cargo of spices came up the Thames only in 1503. Then there was sugar. Arabs had introduced the cane and the manufacture into the Mediterranean area. Well before 1200, both had spread to all suitable places on its shores—Syria, Egypt, Greece, Sicily, North Africa, Spain. 'Nordic' men were crazy for it; paid preposterous prices; and had fantastic structures made of it for their feasts. The Mediterranean trade also brought dates and figs, almonds, currants and raisins, olive oil, rice and the sweet wines. It is not surprising that the Merchant Gild of Southampton, where the galleys called on their way up Channel and where the other Mediterranean ships did a big trade, was rich and masterful. The goods were light and could stand overland carriage to the Thames valley and beyond. With the Mediterranean wines, they came on various routes; but Southampton was the leading port of entry.

As for the imported 'luxury' manufactured goods, they came in endless variety by the fifteenth century. The Low Countries had lost ground to England in the spinning and weaving of wool, but far into the seventeenth they remained supreme in dyeing and finishing (cloth-working): that was why so much English cloth was exported 'white'. The 'fyne cloth of Ipre' sold in the cloth-hall, built there in the thirteenth century and shot to bits in the war of 1914, was reckoned better than the best English, and was still sent to London. So were some other Flemish cloths, 'muche fustayne'—fustian, a mixed fabric of linen and cotton, which probably at this time came into Flanders from Ulm and other South German towns where the industry was well established—the fine linen which took its name from Cambrai (cambric) and the tapestry which took its from Arras. Fustian also came all the way from Italy, where the industry and the name (*fustagno*) had originated.

But it was far more precious things from the Mediterranean, and from its trading areas to the east, that the Venetians mainly brought—gold and silver and jewels; silks, velvets, cloth-of-gold and damask; carpets; Venetian glass; and all kinds of 'mercery' and trinkets. There were also imported Cadiz girdles and Spanish gloves; thread of some sorts from Cologne and Lyons; Rhenish glass and Rouen cutlery; Spanish swords and fine Italian armour and French bonnets. Several of these things are only mentioned now and then, in the records that have been examined, but they illustrate the great range of the luxury trades. None of them would take up much cargo space in the carracks or the galleys, or in the English ships that went up the canal to Bruges.

Scotland was dependent on imports, if Froissart is to be trusted, not only for what luxuries she could afford but for some very essential manufactures. 'There is neither iron to shoe horses', he writes, 'nor leather to make harness, saddles or bridles: all these things come ready-made from Flanders by

sea; should these fail, there is none to be had in the country'.[1]
This is certainly an exaggeration: Froissart was not a merchant
or economist. The Scottish hammermen cannot have been so
incompetent as all that; and the wildest Highlander knew how
to tan. There were certainly tanners and smiths and lorimers—
makers of bits and saddlers' ironmongery—in the Scottish
burghs. What Froissart probably meant, or had been told, was
that the kind of good knightly horse equipment in which he
was interested was not easy to come by in Scotland; and that if
you wanted it you had better buy the Flemish article.

THE PRECIOUS METALS AND THE CURRENCY

Imports of gold and silver, as bullion or coin, or in ware, were
of special interest to the English Government. Once they had
got into the country, they were supposed not to go out again.
There was constant regulation and search to prevent this.
Finally in 1478, the export was made felony and that, so
Erasmus thought, was why England had so much silver. There
is another explanation. England produced a certain amount
of silver from those silver-lead ores which the crown mono-
polised; sometimes we come across a licensed export of silver.
(No doubt both it and gold were smuggled out.) The gold of
the British Isles had mostly been used up in prehistoric times,
though in later centuries scraps were sometimes found, and
oftener looked for, in Wales or Ireland. The imports are hard
to trace. No doubt treasure was smuggled in, as well as smuggled out. Sometimes the customs entries record it. There were,
for example, considerable quantities of 'gold for sale' entered
at the 'port' of Sandwich, that is the whole line of the
coast from Winchester round to Faversham, in 1304–5. Where
it came from originally no one knows. Late medieval Europe
was using mainly its accumulated stocks, melted and remelted,
with small fresh supplies, from various European river washings
and minings in gold-bearing gravels, or brought in stages by
trade from East and West Africa.

As coinage, gold was secondary to silver. Gold coins were
struck at intervals from the reign of Henry III onwards; but
silver was the real standard of value and circulating medium.
Minting was crude and even new coins varied in weight; but

---

[1] Quoted by Miss I. F. Grant, *The Social and Economic Development of
Scotland before 1603* (1930), p. 321.

from 1100 to 1300 the average amount of silver put into a new penny fell by only a small fraction. After that it fell by jerks— 22½ grains in 1100 and 22 in 1300, it was 15 by 1412 and 10½ by 1527. Yet from 1300 to 1500 prices of foodstuffs varied very little. Very little, that is, if averages of what figures we have are taken for whole decades: from year to year and sometimes, in spite of Britain's unusually good coastwise and river communications, from place to place, they might vary frightfully. Wheat in the decade 1451–60 averaged almost exactly what it had averaged in 1301–10: in 1491–1500 it was a little cheaper. The average cost of a group of necessaries—wheat, herrings, pigs, cheese, hens, and so on—does, however, show a rise between 1301–10 and 1491–1500 of 27 per cent, and figures up to 51 per cent for some intervening decades.

If prices had varied with the weight of the silver penny, they should have about doubled in those 190 years. The fact was that, owing to a keen demand for silver and a relative shortage in its supply, its purchasing power was going up. That helps to explain the very great activity in European silver mining towards the end of the fifteenth century; but this activity did not begin to affect the purchasing power of silver, and so general prices, in England until large fresh supplies had got through to her and been coined and put into circulation; and that was well after 1500.[1]

As for that abundance of silver and silver plate which so much impressed Erasmus and other visitors, round about 1500, it is perhaps best explained not by the law of felony but by the fact that England, and Scotland too, exported very important raw materials, and England growing quantities of the manufactured article most widely demanded by her neighbours, cloth. They normally fed and warmed themselves well— by the standards of 1500—and with something to spare. They could afford the wine and the fancy imports, and get, or retain, treasure at the same time. England's position was rather like that of the twentieth-century United States, with their cotton, tobacco, wheat and 'hog products'; their cars, machinery and films. They too were in a position to accumulate treasure—for what it is worth.

[1] See below, pp. 185, 186–7.

THE REVENUES OF THE ENGLISH CROWN;
COMMERCIAL POLICY AND
ECONOMIC DOCTRINE

The crown tried to take care of the treasure, but it is hard to speak, in modern language, of royal fiscal and economic 'policies'. The King got what he could where he could. He was supposed vaguely to 'live of his own', as the late medieval phrase was; that is, of the yield of his lands and certain old undisputed sources of revenue, like court fines and the ancient customs. He was always adding to his lands, when great men rebelled; but he was as constantly granting them away again. His strictly feudal revenue, from reliefs, tallages, wardships over minors—with the enjoyment of their estates—and marryings-off of girls, was never very great, and was also often granted out. Yet his agents watched his great tenants' affairs closely, and one of our most useful sources of information are the *post mortem* inquisitions into their estates, to ascertain what 'relief' might be asked from the heir. The King in Norman times had also been a sort of town landlord; but he granted away most of his rights over town land and town justice when he signed a charter; what the towns paid him in return, being fixed, dwindled in real value.

For warlike emergencies, the Norman Kings had the Danegeld, the right to call up their tenants to fight, and the people in general to resist invasions. This last obligation, home guard, always remained in reserve; but except in the North, where Scots were troublesome, England was remarkably free from invasion, compared with any continental duchy or other province. Knightly military service was bought off, at an early date, by payment of scutage, shield money; and eventually, for the continental campaigns of the fourteenth and fifteenth centuries, the King relied on 'armies of mercenaries', hired direct or by contract with his great nobles. For fortification and castle building he could call up masons and labourers for service—but he paid them Ships also he could requisition, though he usually had some of his own; but the 'conscript' mariners were paid—so far as we know: at least they were fed— and so were the shipwrights.

The Norman Kings, as Domesday shows, had inherited various rights to levy tolls on trade—just as all the towns did— and they had either inherited or developed the right to take 'prise', especially that prise of wine[1] which was no doubt descended from the practice, found among barbaric chieftains everywhere, of laying hands on a share of the good things that traders bring to their frontiers in ships or caravans. It used to be supposed that the customs duties evolved from the right of prise; but though there is some connection, the King having an inherited interest in trade across his frontiers, this theory will not explain the facts. King John is found trying to levy a general 'fifteenth of the merchants in the seaports': it lasted less than ten years and helped to increase the unpopularity of that very able, if unattractive, administrator. But fifty years later we get a 'new aid', in the form of a general import and export tax; and later the 'new', subsequently the recognised 'right' and 'ancient', payment by custom on the main commodities of foreign trade.

By that time, about 1300, King Edward I had lost the King's Jews; whom he probably would not have turned out had they remained so profitable to him as they had been to his great-grandfather. The fines levied in royal courts of justice, once an important source of revenue, came to be balanced by the expenses of justice—stipends of the travelling justices and so on. The yields of the old extraordinary levies—Danegeld, scutage, tallage—were fading out. But there was the precedent of the semi-political, semi-religious 'Saladin Tithe', raised to finance Richard's crusade in 1188: 'everyone shall give in alms...the tenth of his rents and moveable goods'. At the same time the King was becoming the intermittent borrower from foreigners that he remained until Edward III found that, generally speaking, his subjects were rich and complaisant enough to take the considerable risk of lending to him what he needed. He was an expansive King and that was much.

On the analogy of the Saladin Tithe, his grandfather's government had based what came to be known as the subsidy, or the tenth and fifteenth. Like tithe it was a levy on a man's goods, but not, as tithe so often was, on the produce of his land only. If his belongings were worth less than 5*s.* he was exempt: the stools and wooden platters and sacks of straw to sleep on, in a really poor man's hut, would often be worth less than 5*s.*, ten weeks' wages. Other people were supposed to pay on everything from cattle to fire-irons. But in towns a man and wife might have, untaxed, one outfit of clothes each; one bed; one ring; one

---

[1] See above, p. 160.

silver buckle; one silver cup, and one silk girdle—if they were prosperous enough to own these things: it was like the married man's allowance in the modern income tax. On the land, knights and gentlemen had their armour and their plate free. This was in 1297.

But it was far too elaborate a system for the medieval, perhaps for any, administrator to work. A generation or so later, when a subsidy was voted, it had come to mean so much from each county: and the county authorities split it up among those who came to be known in Tudor times as 'subsidy men'—people who could be expected to pay.

The notorious poll-tax tried under Richard II might have been fair enough, with proper grading and proper exemptions, such as a poll-tax (*capitation*) had 300 years later in France. The poll-tax of 1377 had neither. The tax of 1379 was graded, and the tax of 1380 was to be varied by local arrangement according to the taxpayers' means; the strong were to help the weak. Trouble arose none the less, and the trouble was so great that poll-taxes were seldom tried again in England for the same 300 years. The reason for this failed experiment in emergency taxation was that the subsidy, having become petrified at a low figure, was not enough even when voted double, as it sometimes was.

A subsidy was an occasional thing but customs had the great merit, from the point of view of the Exchequer, that they came in every year and all the year round; and that only when they were changed was trouble likely with the rising Parliament of the fourteenth century. The quarrels about old and new custom, and evil custom (*maltote*), and about the tunnage and poundage levied on things not originally on the customs list, are more important in constitutional than in economic history. The crown was trying to get all it could from this steadily flow-ing stream; and when its attempts met with united opposition from great and small men—as when Edward III tried to put the export duty on wool too high[1]—it might have to draw back. In the fifteenth century the crown was not generally thrusting; and so it was poor; and it lost France.

The only 'protective' element in the modern sense in the customs system were the special aliens' customs rates. But these might be bargained away; and the mere fact that so much of the customs revenue came from exports shows how little there

---

[1] See above, p. 142.

was that was nationalistic or modern in the system, such as it was. When the King's advisers saw a rich head they hit at it; but Parliament might parry the blow. It might advise the King, as it did King Henry IV, to meet his needs, not by taxing or by borrowing but by confiscation of Church property. The King was often obliged to borrow from rich Londoners, as Edward IV did; his friendships with grocers and their wives were criticised by contemporaries, but had their uses to him.

Henry V did in fact confiscate Church property, but a compromise was reached about the amount. He took only the property of the 'alien priories'—religious houses in England dependent on the great Norman foundations that had been 'alien' since John lost Normandy. The decision reflects a growing, and a not very attractive, spirit of nationalism. Englishmen lived on and by the manors of Bec; if some money raised from rents and dues and sales of produce was remitted to the Norman abbey—some certainly was—this was a thing that no one should have questioned, supposing the Church was what it claimed to be, and was in words recognised as being, world-wide and above the nations. But the great French Wars were in progress, Crécy behind, Agincourt just in front; average sensual men did not think of the Church like that any more, if indeed they ever really had. They had never liked aliens. How should they when to sell beer 'in foreign parts' ('in the forain'), that is outside your town or your parish, was an irregular act; when the men of the next village were the foreigners, the graceless people, that in some rural backwaters they still are? A few years later, about 1436, a now famous literary attack was made on aliens and England's treatment of them in the 'Little Book of English Policy' written, it is thought, by a Bishop. It shows this spirit.

It is in verse and it is economico-strategic. Keep a strong Channel fleet and have an eye to trade is its refrain—

> Cheryshe marchandyse, kepe thamyralte,
> That we bee maysteres of the narowe see.

Then you will be able to put all aliens, from Scots to Venetians, in their place; 'for they must needs pass by our English coasts'. The trade routes and trades of the aliens are described. Their alleged weaknesses are pilloried—the Scots' boastings, the Flemings' dirty table manners. Why do we treat them better than they treat us when we visit their countries? (This was a fair point: suspicion of the alien and rules to keep him under

were ranker in most places than in England.) Why should
Italians ride about in Cotswold, buying up the wool? What
good is the Venetian trade anyway?: they bring luxuries,
vanities, in exchange for our solid utility goods, our wool and
our cloth.

The Jews had rightly thought it a sign of King Solomon's
wealth and prosperity that his ships brought in 'ivory, apes
and peacocks'; but the author of the Little Book was disgusted
that 'apes' and 'marmosets tailed' should come on the Venetian galleys. 'Also they bear the gold out of this land' was his
worst indictment of their owners. How much gold he does not
say, and certainly did not know. It was a good popular appeal
—wool and cloth and gold for apes and trifles and articles of
vain display; but arguments have been given for supposing
that fifteenth-century England could afford her vanities and
not run out of treasure.[1] Certainly, she did not.

Who read the Little Book and what effect it had, if any, we do
not know. Events show that it at least reflected a common
state of mind. A Bill was introduced in 1439 to forbid Italians
importing any merchandise save that of the countries 'beyonde
the Streytes of Marrok': it came to nothing, and they con
tinued to be great middlemen until the Portuguese cut them
out. Another unsuccessful Bill, in 1455, sought to forbid the
'Merchants Strangers Italians' to ride about buying cloth and
wool. By an Act of the same year the import of Italians'
ribbons was prohibited: the ribbons were 'deceitful': let them
send the raw silk.

Then in 1463, came a more significant Act of Parliament.
Craftsmen, it said, cannot live by their skill because of
foreign competition. The importation of a long list of manufactured articles is therefore prohibited. Wardens and masters
of gilds are to search them out and confiscate them. Where
there are no gild wardens, someone else is to do it. This Act
was not maintained; there is no reason to suppose that it had
much effect. But it registers the entry of an 'employment'
motive into legislation about foreign trade, and the existence
of that 'fear of goods', competing or possibly competing goods,
which a modern historian has placed at the back of much
protectionist legislation everywhere. Fear of goods and dislike
of the alien who sends them.

More than eighty years earlier, in 1376, the employment

[1] See above, p. 173.

motive in connection with foreign trade had come into legislation; but reversed. Knights of the Shire and merchants from the Cotswold country had complained of the growing export of woollen yarn, to Normandy and Lombardy it was said. (It is interesting to notice that this yarn export was important enough to attract attention.) It was forbidden. Why? Because spinsters were so proud that they would not stop spinning to help get in the hay and the corn, as was everyone's duty. We never know, in connection with a medieval or early modern law of this sort, how widespread or important was either the action prohibited or the cause for prohibition assigned. But there must have been some export and some reluctance to turn out into the fields. Perhaps exporting merchants, with wool out to be spun, had, as we should say, been pressing for delivery. There may not have been much of it. About 1376 the parliaments of the Statutes of Labourers were very ready to hit at 'proud' wage-earners: these spinsters were not unemployed but over-employed, by Parliament's standards.

In discussing treasure and the bearing of gold out of this land, the average medieval mind had, so far as can be seen, no thought-out doctrine of money—unless it were Columbus's doctrine of gold: 'he who possesses it has all he needs in this world as also the means of rescuing souls from purgatory'. Gold and silver were beautiful and good: with them things were bought: with them, very literally, kings paid for their wars. All through history, when treasure gave out the war had had to stop—unless it were waged in some especially rich region that could be looted for a long time. In some countries, during the later Middle Ages, there was such obvious and flagrant debasing of the currency—leather coins with a bit of silver stuck through them, for instance—that men began to think about money, its functions, and its abuse. But not, so far as we know, in England. There the penny got gradually smaller, but it remained pure. The reductions in weight were spread over a long period. Often the lighter new penny would be as heavy as the worn and clipped pennies that had once been heavier but had been long in circulation. There was never anything faintly resembling those inflations of paper money, with their tragic effects on prices and society, to which the twentieth century has been forced to submit. The slow shifts in the purchasing power of silver itself that were going on all the time were out of medieval sight, and perhaps of medieval comprehension. In every man's experience, the price changes that resulted from a bad harvest or a devastating campaign were so extreme, and so perfectly explicable, as to make it unlikely that he would think of looking behind them for those slow secular movements that modern men test statistically. And, as has been seen, those movements were in fact very slow. The penny changed at rather long intervals and something, as we argue, happened to the silver;[1] but there was great stability in a country where wheat prices averaged much the same in decades about two centuries apart. We know that: medieval man did not. But if he lived fifty or sixty years and kept his eyes open, he might easily agree—as in fact he did—that there was, and should be, some central permanent semi-natural, and therefore just, price about which, by act of God, yearly prices shifted.

That was a reason why, when one of the earlier lightenings of the new coin (in 1351) coincided with the upheaval in society caused by the Great Pestilence, it seemed outrageous that men who had been accustomed to work for 1*d.* a day— a Scriptural figure too—should ask for 2*d.* In the end they got it or something like it. The economic law, which the medieval mind had hardly begun to think about, that kept food prices in a shrunken population fairly stable, once the short dislocations of the plague years had been overcome, drove up at the same time the 'market price' of labour and, as has been seen, of many commodities into which much labour entered.[2]

It is not to be supposed that the medieval doctrine of the just price, about which doctors argued interminably and often very acutely, had any sort of statistical foundation: it was a problem in ethics, in applied ethics, somewhat helplessly solved as a rule by saying that any recognised customary price, or any price decreed by a competent political authority, was just; what a man might take or demand with a clear conscience. That must have made the action of wage-earners after the Pestilence doubly outrageous to scholars and governing people with a little scholarship: it was both a breach with custom and a defiance of the orders of King and Parliament, authorities unquestionably competent.

To pay or receive anything beyond the just price was a sin; yet some doctors felt bound to admit that if a thing were very scarce it was not sinful to pay or accept something above its central 'natural' price. Whether they admitted it or not, the

[1] See above, p. 173.   [2] See above, pp. 118–9.

plain figures—of which we have abundance—show that everyone did everywhere. Similarly with the medieval doctrine of usury. That thoroughgoing usury, the sort that grinds the faces of the poor in peasant lands to this day, is sinful, anyone who believes in sin will allow. Those who do not so believe may agree to call it one of the worst of social evils, a thing that justifies revolutions and makes pogroms of usurers at least explicable. Condemning it as sin did not however stop the medieval usurers. They ground the face of the poor man to whom they lent when his harvest had failed or his only cow had died, as they have ground it ever since—in Ireland and India and Roumania and China. It was, and is, an unfair contest, an unequal bargain between desperate necessity and greed unashamed. But what of interest between economic equals, the payment which a merchant is ready and glad to make for the use of money? The doctors said that this also was sinful, unless the lender ran a real risk of losing his loan—as when he lent for a speculative adventure overseas. The sin lay in bargaining for a certain yield from your money, risk or no risk. This was sinful because money was barren—Aristotle had said so—and could not breed young monies. If, as actually happened, it was argued that the lender lost the use of his money for a time, although his loan was perfectly safe, and so deserved some compensation—substantially the modern argument in defence of reasonable interest—the doctors differed about the reply, but were apt to fall back on subtle arguments about paying for time which is not a thing for man to buy or sell. Yet some of them allowed that a man might claim compensation for thus losing chances of gain.

Meanwhile kings borrowed and paid high rates; the Pope borrowed and did the same; monasteries borrowed; republics borrowed, and the debts of one of them, Genoa, were still embodied in the national debt of Italy yesterday; by one shift or another merchants paid for the use of money when they needed it. And all the while the one form of investment that was understood by everyone, practised universally, and as safe as any investment could be under medieval conditions, went uncondemned. That was the purchase of a rent-charge—£10 a year for £100 down was about a normal rate—arising from the rents of some manor or bit of urban land.

It was unfortunate that the late medieval teaching about usury took definite shape in a European society already so far commercialised that these refined discussions became necessary. In a peasant society the ethical problem is relatively simple. Among practising Christians, or other disinterested people, the loan yielding no interest, very likely not to be repaid, will often be a duty. But the attempt to make what may be a good man's duty towards those in difficulties an obligation as between commercial lender and borrower was a mistake, punished, as such mistakes are, by the encouragement of deception and by failure.

Book III

FROM A.D. 1500 TO A.D. 1750

Chapter VI

Britain in the Early Modern Period

PRICES AND POPULATION

'History is a seamless garment'; and it is often harder to trace anything like a seam in its economic and social folds than in some others. Changes in the fabric are apt to be very gradual, hardly perceptible. But there is no overlooking the changes—almost suggesting a seam and a new piece—that can be traced early in the sixteenth century. There is that Portuguese spice ship in the Thames of 1503,[1] with the Cape route and the side-tracking of the Mediterranean and Venice behind it. (In Venetian history there was not a seam but a rent.) And within twenty years set in, very slowly at first in England but later with shattering speed, that rise in prices which, by Shakespeare's time, had modified the whole economic and social climate as only a currency change can. A great invention affects these and those, but a change in money affects all. The twentieth century has relearnt this, with its inflations, its wipings out of the savings of whole classes, its Germans or Chinese hurrying to turn money into things because it may have lost much of its purchasing power before night.

The sixteenth century was flooded with silver as the years passed; in England—and in some other countries—the position was made worse by the issue of bad money, only part silver; but paper money not having yet come to bless Europe, she was spared the outrageous extremes of the twentieth century. Prices might rise fivefold or more in a couple of generations, never a thousandfold within a year. And though they rose far faster than they had ever risen continuously before, there was time for a good deal of social adjustment to new conditions. Shakespeare's England was a changed, and in some ways a bad, England. It was certainly not a ruined England, or a despondent.

At first sight, nothing that suggests a seam is apparent in or about the year 1750, here taken as the edge of a certain piece of history. But 1750 marks the approximate turning point in the course of something more vital than prices—population.

[1] See above, p. 170.

About 1500 the population of England and Wales may have been 3,000,000, having perhaps doubled in the four centuries since Domesday was compiled.[1] For the eighteenth century estimates are more certain. Figures of the house tax, figures of births and deaths taken from those parish registers which for the Middle Ages do not exist, and argument backward from the first census, of 1801, can all be used. It is a fair estimate that in 1700 the figure was between 5,000,000 and 5,500,000, and in 1750 about 6,500,000: it had then taken about 250 years for it to double. It doubled again in a little more than seventy years, being 12,000,000 in 1821. The most rapid growth came between 1801 and 1821; but between 1750 and 1801 there was a growth of 40 per cent. After 1821 the next doubling took less than sixty years.

The Scottish figure for 1801 was 1,608,000. If it had moved parallel to that of England and Wales, it would have been about 1,200,000 in 1750 and approaching 1,000,000 in 1700. Its course has not been so carefully studied as the English, but these figures cannot be far wrong.

Had population after 1750 grown only at the old rate, whatever else might have happened, inventions made, continents and islands opened up, Britain would have had a totally different economic history—and perhaps Australia and New Zealand would have had only the economic history of the Black-fellows, the Maoris, and a few missionaries and whalers.

THE COURSE OF PRICES

As price history has here been given such an important place, it will be well to summarise it at the outset. Average decade prices, though not year to year or local prices, had been relatively stable for two centuries before 1500, as has been seen; those prices rising most into which most labour had been put, for wages approximately doubled after the Black Death; then, having doubled, they remained fairly stable.[2] Take the prices of the dozen foodstuffs and animals for food already quoted[3]— wheat, cheese, eggs, oxen, herrings, and the rest—and make a 'cost of living' figure of them—rough, needing comment, but significant. Calling this composite figure 100 for 1301–10, it was only 127 for 1491–1500. By the decade 1531–40 it was

---

[1] See above, p. 77. [2] See above, pp. 118–9.
[3] See above, p. 173.

already 210. Then Henry VIII debased the coinage: the figure rose to 287 for 1541–50. The coinage was not restored until early in Elizabeth's reign and the figure for 1551–60 was 464, nearly four times what it had been fifty years back. In spite of the restored coinage, and mainly because of the fall in the purchasing power of the silver which after 1550 was flooding into Europe from Peru and Mexico, the rise continued; and in Queen Elizabeth's last decade (1593–1602) this rough 'cost of living' figure stood at 700, nearly six times the level of 1491–1500.

Take the case of wheat, the bread-corn of all comfortable Englishmen and of most others when they could afford it: when that was will be discussed later.[1] From 1300 to 1450 its average price was about 6s. a quarter—though in bad years it might be nearly three times as much. From 1450 to 1510 it was rather less, in this being exceptional among foodstuffs. In Elizabeth's last decade, when it is true the harvests were bad and the 'nine mens Morris', whatever that was, 'was filled up with mud' in summer, the average was 34s. 10¼d., showing almost exactly the nearly sixfold rise of the prices of foodstuffs generally.

Prices of foodstuffs are the best gauge of possible social effects of price changes, partly because they are most certainly ascertainable, partly because everyone must eat, and partly because any attempt to ascertain 'prices in general' always has to face the same obstacles—the extraordinary changes in habits and fashions among consumers, from century to century, and the arrival of new articles of consumption, especially luxuries. In 1661, for instance, Mr Pepys paid for a beaver hat a sum (£4. 5s. 0d.) nearly equal to six weeks' earnings of a skilled mason: it is as if to-day a man were to pay £45 or £50 for his fashionable hat. At that time cheese cost 3d. a pound, butter already 6d. Similar contrasts could easily be picked out in Shakespeare's England.

From Shakespeare's later days (he died in 1616) the movements of prices were not again such as to dominate economic history until well after 1750; and down to our own day there has been in Britain nothing comparable with the great change of the sixteenth century. Wheat prices illustrate this. In the late seventeenth or the early eighteenth century, the average price for a decade of good harvests was about equal to that in the bad last decade of Elizabeth (1683–92, 34s. 5½d.: 1703–12,

[1] See below, p. 211.

36s. 8d.). In a decade of domestic upheaval or a spell of very bad harvests it was only some 50 per cent higher (in 1643–52, 48s. 11d.: in 1692–9, 52s.). Barley prices moved along a similar but a less fluctuating line. That, for the moment, is enough. Maximum sixteenth-century prices had become normal in the seventeenth century, but there were not again outrageous new maxima. From generation to generation, under Stuarts and early Hanoverians, men could count on a fundamental stability, with a general upward trend moderate enough not to be disquieting, and never a return to the famine fluctuations of the Middle Ages. The fact may have something to do with the stable confidence and self-satisfaction of the eighteenth century—reasonable prices, reasonable men, a reasonable constitution.

RURAL AND URBAN POPULATION

This country in which population was growing steadily for 250 years, but very little from one generation to the next, remained all the while overwhelmingly rural. Even in 1801 a bare 26 per cent of the population of England and Wales lived in places with more than 5000 inhabitants. In 1750, the percentage would probably have been not more than 20—and it would dwindle slowly, if we had all the figures, back to the perhaps 10 per cent of the years about 1500. There were all the time many boroughs, even cathedral cities, with less than 5000 inhabitants; it was these little towns that retained so often their medieval rural characteristics, their commons, their cow pastures, their 'port meadows' as at Oxford, their open fields as at Cambridge. Even before 1500, highly developed urban life, with extensive subdivision of trades and perhaps well-organised gilds, was mainly found in the places with more than 5000 inhabitants—the Yorks, Norwiches, Bristols and Exeters.

By Queen Anne's day, Norwich and Bristol, the two greatest 'provincial' towns, each had not more than some 30,000 inhabitants. York and Exeter had rather more than 10,000—York having at most doubled since Domesday Book.[1] It is not known that any other town or city had so many as 10,000. The slow growth of the total population of the country would not allow of great increase anywhere down to 1750. Anywhere, except in London which had been sucking people in, at an

[1] See above, p. 57.

extraordinary rate, sucking them in faster than it killed them off—though it is believed that nearly 40,000 died of the Plague in 1603, and it is certain that more than twice as many died in the better known outbreak of 1665. The London to which James I came may have had 150,000 inhabitants. A contemporary reckoned that Queen Anne's London, by the narrowest definition—the City and Southwark—had nearly 250,000, and that Westminster, which started at Temple Bar, had another 113,000; he believed that 'London' in a wider sense, the more or less continuous town, had over half a million. Historians have often accepted this opinion, and statisticians treat it with respect. Probably the figures are somewhat too high; but the statistician would not reduce that half-million below 420,000, at the lowest. It was this gigantic London of Addison and Pope, of the East India Company and the Hudson's Bay Company and the new Bank of England, that men thought of as just Town—very naturally, seeing it was at least fourteen times the size of the next biggest town and must have accounted for something like one in twelve of the whole population of England and Wales. The causes of its growth had been at least as much political and social as economic; but geographical and economic conditions had prevented a check being imposed; and the headlong growth of this greatest capital in Europe, whose people had to be housed and fed and warmed and clothed, was a dominant economic force in the life of England all through these two hundred and fifty years.

INDUSTRY, COMMERCE AND SOCIETY IN THE EARLY SIXTEENTH CENTURY

To the modern mind the urban and the industrial are almost synonymous, partly because it is so easy for some modern industry, or part of an industry, to beget a town—a Swindon or a Port Sunlight. Even to-day, however, there are coal-pits and quarries with no more than pit villages or quarry villages attached. So there were in 1500, though the coal 'delves' were few and small. But all iron was smelted in woodland districts, from the Lake District iron works of the Abbots of Furness to those of the Sussex Weald. And iron was very widely worked outside the towns, and inside many places that were not yet towns. Even in Domesday a few of these village groups of iron workers are found.[1] They are not easy to trace for a century or

[1] See above, p. 66.

two after that, but they were certainly growing up wherever iron was easy to get. The Sheffield 'whittle' that Chaucer's miller carried in 'his hose' was evidently a familiar thing to Chaucer's readers: there must have been plenty of them in use. Fourteenth-century Sheffield was a poor little town; and in any case the 'whittle' was probably made in the country round about and only marketed in Sheffield, as such things continued to be for centuries. Leland, in Henry VIII's time, found the hamlets of Deritend and Birmingham—Birmingham had a single street—full of smiths, cutlers, lorimers and nailers. These people were often, perhaps usually, peasant iron-workers —one foot on the land, one on the bellows—as the German peasants of Siegerland still were in the nineteenth century. Nailers and scythe-makers and other specialist iron-workers, again often with one foot on the land, were widespread in Tudor times in Worcestershire, Staffordshire and about the Forest of Dean—sometimes in chartered towns, more often in places that had not advanced beyond the stage of hamlet, village, or 'market-town', which was not a town but a village with a market: Birmingham had one. As there were blacksmiths everywhere, it is easy to picture the way in which groups of specialists must have evolved from about the village forge, where the raw material was plentiful and as the relatively free trading conditions in England allowed a growing demand to be met. In Scotland it would seem that the more successful monopoly policies of its little towns favoured a greater concentration both of industry and of trade into the hands of their craftsmen and the merchants of their Gildries.

Where all the ships were built we do not certainly know. Most of them, no doubt, in or near ports that had charters and so were boroughs—Southampton, Dover, Boston, Hull, Newcastle, Bristol and the rest. But the actual soil of a close-packed medieval borough was not a good location for a shipyard. Few towns, if any, had shipwrights' gilds, and probably, as in London, the yards generally lay outside the borough boundaries. There must also have been many little boat and barge building sites in coastal and riverside villages.

The most widespread of industries were of course those of cloth and linen weaving. Tudor legislation shows that 'household' woollen cloth, home spun, was made almost everywhere, as rough linen cloth certainly was. Even before 1400 the making of the better cloths, the cloths that were marketed and exported, was extraordinarily widespread. Late in the four-teenth century there were only four English counties from which the royal officials appointed to superintend the trade, the 'ulnagers', did not report a production of broadcloths or their equivalent: these were Cumberland, Durham, Lancashire and Cheshire. Sometimes the cloths are said to come from a city or borough—York, Coventry, Winchester, even London—though that does not prove that they were woven within its bounds. More often they were registered, as we should say, at some rural centre. Somerset and Wiltshire were the leading coun-ties, followed by Devon, Gloucester, Warwick, Hampshire, Kent, Essex, Suffolk and in the North, Yorkshire. The figures do not include the lighter marketable cloths, worsteds and others; so Norfolk, from which the worsteds got their name, comes towards the bottom of these 'ulnage' returns. But we must include the worsteds, in imagination, in any general picture of a wool industry which had grown very considerably in importance by 1500; and went on growing.[1]

The proud spinners of the fourteenth century have their monument in the preamble to an Act of Parliament.[2] They may not have been so proud everywhere as the petitioners said that they were in the Cotswold country in 1376. But they must have existed almost everywhere: a great deal of distaff spinning goes to every piece of cloth. The work would be graded, from the spinning of one's own wool into yarn to be worked up by a village weaver—weaving at home had declined by 1500, except in out of the way places: household cloth is home*spun*—through spinning some neighbouring clothier's wool on com-mission, to the more commercial spinning for market, for sale to a yarn 'brogger'. Whichever it was, there was the market—the weaver's price, the clothier's price, the brogger's price—in the background, or even the foreground. The nation of shop-keepers had gone through a long education in dealing before Adam Smith, not Napoleon, coined the phrase.

Yarn-dealing was only one of many sorts of dealing in which it had practice. As far back as King John's reign we meet a 'cornmonger', though we are not quite sure what he did. The rebels of 1381 wanted, among other things, the right to

[1] As Professor E. M. Carus-Wilson has shown (*Medieval Merchant Venturers*, pp. 279–91), the ulnage returns are a very insecure foundation for statistics; but the general distribution of the cloth industry was probably much as described in this paragraph. [J.S.]

[2] See above, p. 179.

sell their country produce freely on the local market, free that is of those town tolls which were the only obstacles to internal trade. There were no shire boundaries in England, at which tolls might be levied, comparable with the endless continental boundaries of counties and duchies. Broadly speaking, the internal trade in wool and corn and other foodstuffs was free. Nothing had increased its size and importance more than the growth of London. London regulated corn-dealings elaborately; it organised granaries to meet emergencies, though they appear not to have been very important, and their gradual abandonment after 1650 left the huge London of the late seventeenth century at least fed. But the general assumption in London, from the Middle Ages, was that the corn would come of itself—by way of trade. And it did, the trade growing as London grew, aided by occasional imports in years of bad harvest. Before 1500 London relied mainly on the home counties, though before 1400 we meet now and then consignments from Cambridge, Norfolk and Lincoln. By Elizabeth's time there are regular shipments of the plentiful corn from the Ouse and Cam basins through Lynn, and corn comes from so far north as Hull, though Kent is still the great provider. Corn moved also down from the upper Thames and down the Lea from Hertfordshire.[1]

Not only was the trade in wool, corn and cattle free; so was all trade by river. This may seem obvious, but continental history shows that it is not. Continental river traffic was seriously impeded until the most recent times by the tolls and policies of riverside states and cities. Rhenish cities often pursued a 'staple' policy: cargoes had to be unloaded and sold at the local 'dump', to give local men a chance of handling the goods. Corn could not legally get through Paris; whether it came up-stream or down-stream it had to be sold there—until the Revolution. There were no similar obstacles on the Thames. It was natural for down-stream traffic to stop at London, though the wool and cloth and corn unloaded there might in part be shipped abroad; but there would have been a transhipment from river-boat to sea-boat in any case. It was the pride of the western counties that the Severn was a free river. In the sixteenth century Gloucester and Worcester fought hard for the right to levy tolls on passing boats; but they were not successful enough to hinder traffic appreciably.

[1] For the regulation of corn exports, see below, pp. 283–4.

We hear of no serious impediment to traffic anywhere on the Fenland rivers, or on the Yorkshire Ouse or on the Trent; though there was an old controversy on many rivers about the ownership and use of weirs, *kidelli*.

What might be called the commercialising of English life had been helped by the great strength of the medieval monarchy and the absence of any rigid barrier between gentlemen —'armigerous persons'—and traders. England never developed a law for noble families and another for burgesses, as some continental countries did: no English word has the full and real meaning of *bourgeois* or *Bürger*; 'burgess' is a most inadequate translation. Because the monarchy was strong, there were none of those duchies or counties or free cities pursuing policies of their own to hinder nation-wide commercial intercourse. The Scottish burghs were narrowly monopolistic, but were not as yet important in the whole economic life of the island. English merchants, from early days, had bought manors, as has been seen.[1] Great lords, lay and ecclesiastical, had sold the produce of their demesnes. In the fifteenth century many knights were closely connected with 'business': the great Sir John Fastolf, who died in 1459, lent money to merchants at 5 per cent—a very reasonable rate. Younger sons of 'gentle' families constantly 'went into trade', being put into its more profitable branches or apprenticed to members of the 'better' companies. Though the old-style demesne agriculture, with villein services, was dying by 1500, many great men in the sixteenth and seventeenth centuries retained direct control of extensive 'home farms', often added to by purchase or enclosure. Such men were interested in markets for corn or wool or cattle. Late in Elizabeth's reign, for example, the Temples of Stowe sold wool to 'staplers'—the term was becoming used to describe any wool-dealer—and fat beasts to London butchers. They had an agent in London, Thomas Farrington, merchant, who took the proceeds and acted as their banker, paying out to their order—the habit from which the cheque developed—and even lending money of theirs that was lying with him till wanted, like a true banker.

[1] See above, p. 126.

Chapter VII

Agriculture and Rural Society

Although British society was much more 'commercialised', and more industrial, by 1500 than has sometimes been supposed —questions of industrial unemployment in relation to national policy were in the air in Jack Cade's time (about 1450)[1]—it remained throughout a rural society, though with a fast-growing and eventually overgrown Town as its head. The framework of this society was considerably less changed in those centuries than the loud outcries about enclosure in the sixteenth and early seventeenth, and the steady but quieter continuance of enclosure from 1650 to 1750, might lead one to expect.

This is partly because much of the country was already enclosed in Henry VIII's reign; partly because in most of those counties from which the loudest outcries came in the sixteenth century the greater part of the enclosing still remained to be done in 1750. There was enclosure trouble in Nottinghamshire in the sixteenth and again in the seventeenth century, but 32 per cent of the whole county area, not merely of its agricultural area, survived to be enclosed by Act of Parliament after 1750. 'Enclosure', as we know, is a vague word that covers at least three distinct movements—the enclosure of the great open fields characteristic of midland agriculture; the enclosure of the regular town or village commons; the nibbling away of forest, moor, and other waste land by what were called expressively in the North 'intakes'.[2] When a Tudor writer spoke of an enclosed country, he meant one in which most of the cultivated ground was enclosed. Such cultivated ground might lie among great stretches of moorland, as it did in Devon. At the time of the Reformation there was much enclosed country throughout the whole South-West, from West Somerset and South-West Dorset to the Land's End. (There were in fact

---

[1] Compare above, p. 178.   [2] See above, pp. 123–4.

a few, a very few, open fields in Devon.) Hereford and Shrop-shire, with important parts of Worcester and Warwick, were also regarded as enclosed; though there was a fair amount of open field in these western shires. To this list can be added, on that side of the island, Wales, Cheshire, Lancashire, and those opener parts of Cumberland where there might have been much true open-field agriculture but where actually there was little or none. On the east side, Kent was 'enclosed' country, with much of North and East Sussex, South Surrey and East Essex. So too were East Suffolk and parts of East and Mid-Norfolk; likewise the North Riding of Yorkshire, and much of Durham and Northumberland. Scotland was foreign soil, on which agriculture was carried on, as has been seen, entirely without organised open field, though most of it lay open enough.[1]

Nibbling at the waste and forest there had always been—much of it unrecorded. With the fall in population after the Pestilence, there would be less incentive to nibble; but the process seems to have been resumed as population recovered in the fifteenth century and grew slowly but steadily after 1500. It can be watched, though indistinctly, in a typical county of hamlets and scattered farms like Devon, a county in which, as an Elizabethan put it, the 'growndes' were 'for the most part ... devided and severed wth mightie greate hedges and dytches'.[2] The enlargement of farms can sometimes be traced, when records are available, by their slowly increased size across the centuries; often by the names of their outer fields—Furze-close, Broom-brake, Higher New-close. And although at least three-quarters of the existing Devonshire farm and hamlet names are found even before 1350, with the sixteenth century new names appear, 'and this movement', of new enclosure and settlement, 'is continued well into the eighteenth century in the upland parishes',[3] being specially active between 1650 and 1700. By 1750 the work is about done.

All the time cottagers are nibbling at the edges of the moors, especially in the neighbourhood of Devon's growing 'woollen' towns and seaports. Moor to nibble at was never far from the biggest of them, which were not very big.

---

[1] See above, p. 103.
[2] John Hooker, *Synopsis Chorographical of Devonshire* (MS.), quoted by W. G. Hoskins, *Econ. Hist. Rev.*, vol. XIII (1943), p. 80.
[3] *Ibid.* p. 89.

In many districts where waste was plentiful, uplands still to be occupied, and population scattered, the same processes were certainly going on, but in most they have not yet been carefully studied. Often we can only see results in the descriptions of the late eighteenth and the early nineteenth centuries— the poor man's irregular little enclosure on the edge of some forest, the King's Forest of Dean or the forests of Hampshire and the Sussex Weald, that delighted William Cobbett; the enclosures by great men for parks, which we can generally date, and by small men by action that we can rarely date, in the forest area of Nottinghamshire—where much land had already been nibbled into enclosure between Worksop and Retford in Leland's day.

Whatever the tenure, whether important enclosure was done with the consent of some lord of the manor or unimportant enclosure without it, no one objected much to encroachment on the fringes of Exmoor or Dartmoor or the Blackdown Hills; any more than objection would be raised to the creation of a farm called upper so-and-so above one called lower so-and-so in some Welsh valley.

The late sixteenth century planned, and the seventeenth carried out—with many checks and setbacks—one enclosure movement on a grand scale, that draining and enclosing of fenland which is connected with the name of the Earl of Bedford. Commissions for Sewers had exercised local oversight over Fenland rivers and drains since the Middle Ages. Then, in Elizabeth's last years (1600–1), an Act of Parliament made general provision for large-scale drainage and for dealing with the complex legal problems of 'commoning' in the Fens.[1] When work began, all sorts of interests—of fowlers, fishers, commoners—were touched, and there was long-drawn-out trouble. But the drainage of the peaty 'Bedford Level'—from south of Wisbech nearly to Cambridge, and from Peterborough to Brandon in Suffolk, with its 'foule and slabby quavemires... and most troublesome Fennes'—[2] went forward: by 1637 the twenty-one-mile-long Old Bedford River cut off the loop of the Ouse from Earith to below Denver. Fourteen years later the parallel New River, the 'Hundred Foot', was finished. They were controlled by sluices; and just above where they de-

---

[1] See above, p. 83.

[2] William Camden, *Britannia*, tr. Philemon Holland (1637), p. 529; quoted by H. C. Darby, *The Draining of the Fens* (1940), p. 26.

bouched into the Ouse, Denver Sluice kept the high tides from running up the river nearly to Cambridge. Between the 'Rivers' the Washland took, and still takes, flood water too heavy to be carried away between tides.

These were the main water escape and water control works, but there were many others. The peaty fenland dried—and sank. Soon after the century was over the problem of pumping water up into the drains and embanked rivers had to be faced. The destruction of Denver Sluice by tide and flood in 1713 made the position critical. The sluice was not rebuilt until 1748–50. By that time pumping was a recognised cure for the falling surface level that contemporaries hardly realised: up and down the levels groups of landowners were setting up windmills to drive the 'scoop-wheels'—water-wheels reversed—that lifted the water from a lower to a higher channel. There were still big undrained meres, and fens to the north, to be dealt with; but an important agricultural area had been created.

It is easy to exaggerate the geographical importance of the enclosure for sheep-farming that raised such an outcry in early Tudor times—'sheep devour men', 'great men maketh now-a-days a sheepcote in the church'. Perhaps they did, but does parish history contain many recorded church sheepcotes? Though the early Tudor inquiries show declines in village population where sheep-farming on a large scale had reduced the demand for labour in agriculture, deserted villages are singularly rare in England.[1] There is one some ten miles south-west by west of Cambridge, where the church is represented by a grass-grown mound, the manor house by another, with the remains of a moat about it. We know that the gradual replacement of agriculture by grazing was the cause of this desertion. The village had never been big—eighteen tenants in Domesday Book. There is another village with a church a mile or two away. There need not have been grave hardship as population drifted out—the holdings were bought up—though there may have been. And if ever there was 'a sheepcote in the church'—this is possible—it was the only one in the whole county, as this is the sole deserted village.

Inquiry made in 1517, covering the previous thirty years, did show a very considerable number of evictions, though not all carried out to make room for sheep; but the area cleared of tenants was nowhere more than a small fraction of any area

---

[1] But see p. 80 n. 1 above.

reported on. In a large area reported on in Norfolk seventy-six houses and one whole hamlet had been swept away, but no more. What the early Tudor government was worried about, and passed rather ineffective laws against, was such 'putting down of houses of husbandry', 'depopulating enclosure'. There was a political motive, as is shown by anxiety over the Isle of Wight: if population falls how are we to beat off French raids? But that was purely local. At the back of the governmental mind was the simple conviction that a cultivating peasantry, of the old size and in the old places, was 'a good thing'. No one stopped to inquire whether the relatively numerous evictions in Buckinghamshire were not being balanced by the creation of new 'houses of husbandry' in Devon: it was not so that men thought in 1517; though by 1619 King James I was arguing, as a modern economist might, that more land had been ploughed up recently from the waste than had been converted by enclosure from arable to pasture.

As to the sheep; it has never been proved that in the country as a whole their number was increasing rapidly, or that wool prices were so much out of step with other prices that sheep-farming became specially attractive. There was a brisk demand from the clothiers, so brisk that the export was dwindling away;[1] but there is no reason to think that, with exports thus declining, the joint demand of the home and foreign markets was so great as to induce men to keep bigger flocks. All that the facts prove is that, in a considerable number of places and no doubt for various reasons, owners or farmers liked to have more sheep. The London demand for mutton must not be forgotten.

The sheep grievance fades away after Henry VIII; but there is no reason whatever to think that the different sorts of enclosure slackened—though all told they made only a moderate change in the face of the country under the Tudors and the early Stuarts. There were intermittent legal threats against enclosure, but not much administrative action was taken after 1550 until King Charles I, between 1634 and 1639, levied heavy fines from some 'depopulating' enclosers in seven counties, after an outbreak of midland rioting against them. That was the end of the policy; and the King was impecunious. Commons near towns and big villages were often partly enclosed, sometimes without recorded grievances, sometimes with

[1] Cf. above, pp. 164–5.

social friction and riots. More of the moors and waste-lands were brought under the plough, or used for the cow, as in Devon. And there was something of a campaign in favour of the most fundamental geographical change of all, the enclosure of the strips of the open fields and the rearrangement of the holdings. Its best-known advocate was the 'poet' Thomas Tusser whose *Hundred Points of Good Husbandry* appeared in 1557 and was reissued in 1571, 1573, 1577 and 1580, to become a sort of farmer's classic. Tusser was an Eton and Cambridge man, a musician and a farmer in East Suffolk—who died in prison for debt in 1580. He hated the open fields, 'the champion husbandry', because of the time-wasting business of moving from strip to strip, the old-fashioned routine of their agriculture, and—as he believed—their failure to yield a proper return in foodstuffs.

> More plenty of mutton and beef,
> Corn, butter, and cheese of the best,
> Where find ye (go search any coast)
> Than there, where enclosure is most?

But he was fair-minded enough to admit that

> The poor at enclosing do grutch,
> Because of abuses that fall,
> Lest some man should have but too much,
> And some again nothing at all.

If you rearranged fields or commons, the grasping man might come out on top. That, however, is part of the social question, for later discussion.

East Suffolk, where Tusser had farmed, was, broadly speaking, enclosed country. Cambridgeshire was, and very long remained, almost completely unenclosed; so Tusser had knowledge, or at least opportunities for observation, on which to base his strong opinions.

When Queen Elizabeth died, twenty-three years after Thomas Tusser, most progress in the enclosure of midland open fields and commons had been made in Northampton, Leicester, Rutland and part of Warwick. There was perceptible progress also in Bedford, Buckingham, Berkshire, Oxford and Middlesex. In neither group was there any thorough transformation of the face of the country. What the reduction in the total area of common and common-field was between 1500 and 1600, or between 1600 and 1750, it is impossible to tell. (It is not to be forgotten that perhaps not half of the country was cultivated at all in 1650.) East Anglia, which had fields lying open but not the full rigid open-field system,[1] moved faster than the central and eastern midlands. In these, wide tracts still remained almost untouched down to 1750, although the enclosure movement as a whole was gathering momentum after 1700. Under Charles II pamphleteers, writing of 'England's Great Happiness' or 'England's Improvement', had argued for more enclosure, and one of England's earliest journalists, Houghton, had repeated Tusser's song, with a Restoration refrain, arguing for a general Enclosure Act and promising that, if it did not succeed, he would 'be content ne'er to be drunk this seven years'.

There was legislation about enclosure in Scotland a few years later which, at first sight, suggests Houghton's desired policy—a policy not applied in England for more than a century. But Scottish conditions were not English; enclosure in Scotland meant what it says and no more. In most districts no act was needed to rearrange fields, had anyone wanted to do that. Practically all cultivators were tenants: these were not '40s. freeholders'. There were very few commons over which groups of people had rights, so an improving, or greedy, landlord had a fairly free hand at law. But very few landlords went in for improvement before 1750; and 'until well into the eighteenth century by far the greatest number of enclosures' were simply the fencing or walling of land from Scotland's great stretches of moor and waste, to protect young plantations or provide safe grazing ground for cattle.[2]

THE REDISTRIBUTION OF LANDED PROPERTY

An English landlord of the sixteenth or seventeenth century usually had to negotiate or fight—and he might fight without much scruple—to get that free hand to 'do what he would with his own' that the Scottish nobleman or laird possessed long before he had much thought of playing his hand for improvement's sake. There had been great changes in the English landlord class since 1500. The old feudal nobility had long been vanishing. 'Where is Bohun, where's Mowbray, where's Mortimer? Nay, which is more and most of all, where is

---

[1] See above, pp. 89–90.
[2] Henry Hamilton, *The Industrial Revolution in Scotland* (1932), p. 38.

Plantagenet?' Those questions were put in 1625 by a man born in 1558, but might have been put much earlier. Monastic lands had passed, through the King, to Russells, Cavendishes, Cecils or to esquires and rising merchants. The transition had been the easier because monastic landlords, in their somnolent old age, had often let whole estates with their various sources of income to these same local gentlemen, some of whom now acquired what they might already have leased. Queen Elizabeth granted away to courtiers and others a good deal of the Crown lands that remained to her. She did it no doubt the more readily because she sometimes lost on them. Where rents and other payments were traditional and low, as they were on old Crown land, the extra cost of management due to the price rise of her time easily produced that odd situation. The early Stuarts owed some of their unpopularity to attempts to make the remaining Crown lands pay—challenging unauthorised nibblings at waste land, and prying into questionable tenures, especially in the North.

A considerable shuffling-up of landed property came under the rule of the Parliament and Cromwell, when 'malignants' and Papists were fined or had their lands confiscated. Yet there was no sweeping change in the land-owning class. Some got land back at the Restoration. Some utilised neighbours' misfortunes or folly to round off their own estates. Some of the City men who bought, bought as an investment and sold again.

There was all the time a steady filtering-up of new men into the ranks of the squires, from the City and especially from among successful lawyers. A man may go to London, make a fortune, and return to his native county to buy an estate, as Sir Patience Ward bought Hooton Pagnell near Doncaster in 1704. Names of early directors of the Bank of England soon appear on manors. About that time, say from 1695 to 1725, it appears that many small gentlemen, rough rustic Squire Westerns, were being bought out, some by these new men, more perhaps by the great lords who, ruling eighteenth-century England, added to their estates as the small hunting and drinking squire families of £200 to £300 a year died out or had mortgages on their land foreclosed, and were sold up. Rural England still has plenty of old farm houses which were once their manor houses.

BOND STATUS AND COPYHOLD TENURE

There were villeins in Tudor England; bondmen they were generally called; but English writers, accustomed to boast of English liberty, were getting ashamed of them. Harrison in 1577 said there were none; but 'his words were rather prophetic than true'. The courts had held under Henry VII that if a villein got a lease from his lord for a term of years '*cest enfranchisement*', a decision which declared free many rising and lease-taking villeins—reeves perhaps, like the early Pepys.[1] It became easier and easier to run away to Town or to the towns. Or to get ordained: three bondmen of a Lincolnshire manor in 1570 were curates in adjacent counties. Sometimes villeinage survived because a greedy lord found the squeezing of a substantial 'bondman' profitable: he might even seize the land of a freeman who had a bondman's surname and failed to prove the emancipation of his ancestors. The Star Chamber and the Court of Requests had to deal with such cases under Henry VIII and Edward VI. When in 1575 Elizabeth gave instructions for the manumission of two hundred bondmen on the estates of the Duchy of Lancaster, she also instructed her agent to fix the price: if they could not pay it he might seize their lands. That was near the end. The courts always favoured freedom, as they did in the last recorded case about villeinage (1618): they said that the appropriately named plaintiff, Pigg, was free.

Meanwhile the copyhold tenure, which had grown out of villein tenure,[2] was establishing itself, again with the help of the courts. In early Tudor times, there were still plenty of tenants in villeinage—customary tenants, not necessarily villeins by blood—who had no copy of the court rolls, *custumarii sine copia*. That facilitated eviction by a greedy or enclosing lord. But gradually their position was improved; the courts treated all alike; copyholder became the general term; and Sir Edward Coke in his *Complete Copyholder*, of the reign of Charles I, could boast—'But now Copy-holders stand upon a sure ground, now they weigh not their Lords displeasure, they shake not at every sudden blast of wind, they eat, drink and sleep securely; only having a special care of the main chance, (viz.) to perform carefully what Duties and Services soever

---

[1] See above, p. 115.   [2] See above, p. 113.

their Tenure doth exact, and Custom doth require: then let Lord frown, the Copy-holder cares not, knowing himself safe, and not within any danger.'[1] Coke went on to explain the various ways in which the Common Law, of which he was so proud, had secured this copyholders' safety, especially the Action of Trespass which the copyholder might bring in a Court of Common Law against a Lord who 'ousted' him; 'for it is against reason, that the Lord should be Judge [i.e. in the manor court] where he himself is a Party'.[2]

'What Custom doth require': there were various customs. Some copyholds were held to be 'of inheritance': they went automatically from father to son. More, probably, were for lives—that is, they ran for the lifetimes of certain named persons, usually three, and usually members of the tenant's family. On the death of the last of the three, the land reverted to the lord. But when one of the 'lives' 'dropped out' by death, you might bargain with the lord to insert a new 'life'— but you would have to pay a fine for it. When, two hundred years after Coke's day, collegiate landowners declined to go on inserting, they had only to wait until the lives ran out and the copyholds, like 99-year leaseholds, fell in.

Custom also dealt with the fine that an incoming tenant, whether the heir or not, had to pay on a copyhold of inheritance. 'In some Manors Fines are certain, in some incertain', Coke writes.[3] A 'certain' fine was a precise sum of money, usually small, and fixed for ever; so that a copyholder of inheritance with fine certain was in a very strong position, as nearly as possible a freeholder. The prices of his produce were all going up: his son would succeed him at small cost. There never was, or has been, a census of copyholders; but it is believed that this most favoured section of them was a minority. Where fine was 'incertain', the Lord might bargain and press on his tenants, as he might on tenants for lives when they paid to 'insert a life'.

There was most of this pressure during the sixteenth century, while the relations between landlord and tenant—disturbed by the price revolution—were being readjusted. By 1650, and still more by 1750, a copyholder was by no means necessarily that humble tiller of the soil that his villein predecessor had

[1] Sir Edward Coke, *The Complete Copyholder* (edition of 1673), p. 7.
[2] *Ibid.* p. 142.
[3] *Ibid.* p. 154.

been. Anyone could hold by that tenure. A prosperous yeoman might have some land held in 'free and common socage', some leasehold, some copyhold. There were whole groups of substantial yeomen all of whom were copyholders. 'Socage', under the Stuarts, had not quite lost its medieval character. Some little customary 'free rents' survived. 'Reliefs', on inheritance or sale, survived too, sometimes; but they were fixed, like the rents. These resemblances to copyhold might make a yeoman relatively indifferent about his tenure, since copyhold had lost all servile taint. So much so, that it might easily become an urban tenure as towns expanded. The last bit of copyhold to fall into a certain College, by expiry of lives not many years ago, was in an Exeter street.

RENTS AND FINES; ENCLOSURES BY THE PEASANTRY

When Henry VIII, in 1537, defined the duties of his Council of the North, he instructed his councillors to 'make diligent inquisition who hath taken and enclosed commons, called intakes; who be extreme in taking of gressoms and onering of rents'. There, when interpreted, and in a prayer issued by reformers under Edward VI—'O Lord, we pray Thee that the landlords may not rack and stretch out the rents'; there are the sorest places in sixteenth-century agrarian history. Enclosure, of whatever type, affected only people here and there, the rents and the 'Gressoms' affected every cultivator because they were connected with the rise in prices. The Gressom, or Gersum, or *Ingressum*, was the fine paid by the incoming tenant; except for the lucky minority who had 'fine certain', it was one of the points on which a lord, not necessarily a greedy criminal, might most easily press; and fines might be connected with most tenures—for entry into a copyhold or for renewal of a lease. When the men of the North had risen in the Pilgrimage of Grace in 1536, a precise economic demand had been made in their name—that the gressom be limited to two years' rent. That was before prices had gone up much. The men who made the demand did not explain to what tenures it applied—probably to some variants of copyhold of the sort that developed later into the hybrid 'customary freehold'.[1] The Council of the North, reconstituted after the Pilgrimage, was instructed to keep an eye on agrarian abuses.

[1] See above, p. 112.

So was the short-lived Council of the West, set up in 1539; its instructions repeated those of the Council of the North almost word for word.

Among these agrarian abuses came the 'onering' of rents; that is to say, increasing the rents, increasing their burden on the tenants. The rent 'onered' might, one supposes, be either a leasehold rent or one of the surviving payments from a copyhold or freehold. Such increases, and increases of gressoms, might be devices adopted by lords who wanted to get rid of tenants—in order to add the land to their own demesne, perhaps to enclose it, or to let it to a fresh tenant who would offer good terms for a lease. On the other hand, there might be better reasons for the increase. As prices rose, and with them all a lord's living expenses, if he could not make his estate yield more he might be forced into the awkward position of the Crown under Elizabeth. From the beginning of recorded legal history, the villein on 'ancient demesne of the Crown', and with him other Crown tenants, had enjoyed favourable terms— easier services, then low fixed money payments in place of them, or as a freeman's dues. At this very time in France, the general prevalence of such fixed payments was breaking many of the old *noblesse*—lords and gentry the English would have called them—as prices rose. The more commercially-minded English landowners, with some French ones, were using every possible means—legal and less legal—to save their position. Leases were for 'terms of years', sometimes, like copyholds, 'for lives'. In twenty years of the sixteenth century, still more in one or two lifetimes, what had been a reasonable money-rent might become quite unreasonable from the landlord's point of view or indeed from any point of view. The tenant got all the advantage of prices for his produce doubled or trebled, the lord if he did not cultivate got no more money to pay for his horses, his Spanish gloves and his slashed Elizabethan doublet—or even the rough clothes and rough living of a tiny rural manor. So he wanted to revise letting terms as often as possible, and to produce on a 'home farm' all that he could for his larder or for market, like the Temples of Stowe or Justice Shallow, who had a good orchard and a 'score of good ewes' priced for him at ten pounds.

When Queen Elizabeth's Parliament, in 1576, compelled the colleges of Oxford and Cambridge to take one-third of their leasehold rents in corn, marketable or consumable stuff,

it was to their very great advantage. The parson who took his
tithe in the fields, stored it in a tithe-barn and ate it, was spared
some of the anxieties of a squire who had only a few fields
'in hand'.

The enclosing of commons 'called intakes' referred primarily no doubt to that taking in of land from the moors so
frequent in the West and the North. It would not become an
abuse which a Council after making 'diligent inquisition'
might try to mitigate, unless local feeling ran strongly against
it. In the West, where the Council soon vanished, there is no
reason to think that anything was done: the men of Devon
continued to take in from the moors. So did the men of the
North, where the Council had a longer life, though there they
were more liable to 'inquisition'. Indeed, men are known to
have enclosed, from moor or fen or wood, in nearly every county
of England.

Those most active were, in a small way, humble encroaching
'squatters', and, in a big way, the now established and rising
yeomen, that strong agrarian middle class which it is a mistake
to idealise.[1] They were efficient by the standards of their day:
they were also 'land-hungry, profit-hungry'. They had the
qualities and the defects of those eighteenth- and nineteenth-
century ironmasters, coal-owners and mill-owners who so often
—like the Peels—came of yeoman stock. In these earlier
centuries they are connected with the clothing industry and
are pioneers in coal-mining. As cultivators they might inherit
or buy or rent land; they might be leaseholders or copyholders;
they might just be freeholders, as the gentlemen themselves
became when tenure by knight-service vanished at the Restoration. Their holdings were of all kinds, open-field strips or
fields enclosed, mainly arable or mainly grazing land. In size,
so far as has been ascertained, an arable holding might be
counted as a yeoman's from about thirty acres up to perhaps
200: a grazing yeoman might hold several hundreds of acres.

They were just the men to be keen about moderate but
substantial intakes. The general rearrangement of an open-field
village called for planning at 'a higher level'; but the taking-in
of 'furze close' or five acres of waste fen was a yeoman's job, or
indeed a husbandman's. All through two centuries, small and
moderate enclosures by such men are on record: they do more
enclosing of this type than the gentlemen. Often, perhaps

[1] See above, p. 116.

normally, it was by agreement with the lord and with neighbours: scores of such agreements have survived. This being so, it is not likely that even a Council of the North did much to check the movement. Contentious men might take cases before it; but as King James's remark about enclosure shows,[1] level-headed people in authority saw the advantages of a movement which destroyed no houses of husbandry and increased the supply of food.

Enclosure by agreement was not merely a local phenomenon. It is found more or less everywhere. Late in Elizabeth's reign, for example, King's College, Cambridge, agreed with the tenants of a Norfolk manor to enclose the commons. The College, as lord, took so much: each tenant took his share. The bargain was sealed with a dinner in Hall. If any cottagers had a grievance, it is not recorded.

A similar process can often be traced in the seventeenth century. Take the most north-easterly and the most south-westerly open-field areas. Between 1633 and 1700, twenty-eight enclosure agreements, twenty of them involving open fields, were registered in the Palatine Court of Durham. Pembrokeshire, 'bare champion' under Elizabeth, was 'much altered by inclosures' in 1700.

Rising yeomen were likely both to make 'intakes' and to kick against open-field routines that interfered with their plans. Consolidation of holdings in open fields, not a new thing, certainly continued. If a yeoman bought out a small impecunious squire, and we have Harrison's statement of 1577 that he might do so, he might come into the use of a demesne more or less consolidated. After that cases of yeomen exchanging their strips for plots are known; other cases may be inferred. Perhaps Little Garth lying in 'le Middle Field de Knowstrop', in the Leeds survey of 1612, was a new enclosure, not as has been suggested a possible old one.[2] This breaking into the pattern of the fields was of course particularly likely to occur near a growing town; in remoter rural districts the pattern often remained as intact as it had ever been right down to the final enclosure of the eighteenth or nineteenth century: this the abundant surveys made at enclosure time, and now collected into county record offices, make clear.

[1] See above, p. 198.   [2] See above, pp. 123-4.

ENGLISH RURAL SOCIETY; WAGES
AND THEIR REGULATION

That the yeoman prospered with the rising prices is obvious. Whatever his tenure, he worked for the market. If he owned his land, it was an asset that was appreciating. If he were a copyholder, he was not the man to 'shake at every sudden blast of wind'. He knew about the law—his sons sometimes went into it. He could get a writ or fight a case of trespass with any man: he was often a litigious type. If he had a lease he would make the best of it while it ran, and keep his end up in the bargain for its renewal. Harrison is very explicit about his prosperity—his chimneys, his pewter, his clothing and his bedding; how he started his sons in life and dowered his daughters. He—the representative yeoman; of course there were failures—not only did well out of the century of steeply rising prices, but held his own when they were more stable in the century that followed, perhaps riding with Oliver, to be reckoned a bit of England's backbone under the early Hanoverians.

He did well and so did the representative, rather commercially-minded, gentleman—not the improvident one who went under. 'The ancient manors...of our gentlemen', Harrison writes, 'are yet, and for the most part, of strong timber.... Howbeit such as be lately builded are commonly either of brick or hard stone, or both.' After 1577 these 'brick or hard stone' manors multiplied. Not many were built or rebuilt in 'strong timber' in the next century. The stone or brick manors of late Tudor and early Stuart times, like the great places— Hatfield, Burghley House, Audley End—still stand up and down the country, though the smaller manor, of whatever built, has so often become the house of the modern equivalent of the Elizabethan yeoman, the substantial tenant farmer.

The dividing line between yeoman and husbandman was not sharp. But the average husbandman may be thought of as the 'small holder' with twenty to ten acres of land, or even less. He was a 'subsistence farmer', living on his own produce as best he could, and no doubt working his family hard. How he lived would depend on his soil and his crops. He would aim at some surplus, to be marketed and give him the ready money that was essential to meet his modest expenditure on clothes and utensils and the demands of his landlord. Very often he was a copyholder, but he might equally be a small leaseholder or a small freeholder, a tenant-at-will or a tenant from year to year. Tenancies from year to year were something of a novelty in the sixteenth century, but they gradually gained at the expense of tenancies-at-will; partly because they gave the tenant security from Michaelmas to Michaelmas, partly because they entitled the landlord to claim his full rent up to the end of the agricultural year. The farmer's year ends at Michaelmas, after harvest is done. Michaelmas was the usual and convenient season for a change of tenant; it became convenient also for the bigger farmers of the eighteenth century, and so remained in the nineteenth.

In so far as the husbandman's family could live on the produce of his holding, price changes would not much affect them; and if he had a little produce to market, its raised price would meet the raised prices of what he had to buy. He lived a hard life, especially in bad seasons; but from Tudor times onwards there were no instances of that true famine which had haunted earlier centuries and was prayed against in Cranmer's Litany, together with 'plague, pestilence...battle and murder and sudden death'.

There was a more distinct line between the husbandman and the lower ranks of the rural population than between him and the yeoman. They were those who never thought of living by their land, if they had a little, as some few had. They formed a class that was certainly increasing with an increasing population, all through the period; but a class that had always existed since real slavery died out. Any increase in the size of holdings or of the 'home farms' of landlords, by consolidations and evictions, would tend to enlarge the class; but though we often come across consolidations and evictions, we have no statistics that will even begin to tell us what their effects were on the bigger changes of population and classes. It is safest to connect the growth of this class mainly with that probable doubling of total population which these two and a half centuries witnessed.[1] We can be sure that, although fresh land was brought under cultivation, the creation of extra holdings, other than cottagers' scraps filched from waste or forest, was unusual: the fresh land was usually added to a holding that existed already.

When statistical writers began to appear, late in the seventeenth century, they called the members of this agrarian

[1] See above, p. 186.

proletariat 'outservants' (as opposed to male and female domestic servants), 'cottagers', or 'paupers'. They connected them, rightly, with the 554,631 dwellings in England and Wales which the hearth-tax of 1685 registered as containing only a single hearth. They recognised that some of the cottages had 'land about them', and so housed that sort of cottager who could live in part from his land, in part from 'outwork' for farmers or gentlemen. But their calculations suggest that they considered such land-holding cottagers a small minority, though most country cottages had some bit of garden ground.

A comparison of the fairly well-informed guesses of the early statisticians with the census returns of the early nineteenth century makes it quite certain that, taking the whole of England and Wales, this agrarian proletariat was not twice as numerous as the land-holding class—farmers, 'yeomen', husbandmen—in 1750. The probable ratio was about 1·8:1. (The ratio was only 2·5:1 in 1831, and only 2:1 in the Yorkshire of 1911, a county with many small farmers.)

There is no great difficulty in showing that, as a result of the price-rise of the sixteenth century, for members of this class—for Bullcalf o' the green and Mouldy—Shakespeare's England was a poor place. Their predecessors of the fifteenth century had lived rather dangerously but in relative comfort, to judge by the purchasing power of their wages.[1] There is no reason to think that 'housing conditions', in a one-hearth cottage or hut, were much worse in 1485 than in 1685. The widespread anxiety about 'masterless men', rogues and vagabonds in early Tudor times is probably exaggerated in our minds—as all the troubles of that age are—because printing has left a stock of pamphlets and other writings for us to read greater than earlier centuries could furnish. There had always been outlaws and thieves, beggars and folk in the greenwood. But it does suggest that the civil wars of the fifteenth century, the Tudors' scattering of the private armies of retainers, the social dislocations connected locally with enclosure and the dissolution of the monasteries, had added to their numbers. A change of landlords, as at the dissolution, did not necessarily involve unemployment. The importance of monastic charity has been exaggerated; and if a monastery maintained a fair number of hangers-on, so did the swollen households of the Tudor nobility who acquired the Bolton Abbeys and Woburn Abbeys and

[1] See above, p. 119.

Ford Abbeys. The main trouble came from a growing population in a rural society in which the number of separate agricultural holdings was certainly not growing. Many of the new mouths went to Town or the towns or picked up some trade in the country. Some took to the roads or to crime. All who could added to the family earnings by any available sort of by-employment for some member of the family—spinning, nail-making, or whatever it might be. The rest worked for what wages they could get, wages that the State tried to regulate, with fair success—and the agents of the State were mostly wage-payers, local Justices of the Peace. They were perhaps not unusually hard-hearted; but economic conditions were in their favour, as after the Great Pestilence they had favoured wage-earners, who also had taken every advantage of their position.

Between the first and the last decade of the sixteenth century day-wages on the land about doubled. That last decade was an unusually dear one, and is perhaps not quite a fair test: but we have seen that in it a rough sort of 'cost of living' figure works out at nearly six times that of 1491–1500, and at more than three times that of the decade in which the monasteries were dissolved (1531–40), before Henry VIII debased the coinage, and before the great flood of silver came in from the New World.[1]

This sounds desperate and it was certainly very bad. Consider it in another way. That decade 1491–1500, on the average of years and places, was quite abnormally favourable to the pure wage-earner. Supposing that he and his ancestors had lived entirely on wheat, his day's pay would have bought nearly three times so much of that superior food as a day's pay had brought them in 1300. This two centuries' gain he was losing under the Tudors: by 1600 the day's pay would buy just as much wheat as it had bought in 1300. They lived at both dates.

Poor men did not live on pure wheat at either; but Englishmen have always liked it and eaten more of it when they could. As prices rose, they fell back on rougher and cheaper grain— Harrison says so in 1577—on rye, barley, oats, even linseed. Scotland and the North had always used oats freely, and Wales barley. But wheaten bread was what the gentry ate; and so did other people in proportion as they prospered. In Shakespeare's day they had to go back on it. Some evidence also suggests,

---

[1] See above, pp. 186–7.

a thing in itself probable, that the consumption of what was called 'white meat', i.e. the relatively expensive dairy produce, declined.

The situation looks so bad that historians have been on the look-out for extenuating circumstances. A bit of land about the cottage was one such circumstance; but the men of 1491–1500 might also have bits of land. Use of the common—by custom not by right, if you held no land—was another; but neither was that a new thing. There is provision in Tudor law for an employer to feed his man—and to give a higher wage when he did not—but there is again no proof that such feeding was a novelty; the old habit of supplying food on boon-days suggests that it was not; but it would be a help when prices were rising. What does seem probable, though it cannot be demonstrated, is that the spread of the wool manufacture and of other industries that touched village life gave to the agricultural wage-earner's family greater opportunities for earning, and so for adding to the family income, than had previously existed. But when all has been allowed for, it remains certain that the material position of the mere wage-earner deteriorated perceptibly under the Tudors—unless every figure lies.

It has been said that 'the social problem of the sixteenth century was not a problem of wages, but of rents and fines'. Certainly it was of these that parliaments and law courts debated and social reformers declaimed. But few reformers sprang from wage-earning families. Bullcalf o' the green and Mouldy were inarticulate. Those who paid rents and fines were not, and many of them had votes. Often they were an absolute, even a large, majority of the rural householders; perhaps they were a majority everywhere under Henry VIII and Edward VI. It was certainly these occupiers of 'houses of husbandry' about whose fortunes governments were anxious: the others they were in some danger of lumping with the masterless men and vagabonds. As in regions of small farms to-day, in Wales or in Cumberland, the wage-earners were scattered individuals, not groups. There is a parallel in France before the Revolution. Peasants' grievances interested Arthur Young: he has little to say about day-labourers, *journaliers*. Even in parish petitions of grievances in 1789, the position of the *journalier* is seldom referred to, except as a kind of hell into which peasants may fall if things are not bettered. There are explanations common to the two countries in their two centuries. Lifelong agricultural wage-earners, in France certainly, in England probably, were outnumbered by the land-holders. In both they were inarticulate. In both, many actual wage-earners were peasants' or husbandmen's sons, waiting the death of a father or elder brother to take over the family land. Yet as, in sixteenth-century England, the lifelong wage-earners, or wage-seekers, were certainly becoming a more important social group, destined to be a majority well before the next century was over, it is arguable that if theirs was not in fact the social problem of the time it ought to have been.

This Elizabeth's government recognised in a fashion, in its labour legislation. Before prices rose, the policy of legal maximum wage-rates had been no serious hardship. It was retained in 1515; but one or two county assessments that have survived from 1560-1 show that, with the price-rise, local authorities had felt obliged to disregard it. (Individual wage-payers had disregarded it already.) Cecil, coming into power, turned to the precedent of 1389-90,[1] and its 'convenient proportion' of wages. He certainly intended that the general assessment of wages by the Justices of the Peace, provided for in the great Act of 1562-3, should be based on this principle; and although we find complaints, in the dear years of the fifteen-nineties, that wages had in fact not been 'rated... according to the plenty, scarcity...and respect of the times', there is evidence from both the sixteenth and the seventeenth centuries that it was not quite neglected, though Justices were often inert and went on re-issuing old assessments. Those of Kent, for instance, had 'yearly certified' wages 'without any change' from the year of the Act to that of the Armada. It looks as if what rise took place was in spite of, not because of, the Act.

And the Act shows that legislators still thought of all people who had no property as semi-servile. Qualified craftsmen might be compelled to work in their crafts; men not otherwise employed, from the age of 12 to that of 60, in agriculture; women, from 12 to 40, might be compelled to take service. Economic compulsion appears generally to have been strong enough to make men serve on the land, for what they could get, without pressure from the Justices. As the humbler crafts, such as the weaving of 'household' woollen cloth, were left open to them, without the regular apprenticeship which the Act tried to enforce for more skilled occupations, they had at least

[1] See above, p. 121.

alternatives, when they had enterprise enough to seize them. But the combined pressures of a growing population and the law kept enough on the land to rob their labour of that scarcity-value which their predecessors had enjoyed in the later fourteenth century.[1]

It is not surprising that some of the later Elizabethans began to wonder whether population was not becoming, as men would say later, redundant, and to think of overseas adventure and the newly projected plantations as an outlet for it. (Was the 'redundancy' an important incentive to adventure? It has been since.) They took their illustrations rather naturally from the records of crime, arguing that an alleged, but to us not a proved, increase of crime meant that there was not enough honest employment available. Richard Hakluyt, the enthusiastic historian and advocate of adventure, lamented that it did not absorb all those 'able men to serve their country which for small robberies are daily hanged...even twenty at a clap out of some one gaol'.

Throughout the seventeenth and early eighteenth centuries prices remained fairly stable[2] while wages, both on and off the land, crawled up. Wages did not move much until after 1650, though some rise can be traced from about 1630. The pure wage-earner had not yet the numerically dominant place in rural society that he was to acquire later; but it is well not to forget that the half-century that ended with the Civil Wars had been for him unusually harsh.

Wage-assessment by the Justices went on, in places, far into the eighteenth century. Thirty issues or reissues of rates are now known between 1700 and 1750, and a few even after 1750. Here and there in the seventeenth century an issue is connected with some local or temporary scarcity; but the general impression is that the slow upward move of money wages came first, and was then recognised. In 1668, when it had already set in, the Somerset Justices issued a wage-schedule which showed no advance on the official rates of twenty years before. In 1687 the Buckinghamshire Justices enforced in court payment of a wage above their own published rate. Everything, of course, depended on activity in the enforcement of the official rates. This varied greatly; but, owing to the relative stability of seventeenth-century conditions, rates assessed and rates actually paid did not diverge widely, so far

[1] See above, pp. 118–9.   [2] See above, pp. 187–8.

as we know: 'the case for a [general] divergence between assessed and economic rates before, say, the sixteen-eighties is still not proven'.[1] With the eighteenth century very little is heard of court proceedings for infringement of legal rates—of which there had been a fair amount previously—and the divergence between the wage assessed and the wage paid grows. The system was moribund, but it died harder than historians used to think—and the memory of it did not die.

RURAL SOCIETY IN WALES AND SCOTLAND

When King Henry VIII cut up Wales into counties and gave it English Law, he also gave Justices of the Peace, whose business it became to apply his daughter's wage-law. We know that they did assess wages; but their few known assessments have not been much studied. They appear to have dealt mainly with farm-servants, living in, and with harvesters. That is what we should expect. The development of anything that could be called a labouring class was very slow and very partial in Wales of the Welsh. Even in the early nineteenth century 'a kind of feudal connection' survived in places. Whole families worked for a farmer at a fixed low rate per day: he might give them land and gardens and cheap bread-corn, or he might not. Again, a 'labourer' might put in a day's work for each horse that he borrowed from the farmer to plough some scrap of land of his own. This is in the South   South and north, in the eighteenth century, we are told of 'labourers' who gave 'love-reapings', and had in return 'love-ploughings'. It is all very medieval; it recalls English 'boon-days' and the free tribesman with his servile dependants in ancient Welsh law.[2] Wage-rates, when we find them, tell us very little. Those we know most about are for farm-servants living in, and as these were fed the wage is of secondary importance.

Scotland, Low or High, was no better furnished with a labourer class, as opposed to labouring individuals, than was Wales. And the Highlands, at least, were much shorter of cash in which to pay wages: late in the eighteenth century a High-land gentleman might pay his cobbler with an ox-hide and his carpenter with a log. Down to the crofter, nearly everyone had, if not a foot, at least a toe on the land. Each grade

[1] R. Keith Kelsall, *Wage Regulation under the Statute of Artificers* (1938), p. 27.
[2] See above, p. 56.

normally did work of some kind for the grade above it—
farmers for their laird, small or great, or in the Highlands
for the 'tacksman' who held under the chieftain of the clan; cottars for the laird or the farmer; crofters, with their fragments
of land, also for one or the other. All were tenants, except
noblemen and true lairds. All were personally free and all
were socially independent. The lower grades could seldom live
by their holdings: they might serve, or hunt, or fish, or practise
some country craft. But the holding was there—except for
a few beggars, broken men, and destitute women, for whom the
parish had to provide.

Welshmen and Scots, and above all Highlanders, were then
far nearer than the average English to that 'natural economy'
of which economists have written. You paid so often in hides
and oatmeal and days' labour. Before such conditions the
statistician is silenced. Was a cottar better housed, or fed, or
clothed at the time of the '45 than when Queen Mary fled
into England? The statistician cannot say. After 1603 everyone
in the South was safer from Border raids; and after the '45
everyone on the Highland fringe from cattle-liftings and
raidings of barns for corn—in those 'Moray lands', for example,
'where all men' used to 'take their prey'. The Reformation had
come and then the Union, first of Crowns and after of Parliaments. Society was stabler, safer, more law-abiding. Whether
its lower strata had become any more comfortable may certainly
be doubted, but cannot be demonstrated.

AGRICULTURAL TECHNIQUE

Of technical progress in agriculture it is very hard to speak
until we get well into the eighteenth century, and it is not
easy then. The first mention of this working method, or that
new crop, or some improved rotation, can often be traced;
but what the historian most wants to know, and often cannot
learn with any certainty, is how many people adopted it, and
where, and when. What is certain is that, far into the eighteenth century, there were some traditions everywhere that had
not changed, and many regions where little or nothing had
changed. There was the old heavy, wheelless Scots plough that
'made rather a triangular rut in the ground than a furrow'—
with its twelve oxen, its mixed team of oxen and horses, or, in
Ayrshire, its four to six horses. The traditional Kentish plough,

with its six to twelve oxen, was just as cumbrous and un-changed, though technically better. There are the men of Cam-bridge under William and Mary, shown reaping with the sickle in their 'Carme Field', where now a University library stands, precisely as in any medieval illustrated manuscript. And, if the picture is to be trusted, all, on their several strips, are harvesting the same crop: it is Carme Field's turn in the rotation for wheat. There is Devonshire, which in 1750 was said not to have a single wheeled cart, crops and everything else being moved on sledges or on horseback. There are the Welsh, still most interested in their cattle, but driving them more and more for sale into England where, in 1707, 'your *Angleseys* and *Welch*' are reckoned 'a good hardy Sort for fatting on barren or middling Sort of Land'. Hardiest of all are the black Scots which, well accustomed to be driven, were already coming south; and though the drovers' roads through the Cheviots were not so busy in 1707 as they became later, Defoe found 'a prodigious number of black cattle' fattening in the 'vast tracts of meadows' behind Yarmouth, in the twenties.

The teams suggest one change which was certainly going slowly forward, though whether it meant progress or not contemporaries were still not agreed—the replacement on the land, and especially in the plough-team, of the ox by the horse. It has been suggested that the horse was first harnessed to a harrow, perhaps very early. We know that the relative merits of plough horse and plough ox had been debated from the thirteenth to the sixteenth century.[1] One of our earliest field maps, a very charming one embellished with pictures, that of Laxton in Nottinghamshire, shows a single horse dragging a harrow and a yoke of oxen with a horse harnessed in front dragging a wheeled plough. That is symbolic of the compromise then arrived at for the country as a whole. In the eighteenth century there are ox regions and horse regions, but the horse tends to predominate. We most often meet horses on the west side of the island, from Ayrshire downward, including Wales. But we meet them also, from four to six of them to a plough, in Northampton, in Berkshire and in Middlesex; and we meet not exactly horses but garrons, ponies, ploughing in the High-lands. Ox-teams are still easily found; they survived into this present century in Sussex; but by the eighteenth 'progressive'

[1] See above, p. 84.

people are all for the horse. Soon, when Coke of Norfolk wants
to teach Gloucestershire men, he will send a Norfolk plough,
a ploughman and a pair of horses to beat, not oxen, but the
traditional Gloucestershire six-horse team handled by two men
and a boy.

It is with implements as with teams—no striking change
or improvement until well into the eighteenth century, and then
an immense weight of tradition against change, tradition which,
if not always blind, often was.

Changes and progress in cropping are closely associated
with the use of the common fields, though innovation was
easiest and earliest in 'old inclosed' districts like Kent. Common
field routine, we now know, was less rigid than many brief
accounts of it suggest, even before 1500. There were always
more crops to be raised than one of winter corn—wheat, rye, or
mixed grain—and one of spring corn, barley or oats. In a
three-field rotation we should expect to find most uniformity
and routine on the winter-field, the 'white' corn field, as it is
sometimes called. The other cropped field is sometimes called
the 'peas' field, as it seems to be in the earliest known field-
regulating agreement, one of about 1425. In any case, room
had to be found for peas and beans, perhaps also for tares
(vetches) and hemp and flax, though the two last were generally
grown apart in closes and gardens: an early seventeenth-
century writer makes his shepherd grow hemp enough in his
garden 'to make his lockram shirts'.

We know that in early Stuart times crops might be grown on
the spring-corn field of one three-course set 'according to each
man's fancy'.[1] That is at Laxton in Nottingham. Away on
the Berkshire Downs, on a two-course set, Robert Loder in
1610–20 was sowing wheat, barley, beans, peas and vetches on
his strips in the single-cropped field pretty much as he liked;
once, at least, he 'hitched' a vetch crop from the fallow field.
Long afterwards, in 1794, an agricultural expert wrote: 'whoever apprehends that the occupiers of a common field are
necessarily tied down to any precise mode of management, by
the custom of any parish, are grossly mistaken'.[2] That implies
widespread, and not new, free cropping in Lincolnshire, of
which he was writing. Right into the nineteenth century, in
an unenclosed three-field village of Cambridgeshire, one field—

[1] C. S. and C. S. Orwin. *The Open Fields* (1938), p. 168.
[2] Thomas Stone, *General View of the Agriculture of...Lincoln* (1794), p. 35.

no doubt the autumn-sown—had a stated crop; one lay as fallow pasture; one 'might be cropped according to the various owners' pleasure'.[1] Routine plus liberty. How far back did it go in Lincoln or Cambridge or Nottingham or Berkshire?

After Robert Loder's day, there was much advocacy of fodder-crop growing on the fallow field, especially of turnips and clover. Loder, and no doubt many more unrecorded men, had shown the way with his 'hitching' of vetches. The main obstacle was the widespread, but not universal, right to 'common of shack', grazing on the fallow, as in nineteenth-century Cambridgeshire. So far as is known, Barnaby Googe was the first writer to recommend growing turnips in the field, in 1577. (But such recommendations pass most often, at all times, by unrecorded word of mouth.) Googe was translating a foreign book and drawing on the experience of the Low Countries. Other advocates followed him, and before the seventeenth century was over—it was all very slow—a few successful experiments in using turnips for feeding sheep were being reported. But they come from districts where the true open field was rare—from parts of Norfolk, Suffolk, Essex—and turnips are said to do well on 'barren or heathy' land, which suggests fields newly enclosed from the waste. Jethro Tull, 1674–1741, the pioneer agricultural reformer of the early eighteenth century, says that he 'introduced turnips into the field in King William's reign; but the practice did not travel beyond the hedges of my estate till after the Peace of Utrecht' (1713).[2] Note the 'hedges of his estate': he has not open field in mind for his experiment.

The use of the spring-corn field was more elastic than used to be supposed. There were, and always had been, stretches of the country where grazing rights on open-field fallow had never been important, so had not to be dealt with. But some of these 'old enclosed regions' were as intensely conservative as any in the kingdom. Devonshire, with its sledges and pack-horses, was thought by reformers after 1750 to be unusually benighted. Cornwall was not 'progressive'; nor were some counties along the Welsh Marches. Whether on or off land that lay, or had lain, in open fields, progress in getting rid of fallow moved mainly from east and south-east to west and north-west—in Scotland as in England—and it was not until after

---

[1] E. C. K. Gonner, *Common Land and Inclosure* (1912), p. 21, n. 3.

[2] Quoted by Lord Ernle, *English Farming Past and Present* (1922), p. 135.

1750 that the two crops mainly planted on the area formerly left fallow, clover and turnips, came into anything like general use.

Naturally, it was not often in open fields that specialised crops new to England were tried—in comparatively small quantities. Hops first came late in the fifteenth century, a little before that Reformation with which a popular rhyme connects them. They were grown at various points in the East and South-East, but became, as they have remained, a Kentish speciality; it was a Kentish man who wrote a *Perfite Platforme of a Hoppe Garden* in 1574. Saffron was not quite new: it had been known since the fourteenth century, but its use and growth extended in the sixteenth when Walden—'Welshmen's or slaves' valley', an interesting old name—began to be called Saffron Walden. There are many saffron 'gardens', 'closes' and 'grounds' among Essex field-names. Only one of the names, 'saffron shot', suggests that a block in an open field may have been devoted to the crop. About Pontefract they grew liquorice— and 'pomfret cakes' flavoured with it were still so called in the nineteenth century. Various districts specialised in hemp and flax, neither a new crop, or in the oil-seeds, some of which were relatively new, or in the old dye-stuff plants, madder and woad.

What might be tried on recently reclaimed soil is illustrated on the Bedford Level, after its drainage.[1] Blocks of the land had been assigned to the 'adventurers', the people who with the Earl had risked capital in the enterprise, other blocks to those who were losing common rights. This cleared the way for experiment. Land got from the fen had often been first used for enclosed grazing: the cattle or sheep cropped, manured, and improved it. The process was repeated after the great drainage; but all sorts of crops were also sown—flax, hemp, oats, cole-seed (the source of that colza-oil which makes a beautiful soft lamplight), onions, peas and woad. There were willows everywhere, and in places, as the fen dried, wheat.

When Cobbett passed through the more thoroughly drained and improved Fenland of the early nineteenth century, what struck him most were the 'immense bowling greens' covered with fat sheep. This dyke-enclosed grazing had replaced the old intercommoning of village herds in the fen—though bits of old commoning practice survived. Altogether, even by 1750,

[1] See above, pp. 196–7.

Britain had made fairly good use of her grazing opportunities. There was inadequate winter feed, but there were great stretches of good downland, including Epsom Downs on which the godly shepherd and his boy 'brought...thoughts of the old age of the world' to the mind of Samuel Pepys. There were standing pastures and an autumn 'bite' after the hay had been cut in the meadows. Modern enclosure from fields and commons and the old grazing enclosures of the West helped to keep enough sheep and cattle to provide the nation's wool—with meat and dairy stuff enough for many if not for all. A new agrarian class or group had evolved in Tudor times—the graziers. Before 1500 a 'gras-yer' had been a supervisor of forest pasture. By 1525 he was anyone who had many sheep or cattle grazing. In 1611 he is called 'a fattener of cattle'.

The Welsh, Scotch and other cattle that he fattened were presumably slaughtered for the market of the well-to-do; and though the cream was there perhaps not much of it got through to the poor. That fall in popular consumption of 'white meat' —dairy produce—which almost certainly was part of the deterioration of the condition of wage-earners under Elizabeth, seems to have persisted. 'Husbandmen, and such as labour', Burton wrote in his *Anatomy* in 1621, 'can eat fat bacon, salt gross meat, hard cheese...coarse bread at all times'[1]—and it is by no means certain that labourers had bacon or salt meat enough. However, there were conies to be trapped, birds to be snared, and miscellaneous poachings. At the close of the century comfortable people thought that there was 'no Country in the World where the Inferior Rank of Men were better...fed'[2]— which may well have been true, for in most countries they were singularly ill-fed.

There was a possible addition to dietary being considered in the seventeenth century, the potato. It was much written about and it was grown experimentally in some gardens; but it never made an important contribution to the diet of the English rural poor during these years—partly because, to have so become, it would have had to be grown in the fields; partly because few cottagers had knowledge or land enough to make their own experiments; mainly perhaps through that

---

[1] Quoted by Sir Jack C. Drummond and Anne Wilbraham, *The English-man's Food* (1939), p. 121.

[2] Charles Davenant, *Discourses on the Public Revenues* (1698), quoted *ibid.* p. 123.

dietary conservatism so strong in most men. Harsh necessity, and possibly nimbler minds, overcame that conservatism in Ireland; by 1750 the population was multiplying on a diet of which the potato was an important part. In the sixties of the seventeenth century, a literary potato enthusiast had praised the white-flowered 'Irish' potato, which he said was being tried in Wales and the North of England. Rather later, the journalist Houghton said potatoes were 'very numerous' in Lancashire and 'a pleasant food...eaten with butter and sugar'. (That hardly sounds a poor man's dish.) By 1750 their growth was spreading in London market-gardens on the Essex side—Plaistow, West Ham. They had got a firm hold in Wales, the Scottish islands and West, and the English North-West, as a supplementary food for part of the year. Most people had heard of them and many gardens may have shown a few. But that was all. It was long after 1750 that Coke's Norfolk farmers first allowed that perhaps potatoes 'wouldn't poison tha pigs'.

ENCLOSURES: THE EIGHTEENTH CENTURY

The policy of using an Act of Parliament to overcome the legal and personal difficulties connected with large-scale enclosure either of fens, commons, or open fields developed slowly during the later years of this period. Its predecessor was an enclosure agreement registered, to give it binding force, in a court of law—the Chancery or, as has been seen, the Palatine Court of Durham.[1] Almost by an accident, it would seem, a rearrangement of fields in Herefordshire was approved by Act of Parliament under James I. Then comes a long gap. Under Charles II there are Acts for enclosure of fens and wastes, and of Malvern Chace. A few Acts dealing with open fields appear under William and Mary, Anne and George I. The pace quickens under George II, but not markedly until his last decade (1750–60).

Yet by 1750 the method had been worked out by which the great eighteenth- and early nineteenth-century enclosures were effected. This method, the motives at work, and the connection with enclosure by agreement, can all be best illustrated not by generalisations but by particular Bills. Take the Bill of 1749 'for Confirming Articles of Agreement, and an Award, for Inclosing and Dividing the Heaths, Wastes, Fields, and Common-

---

[1] See above, p. 207.

grounds, in the Township of Norton juxta Twicross, in the County of Leicester'—a village of a few hundred inhabitants, five miles north-west of Market Bosworth, between Twycross and Appleby Magna. Charles Jennens Esq. is Lord of the Manor, John Clayton is Rector; a knight, another esquire, 'and divers other Persons are Freeholders, and Land-owners' in the township. You still speak of the 'town' of Norton, just as Chaucer would have spoken.

The township contains about 1744 acres, of which about 377 'hath, for several Years last past, been so over-run with Heath and Furze, that it hath been of little or no Value...; and the Common-fields, Meadows, and Pastures...lie so confused and intermixt, that they are incapable of Improvement'. A survey of 1725 had established the facts, and that the 377 acres 'were chiefly enjoyed by Persons having no Right of Common therein'. (Who were these? Possibly gipsies; much more probably the rightless non-landholding poor of Norton juxta Twycross.) By an agreement of January 1747 a group of commissioners 'were to plot and allot the Share of each Freeholder' in the whole 1744 acres and, among many other things, 'to ascertain and appoint the publick and private Highways and Roads throughout the new Inclosures'. Their award was to be confirmed 'by a Decree of the Court of Chancery, or by Act of Parliament'.

There were some enclosures already, which were taken into account in the award made in September 1748. Land was assigned to twenty-six freeholding people, and to the Corporation of Coventry, as Trustees of a Charity School. The range was from 545 acres 21 perches for the knight, Sir Thomas Abney—*not* lord of the manor—down to 33 perches for Richard Francis. Assignments were made 'in lieu of each Freeholder's Land, Common-right, and Estate whatsoever'.

The award mentions a Mill-field, a Wood-field, a Snareston-field, a Church-field and an Austrey-field; also the Heath-fields and the Heath-field Leys (pastures); an area known as the Shornells, which had 'gorsy Parts' like the Heaths; a Town-meadow; and several Closes and Crofts. It decides who shall do the fencing, but also refers to an 'old Boundary-fence' between Snareston-field and Church-field. The Town-meadow is being cut up, assigned, and fenced; the fencing is everywhere by quickset hedge and ditch.

Various people who would not come into the award at first

have recently executed it. In fact all have done so 'except William Chester, who hath only a Close called Tompson's Close, containing Three Acres Two Roods and Five Perch, antiently inclosed; and John Priestnall, who hath only Thirty-eight Perch, of old Inclosure; and Richard Francis' of the thirty-three perches. None of these had, or claimed, 'any Common-right [of grazing or haymaking] in the open Fields, Heath, or commonable Places, in the said Lordship'. A small stubborn group who, according to the Bill, stand to lose nothing; they will get their little closes and they claim no common rights, but perhaps they farmed under the Knight in the open fields, and feared the consequences of enclosure for the small tenant-farmer.

The work of assignment had begun; but to make it 'absolutely valid' the promoters would now like, not a Chancery Decree but an Act of Parliament. They got it.

Details of Norton-juxta-Twycross geography are for the local historian. The general historian sees an open-field village in its last rather complex phase—apparently with three main fields, two minor fields, some 'antient' enclosures, and some detached fields and leys on the heath. There would be room for considerable varieties of cropping if local men had enterprise for it. But Leicestershire, a very 'open' county in 1600, was going over to the pasture and dairy-farming which would dominate it; so perhaps the crops were of secondary interest, and perhaps small open-field arable farmers were in real danger of being replaced by bigger grazing farmers. Forty-five years later the typical Leicestershire farm was said to be of 100 to 200 acres, of which only some twenty were ploughed, and sown for fodder crops. Over its grass fields the hunts of the nineteenth century would go. It was emphatically part of 'the shires'; Norton-juxta-Twycross lies, as a hunting man would say, in the Atherstone country.

Chapter VIII

Industry, Gilds and Trade Clubs

POWER, MACHINES, IRON AND COAL

All through the centuries since 1100 there had been progress, slow and intermittent but real, in various branches of industrial technique. With the internal peace of Tudor and most Stuart times, with the exciting influence of external discovery and trade, the invention of printing, the growth of population, the fresh influences of skilled aliens—Flemings fleeing before Alva, then Huguenots from Louis XIV's dragoons—the pace of progress quickened. Flemings and Huguenots were followed by Jews and Dutchmen; and although Medina, William III's Jewish army contractor, and Henriquez, an early Jewish discounter of bills at the Bank of England, with Vandeput and Van Neck, Dutch merchant financiers, were not what are called industrialists, their presence helped to keep the economic air stirring.

Before 1500 every 'clothing' region had its fulling-mills,[1] just as every district whatsoever had its corn-mills. Probably water-power had recently come into use for the bellows and the tilt-hammers of the iron industry;[2] it was used to drive grinders' wheels in the cutlery trade, a task for a very simple cheap installation; but that is the limit of our certain knowledge of its use in industry. In the textile industries 'power', well established for fulling, made only slow further progress for a long time. Early in the sixteenth century the 'gig-mill' was invented or imported. In it water turned a rather small wheel, its rim set with teazle-heads which raised the nap on the cloth for shearing. But this might put men out of work and a law was passed against it in 1551–2. The mills went up in spite of the law: King Charles's proclamation against them in 1633—he favoured paternal government—did not stop them. After 1660 nothing did; though as the law was unrepealed it was safest to call them 'raising' mills, not gig-mills. In the early eighteenth century, anyone who wanted one built it.

---

[1] See above, pp. 154–5. [2] See above, pp. 158–9.

A story running parallel to that of the gig-mill is that of the stocking-frame. This hand-driven knitting-machine is credited to a member of St John's College, Cambridge, about the year 1589. Legend surrounds the invention, but it certainly was disliked by the public and at court: knitting supported so many poor women. The inventor was encouraged to try in France, at Rouen; but the enterprise failed. However, the 'frame' was taken up gradually and improved in the seventeenth century. Power was never applied to it; but in the eighteenth century framework-knitters were a recognised, scattered, industrial type in the Midlands, especially Nottingham and Leicester.

An equally ingenious invention, about contemporary with the stocking-frame, was not made in England. The Dutch loom, swivel-loom, or 'engine' loom as it was called later, could weave at the same time a dozen or more narrow things—tapes, ribbons, 'inkles' (braids or the like). It was brought early to London, presumably by foreigners, and became an almost permanent cause of friction there. London silk-ribbon weavers hated it. It was prohibited in 1638; but when rioting broke out in 1675 there was a new spirit in government; the thing was efficient: it provided work and ribbons: let it go on. The same opinion evidently prevailed where there were no remains of such a monopolistic organisation as the Weavers' Company of London to resist mechanism. Somewhere about 1660 the 'inkle' loom got to Manchester, where linen-working was well developed. There in 1683, Ralph Thoresby, the Yorkshire antiquary, 'was most taken with their inkles, eighteen several pieces whereof they can weave in the same loom'.[1] On this loom was founded the very important Manchester 'small-ware' industry of the eighteenth century; also a nineteenth-century Manchester byword—people in a crowded room were said to be 'as thick as inkle-weavers'.

Meanwhile that application of water-power had been made which used to be taken as the starting-point of 'the' industrial revolution. For centuries in Italy silk had been 'thrown' by water-power, i.e. the fibres twisted together into a thread that will stand tension as warp. In 1719 Thomas Lombe, having surreptitiously picked Italian brains, opened his pioneer throwing-mill at Derby. It employed 300 people; was not very widely imitated before 1750; and became the prototype of all

[1] Quoted by A. P. Wadsworth and J. de L. Mann, *The Cotton Trade and Industrial Lancashire, 1600–1780* (1931), p. 103.

the early water-driven cotton or wool spinning mills of the later eighteenth century.

In metallurgy use of the tilt-hammer spread rapidly—not only in the iron industry, but also for hammering copper ingots into plates. Wire-drawing by water-driven rollers, known already in Germany before 1500, passed to England with the erection of wire-mills at Tintern in 1567. The seventeenth century knew rolling mills for metals, an obvious adaptation of the principle of the corn-mill; and also the slit mill in which a knife, falling on the tilt-hammer principle on to the edge of a metal plate, cuts it into narrow rods, 'nail rod' for the savage nailers of Cradley Heath and thereabouts.

Before the century was over, power—and in this case the power of steam—was needed and used in connection with the century's greatest technical development, that of the mines, especially the coal mines. This development was as much connected with the growth of population and above all with the growth of the London demand as with the new uses for coal in industry which had been found since late Tudor times. England's and southern Scotland's widely scattered coal-measures, tapped first by 'delves'—open workings—and bell-pits, had long been of local importance for industrial and domestic use. Midland and Yorkshire smiths had relied on them; so had South Lancashire, the Bristol region and the Forest of Dean. But in very many places defective means of transport limited large-scale industrial or domestic use of coal: not much can be carried far on pack ponies or in country carts. The exceptions, important ones, were coal-workings near the sea and consuming centres on navigable water—Tyneside, Sunderland, Glamorgan, Whitehaven, Flintshire; with London, other cities and Ireland, but London Town above all, London and the Tyne.[1]

In Elizabeth's early days Newcastle was the only important English coal-shipping port. It shipped 33,000 tons—coastwise or abroad—in 1564. In seventy years (1634) the figure had risen to about 452,000. There were 69,000 more from Sunderland, which had grown from almost nothing. Between a quarter and a third of all these coal cargoes from the North-East went to the Thames. For 1580, six years before Shakespeare came up to London from Stratford, London's import of 'sea cole' is estimated at less than 15,000 tons. That would not go far among

[1] See above, pp. 168–9.

perhaps 100,000 people. Wood must still have been the main fuel. But wood also needs carriage; the home counties had been heavily drawn on for London, and Sussex for its iron industry. The Elizabethans were getting anxious about timber reserves. (It is not surprising: between 1540 and 1640 prices of fire-wood rose almost three times as much as prices in general.) When Mistress Quickly spoke of her sea-coal fire, some time before 1600, the new fuel was coming in fast. King James patronised it: he had Scottish coal sent to Westminster. He had been familiar with it in Auld Reekie, where wood was much harder to get than at Windsor. Scotland had long used coal freely, first from the 'delves'—in Scots 'heuchs'—then from pits. Before 1600 her parliament was showing anxiety about coal 'growand scant daily'. The export was forbidden. 'The Scots', it has been said, 'were faced with their long struggle to learn the technique of real mining';[1] but had one mine at Culross which would soon have galleries running under the sea.

Whether King James set a fashion in London or not, by 1605–6 the annual delivery of coal there had risen to 74,000 tons. Before the Civil War it had nearly doubled; by after the Revolution more than doubled again—323,000 tons—and had absorbed two-fifths of all the shipments from Northumberland and Durham. In short, the seventeenth century made London the city of coal smoke. Had all the coal that came in stayed there, each man, woman and child would have had about half a ton a year by 1700. And though a good deal went to industry, none went to raise steam or make gas.

It did not all stay in London: there was an important up-river trade. So there was from many east and south-east coast ports that the north-east coal fleets served, fleets of ships built at many points on the east coast, and containing, in the eighteenth century, up to 400 sail. They put in at ports all the way from Whitby to Plymouth, especially at Lynn which, in 1725, supplied 'about six counties wholly, and three counties in part, with...coals'. That is Defoe who, as he got near to Newcastle, saw that 'inexhausted Store of Coals and Coal Pits' which supplied the South, and especially London, where even the taverns were 'come to make Coal Fires in their upper Rooms'.

[1] Miss I. F. Grant, *The Social and Economic Development of Scotland before 1603* (1930), p. 318.

By that time South-West England had its sea-borne coals from Glamorgan; North-West England from Flintshire or White-haven; East Scotland from Fife. The enemies of England under-stood the significance of the coal fleets; the Dutch—economists and coal buyers—perhaps better than the French. The threat of Dutch fleets might leave London cold; and if Tromp could have held the seas, London might have been frozen out. But the colliers were broken in to risks, and westerly winds often hin-dered the Dutch. After 1688 came a century of Anglo-Dutch friendship during which the passage of colliers, coastwise or to the Dutch ports, was very safe.

Mines were getting deeper, wherever there was a shipping, or a strong local, demand. Pumping became more essential and more difficult. Only on a very steep slope could a tolerably deep mine be drained by 'adits'; a really deep mine nowhere. Men of science and of practice were much concerned with the principles of the pump, wanted to raise water to supply cities and put out their fires as well as to drain pits. The upshot was Savery and Newcomen's steam pumping inventions of 1698 and 1710–12. Both were Devon men. There is no reason to suppose that either thought more of coal-pits than of tin-mines. But it was at a coal-pit that Newcomen's 'fire machine' was first erected and worked, in 1712, at a place near Dudley Castle, probably close to Tipton. Within five years engines have been traced in various significant places—one at a colliery near Coventry; one at Hawarden near the Flintshire coast, and one at Whitehaven, both places from which coal was easily shipped to Ireland, which has none worth mentioning; one at Austhorpe near Leeds; one at Tanfield by Newcastle; and one, one only, at a Cornish mine. The coal-pit demand was the more insistent; and it was in Northumberland and Durham that engineering, mechanical and civil, was most needed to meet it. To move the coal to the water, ground was levelled and embanked and wag-gon roads built. The most remarkable was the Tanfield road, completed before 1725—valleys filled or bridged, and half-mile cuttings, with 'frames of timber laid for five miles to the river side'. These 'frames' made the 'dram-ways' which a century later would be of iron. A train now runs along this Tanfield road using what is claimed to be 'the oldest railway embank-ment in the world'.[1]

Colonel Liddell was a pioneer at Tanfield. South of him, the

[1] W. W. Tomlinson, *The North-Eastern Railway* (1914), plate II.

Bishops of Durham had been 'ironmasters' in the Middle Ages. Dudley Castle also points to the connection between coal and iron and land-ownership; for the Black Country smiths used Dudley Castle coal. It was once usual to give the name of Dudley, 'Dud' Dudley, author of *Metallum Martis* (1665), a prominent place in the story of iron technique; but 'there is no valid reason why this Balliol undergraduate, rather than any one of a dozen other projectors of the seventeenth century, should have been singled out for fame'.[1] The story in outline is this. Starting with medieval iron, mostly wrought for the smith out of the ore by repeated heatings, and a little cast we do not know how but presumably from some primitive blast furnace, we meet the blast furnace in the Sussex Weald in early Tudor times. Cannon were its main output, cannon and pigs to be refined into smith's iron at the forge. In 1573 furnace owners in the Weald included the Queen, Earls, Barons and Knights; most of whom also had hammer-ponds and forges. Iron or cannon-shot they sold where they could find buyers: in 1585 the Earl of Leicester secured an iron contract from the 'King of Barbary'; and sublet it.

Fifty years later there were furnaces in at least fourteen counties. The interval had been one of furious activity wherever iron, water-power and charcoal were available—but there were limits to these possibilities. Charcoal was the main anxiety. The Weald lost ground. Government was anxious about ship-building timber, though coal was solving the domestic fire-wood problem in Town and the towns. The activity, furious down to about 1630, might slacken. Later, it did. That was why projectors like Dudley, who had left Balliol for his baronial father's ironworks in 1619, tried mineral fuel and wrote about it. They may have had a certain success; some coals can be used raw in blast furnaces; but they did not revolutionise smelting or supply the needed iron.

More than forty years after the publication of *Metallum Martis*, in 1708, Abraham Darby, a caster of pots and things in brass or iron, leased iron furnaces at Coalbrookdale in Shropshire. There, some time between 1708 and 1718, probably so early as 1709, he coked coal and fed his blast furnaces with it. He was a Quaker who minded his own business, kept his own counsel; not a literary projector. And he was a caster not a forgemaster. Besides, coke-smelted pig did not at first forge

[1] T. S. Ashton, *Iron and Steel in the Industrial Revolution* (1924), p. 12.

successfully into bar. Charcoal pig was traditional and, it would seem, for a long time better. (Into the present century old-style Sheffield steel-makers liked Swedish charcoal-bar for cutlery steel.) Not all coals make good furnace coke. There were probably discouraging failed experiments. And as the English output of charcoal-bar slackened, the import of Swedish and Russian iron grew. It had been already heavy before the Civil War. For these various reasons, it would appear, Darby's process spread obscurely and very slowly. It was being tried near Wrexham in 1721; but twenty or thirty years later it was apparently confined to that neighbourhood and to Shropshire. Again, there was no revolution; but the wheel was balanced ready to turn.

In another matter connected with coal it had already turned right over. Coal had taken what might be called its nineteenth-century position in innumerable domestic and industrial uses. The details of the story are long and intricate. Here is the summary. Iron-workers, who had always used some coal, made use of it in one process after another. Other metal-workers followed: they even used it at the Mint. For all boiling and evaporating processes it was obviously fit. Salt-makers and soap-boilers, a rising Tudor trade, used it. Glass-makers, growing in numbers, skill and importance, learnt to use it in place of beech-billets, at least for certain purposes. So did brick-burners, partially at first, then totally. The quantities consumed were in some cases very great. When Defoe got near to Shields, he saw the smoke of the salt pans 'ascend in Clouds over the Hills...at least sixteen Miles from the Place'.

The uses to which coal was put seem to us so obvious that it is not easy to appreciate the change. But there exists a report from a Frenchman written in 1738 when the change was about completed, which shows how it struck an observer from a wood-burning people such as the English had been a century and a half earlier. Coal, he writes, is 'the soul of English manufactures'. It 'serves for all the domestic uses for which we employ wood—whether for the hearth, the kitchen, or the laundry'. His list of the people who use it, and whose use of it surprises him, is long. There are bakers and confectioners; whole strings of trades that boil or heat—dyers, brewers, sugar-refiners, soap-boilers and so on. Its use in the glass industry amazes him; for the French still used only charcoal of beechwood many years later. Bricks the English bake by it, as men do in Flanders, he says, 'and even in the neighbourhood of Marly'. 'Coopers have no other fire.' 'All workers in iron and copper make use of coal.'[1] The reference to Marly shows that in each case he has in mind the contrast of fuels, natural enough when France's relative poverty of coal and abundant forests are recalled.

COPPER AND BRASS

Immigrant skill had helped the technical progress of many British industries—among them glass, wool, silk and paper. The immigrants were often refugees, Flemings in the sixteenth century, Huguenots in the seventeenth. But not always. The Tudor monarchs more than once invited capitalists and technicians—Germans or Italians—to develop industries of which they thought the country stood in need. It needed, they held, above all, precious metals and such 'half-precious' metals as copper and the mixture of copper and zinc which is brass. Copper it had, though copper mining had been neglected. Zinc-ore was not known and all brass had been imported— contrasting with the export of that other alloy, pewter.[2] Brass was wanted for war and peace—the 'brass cannon', and the brass wire which made the best teeth when set in boards for carding wool. All relevant mines were declared by the Tudors royal mines; two great companies were chartered in 1568, the Mines Royal and the Mineral and Battery Works—the first industrial companies in British history; and German capitalists and workpeople were invited to develop the industries. Their first main centre of activity was the Newlands valley near Keswick, where copper ore with traces of silver was found.

Zinc ore had been found also—'calamine stone'—in the Mendips and elsewhere; but the projected brass industry grew very slowly. The Mineral and Battery works made iron wire successfully at Tintern, not much brass wire at first. After 1580 the Mines Royal looked south, to Devon and Cornish copper ore, and began to smelt it, at Neath—because 'the soul of English manufactures' was near. At Keswick they had used charcoal and peat.

In the seventeenth century the two companies were involved in the monopolies controversy and were brought low during the

[1] Quoted by J. U. Nef, *The Rise of the British Coal Industry* (1932), vol. 1, pp. 222–3.
[2] See above, p. 168.

Civil War: they had genuine monopolies. They resumed operations after the Restoration, but with no great success. Finally,
in 1689, 'mines royal' were redefined, copper and zinc mining
thrown open to private enterprise. English brass was still
inferior; but the 'battery' of copper ingots into plates, and of
plates into copper vessels of all kinds, had been a success; and
with copper and brass and steel, the skilled smiths, especially of
the Birmingham region, were beginning to make their fancy
'toys'—buttons and buckles and snuff-boxes and the rest. They
were also making cheap jewellery and guns. By 1750 the
Birmingham gunsmiths were an important and growing group.

The end of royal monopoly produced a crop of copper-
mining and copper-working companies under William and
Mary; a more widespread copper industry; and then competition and amalgamations of companies in very 'modern' style.
Brass still lagged; smelting difficulties with the 'calamine stone'
were not finally overcome until 1738; but the country had such
an abundance of worked copper that soon after 1760 she could
get a pace ahead of France in the naval race by sheathing her
warships with it to increase their speed.

SHIPS AND SHIPBUILDING

The immense increase in the use of coal called for those huge
collier fleets on which Captain Cook and other strong seamen
were bred up. There was the Atlantic shipping also, becoming
more important every decade after 1588, with the settlement
of America and the settlement or capture of sugar islands;
though the English were less active fishermen on the New-
foundland Banks than the Portuguese and the French '*terre-
neuviers*'. Before 1500 an English sail had not often been seen
inside 'the Straits of Maroc'. By 1600 the Levant Company,
the 'Turkey Merchants', were at work; and from it sprang the
East India Company.[1] There was the Baltic trade, and the whale
fishery—for both of which Englishmen and Scots contended
long and hard with the Dutch. And there was the West
African trade that Hawkins pioneered on his first slaving voyage,
the trade that later brought gold for the guineas.

What exactly all this meant in tonnage is hard to estimate.
Until the later seventeenth century most ships were small:
Humphrey Gilbert's *Squirrel* that went down in seas 'breaking

[1] See below, pp. 263–4.

short and high, pyramid-wise,' was a ten-tonner. A great ship was one of over 100 tons. Two surviving lists of these 100-tonners suggest that such great ships increased nearly five-fold between 1560 and 1630. By the latter date there were between three and four hundred colliers, a fair number of them over 100 tons, in the coastwise trade from the north-east coast alone. The collier fleet grew with every decade. Smaller ships were used in the general coasting trade—in corn, malt, timber, glass, salt, and other miscellaneous merchandise. They could make most really important towns—Colchester, Ipswich, Norwich, Exeter, Gloucester—besides the more obvious sea-ports; and water transport was vastly preferable to that by land.

The mercantile marine grew at a varying pace in the later seventeenth century, to the accompaniment of much grumbling and legislation, and in the early eighteenth steadily; but there are no comprehensive statistics. In size, ships outside the Royal Navy grew only slowly. When, in 1682, the East India Company sent four on the longest of all voyages, to China, three were under 200 tons and the biggest was 310. Sizes increased in the eighteenth century, but the standard East India-man of the forties, engaged in the China trade, was of just under 500 tons. Only a single ship of more than 500 had sailed in the interval, the *Defence* of 730 tons, in 1689.

These East Indiamen were the great ships of their days. We have no return of ships in general until 1760; but that, though not too satisfactory, will serve. Great Britain was said to own 7081 ships, about one in seven being Scottish, with a 'reputed tunnage' of 486,740. That gives an average of nearly sixty-nine tons. It was believed that the 'real tunnage' was full 50 per cent greater. Tonnage, reputed or real, is a tricky thing, and comparisons of tonnage over 130 years still more tricky; but it looks as if the average ship of the mid-eighteenth century was near to what would have been classed as a great ship early in the seventeenth.

Technically, there is no doubt that in the seventeenth century the Dutch were ahead of the English and Scots in shipbuilding, just as in the sixteenth the Germans had been ahead in mining and metallurgy. Dutch yards were better organised. There was greater economy of labour and some use of the system of alternative parts, spares. The yards had wind-driven saw-mills and great cranes. They had cheaper timber, hemp, flax and pitch—from the Baltic. They paid higher wages, but, as they built all kinds of ships for other countries, they had more continuous work.

Before 1600 they had developed a special type of trading vessel—the *fluitschip* or flyboat or flute—single-decked, a 'mere shell' for cargo, with no forecastle or round-house or guns, and with light simple rigging. She was slender, by contemporary standards—four to six times as long as she was wide. Not made to beat off pirates, less fitted for distant, dangerous voyages, she could be worked with a very small crew. In short, a strictly economic proposition, usually of 200 to 500 tons. She was so economic that in time of war she required convoy; Drake's or Hawkins's ships had not.

In their Dutch wars, the English sometimes captured 'fly-boats', with other types of Dutch ships. More often they bought. This the various Navigation Acts of the Restoration were intended to prevent; but the acts worked slowly and imperfectly. Prizes were of course 'naturalised'. There are incomplete records of 791 naturalisations down to 1676. Add the foreign-builts that got in quietly and illicitly. Note too a possibly exaggerated Scottish admission of 1668 that all Scotland's commercial shipping was of 'outlandish' build; and an estimate that, about the year 1680, at least a quarter of the English mercantile marine was built outside England may not be wrong.

With the close of Anglo-Dutch rivalry and wars less is heard of Dutch-built ships. For one thing, the English had copied the flyboat type, especially for their colliers, which needed exactly its qualities and had not to make ocean voyages. For another, in building for the ocean voyage, the two countries were more nearly on a level. Most important was the fact that England could procure, first great masts and spars for the Navy, and then ships themselves from her American colonies. The 'mast ships' had to be big, 400 tons and upwards even to 1000. They were already running during the Dutch wars. By about 1700 they were the 'regular "liners" of New England, bringing passengers, troops, mail, and later, tea'.[1] They were often built in New England. The colonists had every incentive to become ship-builders. Their inter-colonial relations were by sea. They had the timber. They had saw-mills long before the British. (Down to Nelson's day, the Admiralty did not use saw-mills.) Not all 'colonial builts', as they were called later, were of the liner type. Many were cheap, said to

[1] R. G. Albion, *Forests and Sea Power* (1926), p. 238.

be cheap and nasty—sent across to be broken up, made in a hurry of green timber. Some no doubt were; but what American shipbuilding came to mean for eighteenth-century Britain is shown by the figures just before the Declaration of Independence: the colonies were building over 100 square-rigged sea-going ships a year, with hundreds of schooners and small craft; and the 2343 'colonial-builts' formed a third of the whole British mercantile marine.

There had been revolutionary changes in the design of fighting and long-voyage ships under Elizabeth—and Hawkins —but there was no technical change of importance in the way these ships were built, nor, after early Stuart times, in the design of the King's ships and their cousins the East Indiamen and other great ships of the merchant navy. There was 'surprisingly little difference', even in design, 'between Phineas Pett's *Sovereign of the Seas*, built in 1637 for the Ship Money Fleet, and', not only the ships that Hawke led into Quiberon Bay, but also 'the last splendid creations in wooden warships just before 1860',[1] except that, soon after Hawke's victory, they had been copper sheathed.

Shipbuilding, especially the building of smaller vessels, continued to be carried on at many points on the coasts; but the great ships of the late seventeenth and the eighteenth century were built on the Thames. When Defoe stated, without figures in support, that not a fifth of England's ships were built there, he was evidently thinking of number not tonnage. The Blackwall yard—Sir Henry Johnson's in the seventeenth century and later Wells and Company—was bigger than the neighbouring royal yards. Several others in private hands rivalled them in size. Defoe thought that London, 'sucking the Vitals of Trade in this Island' into itself, had injured both trade and shipbuilding in a number of south-eastern and southern ports—Ipswich, Southampton, Weymouth, Dartmouth, and others. His account of Ipswich bears this out, and also has a place in the general shipping story. Before the Dutch wars of Cromwell and Charles, Ipswich had built the biggest colliers, 'so prodigious strong' that they 'reigned' for forty or fifty years. They were cut out, so Ipswich said, by the Dutch 'flyboat' prizes, 'made free ships by Act of Parliament'. There was fine timber all about, 'an inexhaustible Store-House' of it. There were still colliers in the river in 1725, but forty

[1] R. G. Albion, *Forests and Sea Power* (1926), p. 5.

where once there had been a hundred; and, instead of building more, Ipswich men were sending their timber on the short run to Thames yards.

THE DOMINANCE OF ENGLISH WOOL MANUFACTURES

A Tudor, Stuart, or early Hanoverian writer on economic affairs, or a statesman considering policies, when his mind turned to industry thought first, almost invariably, not about coal or iron or even ships but about wool and its manufactures. Throughout the Tudor century, the exports of wool were dwindling and the Merchants of the Staple dwindling with them, into wool-staplers, merchants but not exporters of wool. If the office of Lord Chancellor had first assumed importance in late Tudor times, the Chancellor—it can hardly be doubted—would now sit not on a sack of wool but on a bale of broadcloth. The loss of Calais under Queen Mary hit an already declining wool-export trade. Under James, the export was prohibited by proclamation, in the interests of the manufacturers. With the Restoration, the prohibition reached the Statute Book—for England. Not yet for Scotland; but there too native industry was evidently using up most of the home supply. Some wool was sent to England and, in the sixteenth century, a little to the Low Countries; but wool was never a 'staple'—that is a taxed—export. A definition of 'staple' goods, made in 1669, which includes 'plaiding and all that is made of wooll', together with much earlier complaints from Bruges that Scotland was sending not the wool that Flanders wanted but things made of it that she did not want, shows that the Scots were moving parallel to the English. But the exclusion of wool from the 'staple' list—a list of attempted public control—left export free; and there was still enough of it to claim and receive compensation when, at the Union, Scotland had to adopt the English export-prohibition policy.

That policy was never completely effective. In Defoe's journalist's superlatives, 'Smugling and Roguing' was 'the reigning Commerce of...the English Coast, from the Mouth of the Thames to the Land's End'. 'Smugling' mainly of imports —silks, brandy, and such—but also the outward 'smugling' of wool, by the 'owlers', especially on the short run to France from the grazing grounds of Romney Marsh, where sheep were many and their wool good.

Prohibition of wool export was followed by a cold-blooded attack made in 1699 on the woollen industry of Ireland. All export from Ireland of wool or yarn or cloth was forbidden—except to England. She was to have no part in the markets that England supplied or coveted. In the home market English clothiers did not much fear Irish friezes and other cheap goods, but they were determined to choke competition in the Plantations and the Levant.[1] Scotland they feared less. Her specialities were non-competitive and generally inferior; but when, towards the close of her separate parliamentary existence, she began to nurse a higher-grade woollen industry, prohibiting in 1681 the export of yarn and unfulled cloth and the import of a long list of woollen and other finished goods; founding in the same year the privileged Woollen Manufactory at Newmills near Haddington—one of whose duties was to make uniform cloth 'to distinguish sojers from other skulking and vagrant persons';[2] following this up by eight more organised 'manufactories' between 1683 and 1704; then any jealous Englishmen who knew the facts had an additional motive for advocating parliamentary Union. The Union operated precisely as he would have wished. The Newmills put up their shutters; sold their hall and their considerable equipment, also 'Spanish wool dyed several mixtures'; and sold their land to a Colonel in 1713. Other 'factories' abandoned the attempt to turn out high quality cloth, falling back on the plainer sorts.

Defoe found 'still some Business' in the neighbourhood 'to the Advantage of the Poor'; but noted that the 'Manufactories' had not been able to stand English competition. The Scots, he thought, were 'not quite destitute in the Woollen Manufacture, though that is the principal Thing in which England can outdo them'. They had 'the Cloths, Kerseys, Half-thicks, Duffels, Stockings, and coarse Manufactures of the North of England, as cheap brought to them by Horse-packs as they can be carried to London'. Yet they had some things of their own—Sterling serges, Musselburgh stuffs, Aberdeen stockings, Edinburgh shalloons and blankets. So Defoe, reporting what he was told or what his observant eye noted—not necessarily the whole truth.[3]

---

[1] See also below, pp. 284–5.

[2] Quoted by W. R. Scott, *The Constitution and Finance of...Joint-stock Companies to 1720*, vol. III (1911), p. 144.

[3] See also below, p. 272.

Late seventeenth- and early eighteenth-century legislation in favour of the cherished industry did not stop at the bludgeoning of Ireland or the more decent commercial conquest—not permanent, but for a generation or more effective—of Scotland. There was also the English consumer to be taught his place in a scheme for state-encouraged consumption. Hence the notorious Act of 1678 ordering everyone to be buried in a woollen shroud and all parsons to certify that they were. There was a drawn-out campaign against printed calicoes and muslins from India resulting in the Calico Act of 1720. These Indian novelties had attracted women who, in the opinion of Parliament and the manufacturers, ought to have dressed in the lighter fabrics made all of wool, or at least in fabrics with a warp of wool and a weft of cotton or silk spun honestly from the raw materials in England. Pamphlets were written; agitations were raised; 'calico chaces' were organised—or perhaps started as rowdy larks—to slit or foul the calico frocks. In the end imported calico was permitted, provided that Englishmen did the printing. There is reason to think that this restrictive act gave an important, and it may be argued a useful, stimulus to textile printing in Britain.

THE ENGLISH WOOLLEN AND WORSTED INDUSTRIES

Wool was spun almost universally, except where, as in much of seventeenth- and eighteenth-century Scotland, its place was taken by flax. In the greater towns, unless they were actual textile centres, spinning tended to decline. We do not hear much about it in London; but a census of the poor taken at Norwich in 1570 reports many women 'that spin white warp'. In the country it was found everywhere. The spinning-wheel—the big single-thread wheel still used in Harris and Donegal—known before 1500,[1] was steadily displacing the distaff, with which most medieval spinning had been done. In 1502 already, weavers at Norwich are using wheel-spun as well as rock (distaff) spun yarn. Yet though by 1700–50 the wheel may be said to have won, and to have completely conquered some districts, it was a partial and incomplete victory. The distaff is found even in East Anglia long after 1750. Its rival had been encouraged sometimes by official or philanthropic action. When poor-houses came, women and children were set to spin

[1] See above, p. 154.

in them. Wheels might be supplied by the charitable to alms-house inmates and other deserving persons. In Cambridge, in the eighteenth century, the much less deserving were committed by the University authorities to a building that came to be known as the Spinning House.

Weaving was still carried on in Welsh farm-houses and Highland crofters' cots, as a by-employment, long after 1750. In southern England not much is heard of this. It was certainly of no general importance. What was both general and important was the survival of the village weaver—it might be of wool or it might be of linen; the man whose trade of making 'household cloth' was, in Elizabethan labour law, open to the humblest without apprenticeship.[1] It is clearly contemplated as a general thing. From the weaver's point of view there was no great difference between working up yarn for a consumer and work-ing it up for an employer; and one gets the impression that the latter often ousted the former, particularly in the many specialised manufacturing regions. It is a point on which exact knowledge and general conclusions are not likely to be available: we may know that a clothier paid a weaver so much: we are never likely to know whether the weaver put in half of his time, or none, in working up Mrs Poyser's yarn. We do know that even in Mrs Poyser's day, in the nineteenth century, the 'customer weaver', as he was then called, was still familiar in North Midland England. He seems generally to have been a linen-weaver at that time, as those 'websters' were who were so general in Scottish clachans of the seventeenth and eigh-teenth centuries—and one supposes, though records are scarce, of the sixteenth also—people who, multiplying, became the outworking employees of the 'manufacturers', or sellers to the merchants, of Dunfermline and Dundee. In spite of the efforts of the late seventeenth century; in spite of the modest achievement that Defoe reported on; woollen weaving, whether for the consumer or the market, was a relatively unimportant thing even in the Scottish towns. There were only twenty-six websters in Edinburgh itself in 1558, and only thirty in Glasgow in 1604.

For the great English industry, the main technical points must be recalled. Whether a reference to 'cloths of Worth-stead' in 1301 means what were later called worsteds, that is, fabrics made of combed wool, cannot be known; but the

[1] See above, p. 213.

fifteenth- and early sixteenth-century Norwich records show the two branches of the industry quite distinct. We have ordinances for the worsted weavers of Norwich, Norfolk, Suffolk and Cambridge—a comprehensive set of rules of 1511—and local rules for Norwich fullers and other woollen workers. The worsteds were never fulled or raised; they were dyed, calendered, i.e. pressed between rollers, and then sheared—to clear away loose fibres of wool, not to make a regular nap on the cloth, as shearing (after fulling and raising) did, and does, with true 'woollens'.

There is a Norwich document of 1564 which says that the worsted industry was 'much decayed'. There had been a heavy decline in exports as a result of the rapid growth of the 'new drapery', light fabrics of the worsted type, in rising Flemish towns such as Armentières outside the deadening old-fashioned rules of such declining centres of the old high-grade woollen-cloth industry as Bruges and Ypres.

Three years after the Norwich lament, Alva went to the Netherlands, and soon the emigration of refugee Flemings to England set in. They were welcomed by Elizabeth's government and, generally speaking, by the East Anglians. The term 'new drapery' crossed the water. Very shrewdly, the English government exempted those who made it from the apprenticeship rules recently generalised by statute. Not until 1594 was any inspection and taxation of the new fabrics organised, such as had long existed for marketable cloth, under an official known as the 'ulnager'—who did not inspect, but farmed out his duties to inspectors.

Norfolk had never done a great deal of woollen-cloth manufacturing, but Suffolk had. In 1500 it was one of the leading counties—as Lavenham and Kersey and the Suffolk churches witness. But from late Elizabethan times onwards woollens almost died out in the East and South-East, giving way to worsteds and mixed fabrics in Norfolk; dying out in Essex and Suffolk, or represented by an industry of worsted type; disappearing almost entirely from Kent where in early Tudor times they had still been important. Defoe thought that there were not 'ten clothiers' left in Kent. In Essex the manufacture of bays (baize) occupied Colchester, Braintree, Bocking and other towns, for which the 'whole County, large as it is', span. 'Bays' were cheap and unfulled, with a worsted warp of combed wool, and a 'woollen' weft that gave the loose, hairy surface. In

Suffolk Defoe has scarcely a word for Lavenham; but he found grinding poverty and a manufacture of 'Says and Perpetuanas' at Sudbury, hard-wearing worsted materials, as one of the names implies; and he found the same, with less poverty, at Long Melford. But in East Norfolk he saw 'a Face of Diligence spread over the whole country', from the 'vast manufactures carried on (in chief) by the Norwich Weavers'.

Norwich goods were by this time classed as 'stuffs'. They were the light, and very often fine, materials with which the calicos competed. They might be all fine worsted, or they might have a silk or a cotton weft—the 'bombazines' so much used by eighteenth- and early nineteenth-century widows, middle-class spinsters, and respectable women not of the first elegance.

In dealing with the location of the industries, the various types of worsted yarn and fabrics must be considered. The worsted processes, as originally carried out, are simpler and shorter than the woollen. To comb longish wool, spin it into a strong firm yarn, and weave it into a fabric that does not require further treatment if the wool or the yarn has been dyed, is relatively straightforward work. It may well have been the primitive textile process. The yarn need not be woven: it may be knitted into stockings, for home use or the market. Stocking-knitting for market was so widespread in relatively backward regions in the seventeenth and eighteenth centuries —the North Yorkshire Dales, for example, or the country behind Aberdeen—that this suggestion that the worsted processes were perhaps older than the woollen processes gains in probability.

Similarly, the hard, thick worsted material from which rain cloaks and working women's frocks were made was woven in many places. In these centuries it was called camlet, one of those 'trade terms' stolen from something far more delicate, a soft cloth of camel's hair. Equally widespread, from the fourteenth century or earlier, was the making of 'worsted' coverlets—chalons, shalloons. They were not liable to taxation, apparently because they were so common. Manufacturing districts on the decline fall back on these plain worsted fabrics, as Suffolk did. Rising districts, like the West Riding, improved on them, or turned from rough woollens to fine improved worsteds.

Widespread as both sections of the industry still were in 1750, they had been more widespread still in 1500. A process of concentration had been going on. Kent was not the only county from which clothiers had almost disappeared, nor Suffolk the only one in which decline was conspicuous. By 1725–50 there were only remnants of an old clothing industry about Haslemere; the same at Reading; at Newbury an ancient and famous fine-cloth industry, which in Tudor times had maintained Jack o' Newbury (and perhaps his legendary factory), had been replaced by the inferior making of shalloons—now used only for linings.

West of Newbury, over the Wiltshire border, a traveller entered the region in which all through this period the woollen industry was a main source of wealth. Wiltshire, Gloucester and Somerset had been the leading producers in 1500—with Suffolk, and already Yorkshire. Suffolk fell away. Yorkshire went forward. Wiltshire, Somerset and Gloucester held their ground. Salisbury, and all the country round, were busy in 1725 with fine flannels and 'Salisbury Whites', unfinished long-cloths for the Levant market. The making of 'Whites' and 'Medley' cloths, this 'richest and most valuable manufacture in the World', extended into North Dorset, around Shaftesbury and Sherborne. It spread all over East Somerset—Wincanton, Frome, Bruton; all over West Wiltshire, from Warminster north to Malmesbury; and in Gloucestershire northward on both flanks of the Cotswolds to beyond the Stroud valley, and eastwards to Cirencester, almost into Oxfordshire at Fairford, and well into the shire at Witney—where blanket-making survives to this day.

Round about the rather widely scattered towns, in which the master clothiers generally lived and had their warehouses and perhaps their finishing shops—fulling was outside, where the power was—the spinning and much of the weaving was done in innumerable villages and hamlets in the combes of the hills.

The excellent local wool had ceased to meet all these needs: from the seventeenth century at latest they were drawing on counties so far north as Lincoln and so far east as Kent; sometimes also on Ireland and, an important development, on Spain.

Wool-working did not stop south-westward of this woollen cloth region: it merely changed character. There was a village knitting industry in Dorset and on the Somerset flats in the seventeenth century; and though stockings were still being shipped from Bridgwater to Spain in the eighteenth, the trade was yielding under pressure from the stocking-frames of the

Midlands. Apart from that, there was no trace of decadence in West Somerset and Devon, from Taunton to Exeter. The region's activity was not in the fine woollen broadcloth, but in lighter and narrower fabrics of worsted, or mixed woollen and worsted, yarn, like the baize.

Devon had made and exported cloth long before 1500. By 1600 or 1650 it had concentrated on the lighter sorts, especially serge, one of the fabrics with worsted warp and woollen weft—described in 1728 as 'a Woollen cross'd Stuff' (stuff equals worsted). The name is another of those trade terms that complicate technical history. It comes from *serica*, silken. Who first said that his serges were silky is not known—probably not an Englishman, certainly a liar. In any case, they were Devon's pride for a century and a half. Defoe arrives at Honiton: 'Here we see the first of the great Serge Manufacture of Devonshire, a Trade too great to be described in Miniature...which takes up this whole County, which is the largest and most populous in England, Yorkshire excepted...so full of great Towns, and those Towns so full of People, and those People so universally employ'd in Trade and Manufactures, that not only it cannot be equall'd in England, but perhaps not in Europe.' A journalist's outburst, but there was occasion for it. So, such a man on a nineteenth-century visit might have written of South Lancashire. As to the weekly serge market of Exeter, it was 'very well worth a Stranger's seeing, and next to the Brigg-Market at Leeds in Yorkshire, is the greatest in England'.

Note that by Defoe's day Irish wool and Irish yarn were coming into Devon through Bideford and Barnstaple. Ireland might not manufacture for export but she might supply the 'universally employ'd' men of Devon.

'Next to the Brigg-Market at Leeds.' There were important wool-textile centres between Gloucestershire and Yorkshire; but Yorkshire was the next textile county. Ever since they secured a charter in 1462, the Drapers of Shrewsbury had been important customers for the rough woollens of Wales. They employed shearmen and other finishers. By the reign of James I they had acquired for their market a monopoly of buying and selling Welsh cloth. Naturally Welshmen and London clothworkers fought it. There were ups and downs all through the Stuart era. But 'in the middle of the eighteenth century the Shrewsbury Drapers' monopoly was still intact'.[1]

---

[1] A. H. Dodd, *The Industrial Revolution in North Wales* (1933), p. 12.

They all spoke English in the town, Defoe had said, 'but on a Market Day you would think you were in Wales'.

Coventry had been a great wool-working town in early Tudor times, a town of many gilds, in which six capitalist clothier Drapers had oversight of the Weavers and the Fullers. But it was one of the towns that was losing ground to the country districts between 1525 and 1700, when its wool industry was moribund. But it got silk instead, started in 1696 and soon flourishing; also watchmaking, started in 1710. No town in Britain has had so varied an industrial history.

There were other midland towns that retained some wool manufacture for market after 1700, among them Kidderminster. But there had never been much in the North and East Midlands up to Lincolnshire. One pictures that country with its regular sprinkling of parish weavers, customer-weavers, of the race that runs in literature from Bottom to Silas Marner. It was certainly there—in Nottingham and Lincoln—that 'the weaver' survived with the blacksmith and the wheelwright as a village craftsman farthest into the nineteenth century. In his last days he generally wove linen.

No doubt he also survived all through the sixteenth, seventeenth and eighteenth centuries in the North Riding of Yorkshire, where what might be called Scottish conditions set in; probably also in the East Riding. It was into the West Riding that Yorkshire wool-working industry, important long before 1500, had concentrated and grown. York and Beverley, Whitby and Selby, all once 'clothing' towns, had fallen into the background before 1550; but Leeds, which had its weavers and dyers in the thirteenth century—and no doubt earlier—had more than taken the place of them all. To its market, held first on the bridge and then all the way up Briggate, held latterly twice a week, came those famous 'domestic clothiers', most of whom in Defoe's day brought only one piece of cloth. They were small farmer-manufacturers in direct economic descent from William Webster, cottar tenant of the lord Eadmund de Lascy in 1258. Their speciality was true woollen cloth, generally 'in the white', i.e. undyed and unfinished.

But Yorkshire was not, and never had been, confined to the making of that material or to its making by that famous class. Worsteds of some sort had been produced in medieval times, and there was great activity in making finer worsteds, especially about Halifax, from the late seventeenth century.

But the abundance of water-power favoured the woollen process, with its fulling mills; so that woollens of one sort or
another, generally rather rough and coarse—'kerseys' and
'dozens'—dominated the West Riding trade throughout. That
the goods were inferior to those of the West of England was
admitted in a court of law in 1638; and in 1725, though it
was claimed that the colour was as good in Yorkshire as in the
West, it was held that the fabrics were not so fine. About the
same time, in 1737–8, Sam Hill of Halifax was struggling in
Yorkshire fashion 'to outdo all England', to beat Exeter and
to beat Norwich, in the making of worsted and part-worsted
fabrics. 'I think it now evident', he was able to write, that
'in spite of fate' the industries would come into 'these northern
Countrys'.[1] They came. Yet down to 1750, in the West Riding
as a whole, the making of woollens greatly predominated.

So did the domestic clothiers, immensely in numbers, greatly
perhaps in output. But a successful working clothier could
prosper until his main business came to be buying, directing,
and selling. He always had spinning done 'out'. Weaving
might follow, or he might collect a few men into a small
'weaving shop'. Or the big clothier might develop, as he had
developed elsewhere, from the merchant of wool or of cloth—
who got his wool worked up in stages, or his cloth made to his
order. There were certainly big Leeds clothiers under Cromwell
who disliked the competition of the small country men, aimed
at legislative control, and played an important part in the
parliamentary and local history of the industry for the next
half-century. They had fellows at Wakefield. In worsted the
big man predominated from the seventeenth century, when it
was being so to speak re-acclimatised in Yorkshire. Re-
acclimatisation cost money as well as pluck. So, in the period
when the industry was taking its modern form, 'the small
independent clothier never existed in it'.[2] We even meet,
shortly after 1750, forerunners of the later capitalist spinner,
'master woolcombers' who bought wool, combed it, aided by
journeyman combers, had it spun, and sold the yarn.

[1] Herbert Heaton, *The Yorkshire Woollen and Worsted Industries* (1920),
p. 270.
[2] *Ibid.* p. 297.

THE TEXTILE INDUSTRIES OF LANCASHIRE

Like every other region, Lancashire had its rough, local and customer weaving of flax and hemp and wool before 1500. Its woollens were so inferior that it fell outside the purview of the tax-gatherer—with Westmorland, Cumberland, Durham and Cheshire. We know how many taxable 'cloths' every other English county wove yearly late in the fifteenth century, and so can grade roughly its manufacturing importance. Sixteenth-century Lancashire 'clothiers' called themselves 'cotegers'. They used rough wool or local flax or Irish linen yarn. Bigger men sold in London and elsewhere what these 'cotegers' made. They might do well out of it. In the late sixteenth and early seventeenth centuries the trade made the fortunes of the Mosley and Chetham families—names notable in Manchester history. Some time in Elizabeth's reign people of their type thought of establishing the fustian industry in England, first in East Anglia, then in Lancashire. The industry was well grown on the continent, and the impulse probably came from or through refugees. For fustian you used cotton, that grew 'upon little shrubs or bushes' and was 'brought into this Kingdome by the Turkie Merchants'.[1] Things called cottons had been made before that, but they were certainly woollen fabrics: the verb to 'cotton' was used to describe a manufacturing process.

Cotton might be mixed with flax in fustian making. It would not be easy for a 'coteger' to get. Some mercantile person would have to supply it. This no doubt helped the rapid growth of the 'putting out' system in the new Lancashire industry, capitalists generally known as mercers or linen-drapers buying the raw material from the Turkey merchants in London, and getting it spun and woven locally.

Lancashire industry was, on the whole, as free as it was various—woollens, linens, fustians, and the 'inkles' which might be of linen or cotton or mixed. Besides the great 'linen drapers' there were various grades of middlemen; and not all the cottage workers remained permanently at that level. For the reason given, they were most likely so to remain when their material was the imported cotton. There were 'Manchester men' who moved about selling the finished goods, smaller and perhaps more stirring than the great linen-drapers. But as linen

---

[1] Quoted by A. P. Wadsworth and J. de L. Mann, *The Cotton Trade and Industrial Lancashire, 1600–1780* (1931), p. 15.

has to be calendered, fustian cut and dyed, the man with appropriate installations, or the capital to hire those who had, was in a strong position.

Up to 1700 all-cotton goods were not much made. Cotton yarn was normally a weft to a linen warp. But the age of the 'calico chaces' provoked first, it seems, Spitalfields then Lancashire to imitate India. Lancashire had begun earlier with rough cotton checks: it went on to calico for printing. By 1740–50 both trades were well established side by side with the fustians and the inkles.

CAPITAL IN THE WOOL AND SILK INDUSTRIES

What a modern writer would call the capitalist clothier type, the type of which Sam Hill of Halifax was an eighteenth-century representative, was well established long before 1500, as has been seen:[1] he remained dominant. The 'clothier that doth put cloth to making and sale', the putter-out, was a recognised member of the highest industrial and commercial grade of society in Elizabeth's labour code. He was classed with the merchants and the goldsmiths; above textile craftsmen whom he might employ—weavers, fullers, dyers, shearmen; far above the humble weavers of household woollens; very far above the innumerable spinsters who were not even mentioned in the code—spinning was not a craft: those who span were not 'artificers', nor did they take 'apprentices', the two classes from one of which the Statute of 1562–3 is generally nicknamed.

These clothiers had long dominated the West Country industry, from Wiltshire to Devon. Living mostly in the towns, they 'put out' over the whole adjacent countryside wool, some of which they might have bought from great distances through wool staplers and wool 'broggers'. The woollen cloth processes subsequent to fulling were generally done in the towns—raising, shearing, perhaps dyeing. 'Perhaps', because until far down the seventeenth century a great deal of the best English cloth was exported 'white' to be dyed and finished, in ways that would meet the demands of particular continental markets, at Antwerp or Amsterdam or Hamburg. This 'white' export never quite died out, but it became unimportant after the decades 1660–80.

[1] See above, pp. 156–8.

In Devon the clothier type was represented in the sixteenth century by Peter Blundell (1520–1601) who by building up a 'manufactory' of kersies—that is, getting them made—left, when he died a bachelor, £40,000 to education and charity. The type did not die with him, if few later clothiers could rival his accumulation.

The 'putting out' employers continued to dominate the East Anglian trade—with their workpeople, or the small masters who jobbed for them, crowded in the towns or scattered over the country. So fully occupied were these people, that Defoe said you might have thought Norwich on a week day 'a Town without Inhabitants', they being all 'in their Garrets at their Looms, and in their Combing-shops, so they call them, Twisting Mills, and other Work-Houses'. He is in worsted country, worsted and silk.

Direction of the silk industry proper, with its exotic raw material, tended to fall into 'capitalist' hands. It was small and hot-house raised, by taxation or prohibition of competing imports and by royal patronage. A London trade almost entirely before 1500, its headquarters remained in London, where the 'throwsters', who with a simple mechanism twisted together fibres for the warp, were incorporated in 1629. Reinforced by Huguenot immigration, the weaving industry became more important in the London area, with offshoots in Kent and Essex, and for ribbons in Coventry. The Norwich district became an important consumer. There, Defoe's 'Twisting Mills' were probably twisting silk. Lombe's great experiment of 1719[1] eventually took silk throwing to places with easily utilised water power, to which in time the manufacture would follow. But there was still manual 'throwing' in London in 1750 and Spitalfields was England's chief weaving centre, the weavers working mainly for substantial master-manufacturers, though a weaver might occasionally deal with a warehouseman direct.

THE ENGLISH WOOL INDUSTRIES: THEIR FOREIGN MARKETS AND THEIR FORTUNES

The creation or improvement of luxury and munition industries—fine paper, silk, glass, cannon, gunpowder—was an essential aim of Tudor and early Stuart policy. But important as the munition industries were for national independence, the

[1] See above, p. 226.

luxury industries for national culture and the welfare of the small groups engaged in them, neither set affected the welfare of the country at large as the fortunes of the wool industries did. In the thirteenth and fourteenth centuries fluctuations in the price and export of wool might touch little flock-masters in remote shires. From the mid-fifteenth century, if not earlier, similar fluctuations in the demand for the various wool manufactures, affecting directly the many concentrated manufacturing areas, might have their repercussions on poor spinners in distant villages. A great export industry, always eager to find 'vents' for its goods, the wool manufacture of the sixteenth and seventeenth centuries was in the position which the Flemish industry had held before it: it was dangerously dependent on the vicissitudes of international politics. English writers were proud of this great industry of theirs. The period ends with the publication, in 1747, of the Rev. John Smith's *Chronicon Rusticum Commerciale* or *Memoirs of Wool*, one of the earliest of industrial chronicles. But English statesmen, and common men up and down the country, had learnt its dangerous connection with unemployment. At every critical phase of politico-economic affairs, phases in which a purely economic cause occasionally predominates, a political cause much more often, it is the wool industries from which illustrations are taken by the statesman, or shouted on behalf of the people.

If Wolsey's international policy interferes with the cloth-export to the Low Countries, the ballad-writer cries

> By thee out of service many are constrained
>> And course of merchandise thou hast restrained
> Wherfor men sigh and sob.

And Shakespeare in *Henry VIII* recalls those who were then 'constrained out of service', thrown out of work: 'the clothiers all, not able to maintain the many to them 'longing, have put off the spinsters, carders, fullers, weavers'.

Some twenty years later the author of the most remarkable social pamphlet of the century, *A Discourse of the Common Weal of this Realm of England*, notes concisely that 'when our clothiers lack vent over sea, there is great multitude of these clothiers idle'.

When the great Sir Thomas Gresham reported to Queen Elizabeth early in her reign how, by operating on the exchanges, he had been able 'by artte and Godes providence' to reduce the burden of interest on royal borrowings in the Antwerp money market, his 'artte' had consisted in throwing the burden on to exporters of cloth who were obliged to take sterling at a fictitious value in exchange for their debts in Flemish money. There were heavy losses to both merchants and clothiers with resultant unemployment.

A few years later (*c.* 1564) Cecil is found actually regretting the growth of the clothing industry, for various reasons—of which the alleged unruliness of the 'clothing' population is one. He hankered after stable society—steady agriculture, conservative corporate towns—and he had been obliged to face and legislate about poverty and unemployment. Quite rightly, he saw that this great and always growing industry, subject to uncontrolled vicissitudes, bred that uncertainty and irregularity of life which breed discontent.

The final struggle with Spain, in control of the Netherlands, made him anxious about 'this great matter of the lack of vent, not only of clothes [cloth] which presently [at the moment] is the greatest'. It might make Englishmen 'fall into violence'; and in fact, next year, men in Gloucestershire and Wiltshire were said to be ready 'to mutiny'. The victory of 1588 did not cure the evil, for war with all its economic consequences dragged on through that gloomy final decade of the century, in which—to deepen the gloom—food prices were abnormally high, as a result of bad harvests.[1] Of military and political obstacles to the external 'vent' of cloth, statesmen were well aware: they did not, so far as is known, note what always happens when food is very dear—that the demand, the 'vent', for clothing falls away. Shakespeare's picture of Wolsey's day may well have been coloured by personal knowledge of the 'putting off' of 'spinsters, carders, fullers, weavers'.

Under James I an economic cause started the trouble. Alderman Cockayne, an ambitious business man, said he could provide employment by developing the dyeing and finishing industries so as to put an end to the export of 'white' cloth. To help him, that export was prohibited in 1614. Exporters and West Country clothiers were furious. The Dutch retaliated with prohibition and a development of a 'white' manufacture of their own. The Alderman was unable to carry out his scheme in time. By 1620 the export of the Merchant Adventurers was barely half what it had been before 1614. The thing had to be

[1] See above, p. 187.

abandoned: but, in combination with other causes, it started a trade depression in the early twenties from which recovery was slow. Depression was not confined to the West Country. There were accumulations of unsold frieze and 'cottons' and baize at Manchester, in 1622, which might have been sold 'if the market were not so bad'.

Civil War was inevitably dislocating; and the King did what he could to humble rebellious London by stopping the free movement of cloth to it—the great centre of export. There was much distress and actual emigration of unemployed weavers to the Netherlands.

Oliver's Dutch and Spanish wars did no good to the staple industry. Besides, bread was again dear. On the eve of the Restoration there was a crescendo of complaints about depression in it. The Yorkshiremen said that their trade was 'dead by reason of the wars with Spain'. No doubt there was some overstatement on political grounds; but 'there can be little doubt that the crisis was a serious one'[1]—and not much doubt that it helped the King to enjoy his own again after 'Protector and Rump had put us in a dump'.

The later Stuart and the early Hanoverian parliaments took every care of the great industry—with their vicious attack on Ireland, their law about woollen shrouds, and their Calico Act. Yet it had its crises, now mainly connected with newer and more remote trades—especially the great Mediterranean trade of the Levant Company.[2] The East India market had proved disappointing: the Hindu was no great consumer of cloth. It was partly in hope of finding another 'vent' that the Company pushed on to China—again with indifferent success. But technique had improved. Though Alderman Cockayne failed, his successors mastered their crafts, so that the export of cloth 'white' fell away. New markets had been opened out. The Russians, unlike the Hindus, liked fine stout cloth. The Hansards, pushed out of their Steelyard under Elizabeth, had been obliged, after long struggles, to recognise the monopoly of the export of cloth to all points between the Somme and the Skaw given to the Merchant Adventurers by charter in 1564. The Adventurers were invited to Hamburg and given 'magnificent' privileges there in 1611. Germany's ruin in the Thirty Years' War (1618–48) made her a poor market but left the English in

[1] W. R. Scott, *Joint-stock Companies*, vol. 1 (1912), p. 261.
[2] For the new trades, see below, pp. 262–4.

a very strong position when she recovered. In Hamburg they had not only their own church but their own parish, from which they could feed inner Germany with cloth: they came to be known later as the Hamburg Company.

Then there were the Plantations with their growing demand. Excellent markets for the lighter goods of East Anglia and Devon were available in the Peninsula and round the Mediterranean: Spanish nuns learnt to wear heretical fabrics. When Defoe travelled and John Smith wrote, the industries, in all their branches, had never been stronger at home or abroad. No home manufacture was in importance comparable. Abroad, Bruges and Ghent and Ypres had been sleeping for centuries. The Dutch were excellent workmen, but not to be feared in general competition. So when, in 1757, John Dyer celebrated the industries in his poem *The Fleece*, he was justified in making that fleece golden.

GILDS AND APPRENTICESHIP

Mining and quarrying and smelting, and every form of transport work, had always lain outside the authority and jurisdiction of urban gilds and companies: only at one spot in Western Europe was there even a coal-miners' gild, at Liège where, by a geological accident, the pits were inside the town boundaries. Masons, when localised, might belong to a company; but most of them were not localised. Water-power had been a solvent of gild-power from the days of the first rural fulling mill. There had been gilds enough in the iron-working trades; but, as it happened, the great developments of the seventeenth century took place outside those towns where they were numerous. It was not in or even about York, with its ten specialised gilds of ironworkers,[1] that the trades expanded. Although they expanded not far from Coventry, whose smiths' fraternity had some industrial rules in 1540—besides many social and fraternal rules—Coventry did not become their centre. Nor did Ludlow whose 'hammermen' got a charter in 1511. There were also organised crafts at Walsall, about which little is yet known. But it is certain that neither in Birmingham nor at Wolverhampton, nor in the villages and on the heaths where nailers' cottages stood, was there any organised local regulation of industry—and no more observance of national regulations than was convenient.

[1] See above, p. 143.

Manchester, with the organisation only of a village, could not have had gilds or companies even if it had wanted them. On the other hand, at Leeds an attempt was made, late in the seventeenth century, to establish company control and monopoly in the sole section of the wool-working industries which, by that time, was still within the effective range of any town authority—cloth-working. The Clothworkers of London were still a powerful corporation. Leeds wanted a similar body. But 1661 was late for a start. The Clothworkers' 'Guild or Fraternity' was both created and controlled by the corporation of the town. We hear, in 1690, of the Leeds Clothworkers trying to stop cloth from leaving the West Riding before it had been dyed and dressed: they wanted the business. We do not hear that they succeeded. By 1720 the corporation is complaining that, 'by a long disuse and failure', the Company's rules are become dead letters. Five years later general supervision of the broadcloth industry is transferred—with how much success has yet to be discussed [1]—to the J.P.'s, a final recognition that the industry was a county, a regional, not a mere urban concern. So it was in all its branches, and in every county of the many in which they were practised.

Urban gilds and companies had certainly been hit by the legislation of Edward VI's reign that 'nationalised' their many 'superstitious' endowments. This legislation killed the purely religious gild and undermined the social gild whose main activities, as set out in its rules, were 'superstitious'—masses and processions and the keeping of saints' days. Legislators took care not to condemn, or as they supposed endanger, the economic activities of traders' or craftsmen's companies; but this confiscation of property in uncertain times must have done them injury. The strong London Companies, composed of or dominated by mercantile capitalists, came through better than others. Mercers, Drapers, Goldsmiths, Clothworkers are full of important men in Elizabethan times. Not necessarily important mercers, drapers, and the rest, since the custom of London had always allowed freemen of one Company to practise the trade of another—or no trade at all.[2] The twelve Great Companies formed a sort of municipal plutocracy that supplied the Lord Mayors and directed City policy.

Companies below them, still full of actual craftsmen or craftsmen-shopkeepers, were greatly weakened in their ad-

---

[1] See below, pp. 292–3.   [2] See above, pp. 126–7.

ministration of trade discipline by the incessant growth of London. Their own apprentices, 'foreign' tradesmen from other towns, illegal unapprenticed men, all could so easily set up in the suburbs out of the reach of wardens and search. Search for 'falsely made' goods became harder, though, partly as a result of measures taken after 1550 to overcome the suburban difficulty, goods were still sometimes destroyed in London because they were ill-made, even in the early nineteenth century.

Outside London, there is a marked tendency in late Elizabethan and early Stuart times towards amalgamation of companies, a movement the cause and results of which are not easy to determine precisely but may be suggested. Amalgamation was not new: in several towns before 1500 companies with no special trade connections had been amalgamated for financial reasons—being too poor to pay for their share of the town pageant, generally. The practice grows. At Northampton in 1574 seven trading 'crafts' are lumped together. A year later at Ipswich a series of amalgamations results in four, but only four, general companies each containing a number of trades. At Hull in 1598 a most miscellaneous group of trades, including plumbers, musicians and basket-makers, are all absorbed into the respectable company of the goldsmiths. This sort of thing had been anticipated in the 1511 charter of the Hammermen of Ludlow; for besides smiths, ironmongers, pewterers and armourers the Company admitted coopers, masons and others. Norwich, a city in which specialised trade organisations had never been much encouraged, grouped all that had been permitted into twelve 'grand companies' in 1622. When Leeds made its belated and unsuccessful effort to organise companies after the Restoration, it grouped several distinct crafts under the Clothworkers; several more into a company for the building trades; put the glaziers in with ironmongers and 'hammermen'; made a small company of shopkeepers; and left only the cordwainers and the tailors as single-trade companies. It is possible that in 1661 cordwainer had become only a trade name for leather-worker. Leeds long remained a leather-working town. On the evidence available there is no reason to think that these different companies were much more effective than that of the Clothworkers.

Nor is there reason to think that these *omnibus* companies could exercise effectively that supervision over materials, methods of work, working hours, and the quality of the output, at which the specialised gild had aimed—with how much success we are never sure. The 'goldsmiths' of Hull could hardly be expert plumbers, though they may have backed the expert opinion of their plumbing members: we do not know that they did. That a Ludlow pewterer would be a good judge of mason's work is unlikely; and in any case 'search' was on a decline even in specialised companies. The Courts were against too much economic interference: from James I's day they held that the Common Law stood for freedom.

What the *omnibus* type could do was to exclude outsiders from its constituent trades and enforce apprenticeship in all. Exclusion was hard or easy in proportion to the size of the town and the trade. The enforcement of apprenticeship was easy, because all skilled trades need something of the kind and because the law of 1563 put the Justices of the Peace behind the coercive power of a company. Indeed, there is no doubt that the law of 1563 was only a true success when one or both of those two things were present, technical need and an interested company. On the face of it the law covered every kind of employment, but it was never so applied. You could be apprenticed to husbandry—but the evidence shows that only two classes of people were: pauper children whom the Justices apprenticed out, like the Lincolnshire poacher in the ballad who was bound to serve a master seven year; and a few, occasionally met with, who resemble the modern farm pupil. Yeomen and husbandmen's sons picked up knowledge from father.

Outside agriculture, the view soon prevailed that apprenticeship was not needed for an unskilled job. In 1600 the courts ruled that a costermonger need not have served an apprenticeship—'because his art was in the selling of apples, which required no skill'. So, the commentator adds, 'an husbandman, tankard-bearer, brickmaker, porter, miller and such like' are outside the law, for the same reason. Was it, at bottom, because there had never been a company of husbandmen or millers? As classes they are not exactly unskilled. The original law left the custom of London untouched: there was no need for a freeman of the City to serve seven more years, like Jacob, if he wished to change his trade. Before 1600 the Court of King's Bench had applied this generally—a man who had been apprenticed to any trade named in the Act might practise any other.

Naming in the Act became important, with a characteristic lawyers' respect for the letter of the law: the Act spoke of trades 'now used or occupied within the Realm', and it began to be held that new trades, new to England since 1563, lay outside it. No doubt there was regular apprenticeship in new skilled trades. Many of them got companies chartered to enforce this and other 'gild' rules during the seventeenth century—Spectacle-makers, Coach-makers, Gun-makers in London—but the law was interpreted so as to render this optional.

There were also local prejudice and local independence to be considered. People who, like some Yorkshire petitioners of 1640, coolly stated that certain important clauses of the Act of 1563 were 'never observed...in the said countie, nor can be' were not likely to enforce the apprenticeship clause except when it suited them.

Companies could enforce it in their own way. By tradition, a freeman's son could become free of a company by patrimony, by being a son. Probably, where there was much to be learnt and when he wished to maintain paternal discipline, the gold-smith or ironmonger father, still more probably the butcher or carpenter, might require his son to serve his time; but the law did not require it. There was nothing in the law to prevent an ambitious Cordwainer's son from taking up his freedom by patrimony and then setting up as a wine merchant with the Vintners. There was in London the steadily growing group of people who might be Mercers or Fletchers because their fathers were, and might themselves be lawyers or idlers or politicians. All through this period men were entering the greater London Companies by redemption, paying their way in, without any necessary intention of practising the trade. Under Charles II Francis Millington, an early member of the Hudson's Bay Company, was a Draper. He may have dealt in cloth—we do not know—but his main business was that of a farmer of the taxes: he was what would to-day be called a financier. As for heredity, the Socialist Chancellor of the Exchequer[1] is an hereditary Draper to-day.

The early Stuarts, with their relatively backward Scottish economic antecedents and their paternal views of a well-ordered society, were favourable to strict company organisation. Besides authorising London Companies for new trades when these rose to significance, as Elizabeth had before them,

---

[1] At the time of writing, Dr Hugh Dalton. [J.S.]

they favoured the specialisation out from existing Companies of groups nominally under them who were developing new processes. Haberdashers had sold imported felt for hats. Some aliens came under Henry VIII and made it. After a long fight they got a separate charter of incorporation in 1604. Similarly the Clock-makers were, very reasonably, taken from the control of the Blacksmiths in 1631. From the Blacksmiths also the Gunmakers broke away; the Tinplate-workers from the Ironmongers. And there were others.

These, however, are hardly instances of working craftsmen getting free of the control of such dealers' Companies as the Haberdashers and the Ironmongers. Felt-making is more industrial than haberdashing, but clockmaking is not more industrial than blacksmithing. However that may be, it is certain that no new Company was chartered unless some of its leaders were men of some substance: a charter was never cheap. How much a leading early master clock- or gun-maker worked with his hands we do not know. Perhaps a good deal. Probably he worked when young and directed when older, as men have done since in many similar trades. The fight was for control, by comparatively small masters no doubt, of their own specialities which they understood; not a fight of 'labour' against 'capital'. But it is fair to Kings James I and Charles I to add that their governments more than once showed a genuine care for the interests of 'labour'.

The difficulty which the London Companies had faced before 1550, when attempting to control a whole range of growing suburbs from their old monopoly area—the City within the walls, plus four wards without—was met by giving the new Elizabethan and Stuart Companies a wider jurisdiction, and by widening the area under those old Companies who asked for it when charters were renewed. On those occasions such widening was almost invariable. Early charters of that type might formally cover Southwark or Westminster; but even under Elizabeth the simple device was hit on of giving a monopoly radius—two miles, or four, from London Stone. In the seventeenth century the radius might be extended to seven miles, or even ten. But could the Poulterers really control the area fourteen miles across that Charles II gave them? And what of the poultry dealer at seven miles one furlong?

The maximum area of control was given, nominally, by James I when he incorporated the shipwrights of Rotherhithe in 1605 as the Shipwrights' Company of England. They were given power to imprison Wapping wrights who were actually freemen of London; but there is no other evidence that 'of England' was more than a flourish. Their economic position is made clear by certain episodes in their seventeenth-century history. Under Charles I, the calkers who worked for them asked to be made a distinct corporation. (There had been master calkers and 'meane' calkers before 1500.[1]) The Star Chamber would not go so far; but it did instruct the Shipwrights to give the calkers a seat or two on their governing body. Sawyers tried to secure incorporation in 1670: they worked for shipwrights, joiners and carpenters, their wages being set by the Carpenters. Their attempt failed. Much later, in 1704, a desire for incorporation is stirring among the working shipwrights. Here 'capital' and 'labour' are clear to sight, and subcontract too, by the master calkers and perhaps by master sawyers. With the eighteenth century the Company remains Shipwrights; but its leaders are called shipbuilders.

There were still a few charters of incorporation issued to Companies 'on the make' after 1660—the Fanmakers' is of 1709—but the chartering age is really over with Charles II, and one of those charters is to a very ancient trade which looks odd as a Corporation, the Fishermen of 1687. The Fanmakers raised the total to ninety, of which more than half (forty-nine) had been chartered since 1550—new trades, or old ones finally given rank. But the spirit of the times was swinging against them. There is a note in the Privy Council records of 1669 that the Elizabethan apprentice law had 'been by most of the judges looked upon as inconvenient to trade and...inventions'. About 1700 more than one legal decision declared seven years' practice of a trade as good as an apprenticeship.

The system had been shaken when Oliver's government suspended apprenticeship law to help demobilised soldiers into industry. It was undermined in Town—towns were quite secondary, and it had never meant much in country districts—by the Great Fire. That ancient Companies lost their halls did not make much difference. Some housed dead trades—Girdlers, Bowyers, Fletchers; few had much direct economic significance for live ones. What mattered was the suspension for seven years of all rules against 'foreigners' in all the building trades, a group which had been in a position to fight against

[1] See above, p. 134.

'illegal' men, or at least, when active, to convict them of 'false work' if they got in. The exact situation is revealed by a request of the Carpenters that, if 'foreigners' were admitted, it should be only as journeymen not as master workmen or undertakers [contractors]. One sees what sort of men dominated the Carpenters. But Parliament put them aside: craftsmen who immigrated to help rebuild London were to enjoy all privileges of freemen of the City.

The dislocation of the Fire left many London crafts shorthanded besides the building trades, just as the Civil War with its social unrest had interfered everywhere with that society of order and privilege at which the early Stuarts had aimed. By 1670 there were 'illegal men' in every town of England and in every trade. No doubt small, compact, skilled London crafts, fanmakers or clock-makers, could carry on in much the old way: it suited their conditions. But there were general complaints of the breakdown of apprenticeship. Young men, the complainants said, were marrying too early because the disciplinary apprenticeship indenture, with its 'fornication he shall not commit, matrimony he shall not contract', now bound so few of them up to the age of twenty-four.

It had never bound the unskilled, the miners, the nailers, the carters and bargemen, the average agricultural labourers, the husbandmen's children, the Yorkshire children who, to Defoe's great admiration, were picking up some childish textile skill from four or five years of age: in short the very great majority of those who in England and Wales did manual work. If the Thames and London had their Companies of Watermen and Porters, the other rivers and towns of England had not. Among such people, the occasional company fighting for a privileged position was an anomaly; and by 1750 sturdy Irishmen were coming to London to carry the sedan-chairs.

TRADE CLUBS

There had been evidence of some class consciousness, as opposed to what might be called craft consciousness, far back in the history of the companies and gilds. Where small masters —calkers for instance, or sawyers—worked for strong employers they would easily acquire the wage-earner's point of view and begin to identify their interests with those of apprenticed or unapprenticed journeymen. Late in the seventeenth century this comes to light in widespread evidence of clubs and organisations which soon arouse the suspicions of Parliament. Mr Pepys once attended a carpenters' 'yearly club' which was obviously not a meeting of the Worshipful Company of Carpenters. Clubs among the London feltmakers of the 1690's have all the characteristics of trade unions. Before 1726, when Parliament legislated against 'unlawful clubs and societies' among wool workers in the highly capitalistic West Country, similar associations have been traced among wheelwrights and tailors. As labour becomes more mobile, the tramping card, to introduce a man in a new town, and the house of call where he can present it and learn the local prospects, begin to appear faintly. In Sheffield, an immobile place, many clubs, 'ostensibly friendly societies', are reported on with suspicion in 1721. A Newcastle shoemakers' society of 1719 has its sick and funeral benefits and may well have discussed over its beer the prices to be charged for cobbling: we are here among small masters who in effect are jobbing workmen. Later, a woolcombers' club comes to light: by 1800 it was very strong. Next, a book of agreed silk-weavers' wage rates in Spitalfields, apparently the result of some sort of collective bargain. And in 1749 Parliament, growing more suspicious, extends its law against clubs in wool to cover the silk, flax, iron, leather, and some other trades. But did that kill the club at the Bricklayers' Arms or the Six Jolly Fellowship Porters? Nothing suggests it. Law in the eighteenth century relied for its enforcement on the 'common informer'. In Sheffield, among other places, his career might be a dangerous one.

Chapter IX

Trading Companies, Finance and Public Policy

REGULATED AND JOINT-STOCK COMPANIES

It was in the last decade of the seventeenth century, when the company that had grown out of the gild was moribund as an economic force of national importance, that, in a boom of investment in another sort of company, 'all the modern organisation of the stock exchange (but in a primitive form)' was at work in London. In that boom the Bank of England and the Bank of Scotland were both born, with many other shorter-lived joint-stock companies.

The roots of the joint-stock company ran back behind the sixteenth century, in which it first appears. It had links with the gild: merchant gilds and other gilds had sometimes made collective purchases—acted as buying units as the joint-stock company would. When incorporate, a company could hold property; it had its seal.[1] Companies handed on to the joint-stock company an aiming at monopoly and, for a time, the practice of apprenticeship. The joint stock was anticipated in the Italian *societates*, which traded as units, and into which investors other than the main partners put money. It was anticipated also by the joint ventures of medieval merchants, and by the practice in England of owning ships and mines in fractions, halves and eighths and up to sixty-fourths. The first English chartered company trading on a joint stock, the Muscovy Company, which had essayed the dangerous voyage to the White Sea in 1553, was so arranged as a matter of convenience and safety. The risks were too great for any few individuals; so a fairly large group agreed to risk each so much, to take a share.

Had the venture not been novel and dangerous, the natural thing at the time would have been to organise these Muscovy Adventurers on the lines of the existing Merchant Adventurers, that is, as what was called later a regulated company. The

[1] See above, p. 144.

regulated company was a gild for foreign trade. It aimed at a monopoly area—the Somme to the Skaw in the case of the Adventurers—as Grocers aimed at a monopoly of 'grocery'. It made rules about admission and trading, as they did. Inevitably it 'stinted' the ships that it hired, that is, assigned space in them to its members. The fleets and sailings it had to control if its authority was to remain real: a member's ship could not be allowed to slip out ahead of the market to an unknown destination. But, subject to the rules, each member shipped his own goods at his personal risk and for his private profit.

The story of the Muscovy Company is fascinating. There was tragedy on the first expedition, death in the frozen North. Later the Company's great agent, Anthony Jenkinson, visited the Czar—the Terrible Czar—in Moscow and went on to argue theology with the Shah in Kazvin. During a short period, between 1566 and 1581, the Company brought Asiatic luxuries to England by that roundabout route—Persia, the Caspian, the Volga, the Northern Dwina, the White Sea. But its career was uncertain. By 1604 critics were complaining that its membership was only about 'eight-score'; and that fifteen directors 'managed the whole trade'.

Asiatic luxuries were more accessible to the Levant Company, the Turkey Merchants, who, starting with a joint stock in 1581, settled down later into the 'regulated' type as their members learnt to take the whole risk of voyages on what became the well known and fairly safe route to Smyrna. There was a controversy in Elizabethan times as between trading companies, normally thought of as monopolistic and regulated, and the free privateering 'merchant' of which Hawkins was a type. Walsingham leant towards freedom. So did the parliamentary critics of all monopolies in Elizabeth's last years. Cecil, a more authoritarian type, relied on the conservative monopoly-minded Londoners, in whose interest he reorganised Baltic trade under a regulated Eastland Company in 1579.

From among the Turkey Merchants, who had received reports from the first English travellers in India, a group of a hundred and one 'adventurers' with fifteen 'committees or directors' prayed for a charter to trade to the East Indies in 1599. Next year they got it—the freemen of the new Company then numbering two hundred and eighteen and their 'committees' twenty-four. They were given the right to organise four voyages to the East, paying no export customs on their cargoes, and to take bullion out of the realm; for though men hoped to find a 'vent' for British goods, they knew that since Roman times the spices and silks of the East had seldom been exchanged for anything but treasure.

The Charter said nothing about a joint stock; but it was evidently necessary. For the early voyages one was raised among the freemen. The original dividend was what the word suggests, return to the subscribers of the capital put in plus an appropriate share of any profits made on the voyage. You divided up. Then, with very complex accounting, freemen began to leave their money, or some of it, in with the Company for the next voyage. A 'general stock' grew up. But it was not until a New General Stock was established, after the Company had managed—with difficulty—to get its Charter renewed under Cromwell in 1657, that its finance took a completely modern form. From 1661 an annual dividend was declared from the annual profits, and—even more important—if a man bought a share, he bought freedom of the Company.

A patent granted to the new Africa Company in the previous year had recognised the convenience of this easy transferability. Before 1661 an East India freeman who wanted to sell out had to find a freeman buyer or arrange for the buyer to become a freeman.

The joint-stock principle had already been applied to the extractive and metallurgical industries with the Mines Royal and Mineral and Battery Works.[1] Their financial history is complicated and not important. Neither had the great future of the East India Company. But the Mineral and Battery had one uncommonly 'modern' feature. It was what to-day would be called an integrated concern or, had it been built up of several, a vertical combination. It raised raw material; it smelted; it had 'battery works' at London and in Nottinghamshire, a wire-drawing mill at Tintern. Had it been as well managed as it was designed its story might have been different. But it was not easy to run such a dispersed concern effectively under sixteenth- and seventeenth-century conditions of news and transport.

Only the Crown could create corporations; but groups might combine in various ventures or in owning fractions of ships without ever asking for a charter of incorporation. They adopted the modern style 'A.B. and Company'. We hear of

[1] See above, p. 232.

Samuel Vassall and Company, Samuel Lemott and Company, both in the African trade; of John Jervase, Molyns, Richardson and Company, who owned the mills which supplied Oliver's government with gunpowder; and of many others.

Company history under the early Stuarts is closely connected with that of monopolies. Those who tried for a patent of monopoly were normally groups who, in the event of success, might ask for a regular charter of incorporation. They called themselves 'societies', as the old Italians had. The salt monopoly, two soap-making enterprises, and a fishery enterprise all used this description. Among them, the Soapers of Westminster were very nearly a joint-stock company, though not quite: capital was owned by individuals who sold to the Company at a fixed price and the Company divided the profit among all its members. Companies of adventurers with shares were very common—the Earl of Bedford's draining adventurers,[1] or the twenty-nine adventurers who, headed by Sir Hugh Middleton and getting half their capital from the King, had brought the water of the New River into their reservoir at Islington in 1613.

The Monopolies Act of 1624, which ended the early phase of royal monopoly experiments, is of the greatest importance in general economic history. By allowing monopoly for inventions for a limited number of years, it has been called 'the first national patent law which contains all essentials': some foreign scholars have seen in it the base of England's later technical progress. In the history of companies, its exceptions to the general rule against monopoly are its most important part. These included all chartered corporations, such as the East India Company was and the Bank of England would be. They included what to-day would be called the munitions industries, for the safeguarding of the nation's body, and printing, for the control of its mind. This last allowed a monopoly of Bible printing to continue which continues still—in the hands of the two ancient Universities and the King's printers. Monopolies were also allowed for glass-making, tavern-licensing, and to the Hostmen of Newcastle.

These last were not a joint-stock company, but they anticipated policies of which some such companies have since been accused. They were freemen of Newcastle who had got from Queen Elizabeth in 1600 a monopoly of the coal trade from the Tyne, in return for accepting a tax of 1*s.* per chaldron (about

[1] See above, pp. 196–7.

40 cwt.) on all coal shipped coastwise. (The Queen's advisers had noted this new and growing possibility of revenue.) The inner ring of the Hostmen, 'the Lords of Coal', had a lease of Crown coal measures; enough 'parts' (shares) in the bigger Tyneside collieries to dominate them; and enough control of the keels and waggons to exploit their monopoly and squeeze out the weaker 'Hostmen'. At one time they practised a 'limitation of the vend', i.e. sale, of coal to keep prices up, just as De Beers does to-day with diamonds. But demand for coal was so good that this was not a permanent necessity or temptation.

Companies, whether chartered, joint-stock, regulated, or informal, were not usually prosperous between 1625 and the Civil War. The Merchant Adventurers were suffering from the backwash of the depression of the twenties,[1] the East India from the licensing of an informal unchartered intruder on their monopoly by King Charles in 1635. Its name was Courten's Association.

Perhaps it was this depression that led to some faint beginnings of limited liability. The Fishery Society had made losses in 1633–4. Asking for more capital, it promised that this should not be liable for the old deficit. The Mosquito Islands Company promised all subscribers of £1000 that no further calls would be made on them in any event. Normally, in all sorts of trading partnerships liability was absolutely unlimited.

The troubles of the forties were not favourable either to foreign trade or to 'company promotion'. But insecurity favoured one group of business men, the goldsmiths. Merchants of various sorts, with the notaries who found money for mortgages and mortgages for money, had done some kinds of banking work long before; but it was from among the goldsmiths that the regular private bankers of London finally emerged between 1640 and 1675. When King Charles closed the Mint in 1640 and seized the bullion, treasure found its way into goldsmiths' strong rooms for safety. They kept it at call as 'running cash' (our current account) and found they could afford to pay interest on it. Until it was wanted, they could lend it out or buy (discount) bills of exchange. A series of these—say, three months' bills—due for payment one after another, provided a steady inflow of cash to meet depositors' demands. The goldsmiths then began to give people their promises to pay, the

[1] See above, pp. 251–2.

first bank notes; and people often wrote notes telling the gold-smith banker to pay, the early cheque, of which a Temple note to Mr Farrington was a forerunner.[1] So by 1675–80 what came to be considered the classical functions of a banker—deposit, discount, note issue—were all being performed in London. Ten years before 1675 Mr Pepys had been grumbling at the Admiralty's dependence on 'these bankers', men who had done well out of the troubles.

Public 'banks', of very different kinds, had long existed in Italy; and since 1609 the Bank of Amsterdam had been a standing illustration to Englishmen of their uses. That Bank neither discounted bills nor issued notes; it merely kept every-one's money, credited commercial customers who were paid in a bewildering variety of currencies with their full value in Dutch money, and transferred funds from one customer's account to another as instructed. In England, men were discussing the case for some public bank during the Civil War; a great deal in the ferment of notions about government and economics that followed it; and again in the seventies and eighties, after Charles II's 'Stop of the Exchequer' in 1672 had broken two or three of the leading goldsmith bankers. The Crown did not repudiate its debts: it merely said it must defer repayment of some of its debts as they fell due, and defer paying the interest. But they had overlent to it so heavily that this was enough. Their fall increased the need for something safe, with some kind of guarantee for its safety. Various pro-posals and experiments came to nothing until the Bank of England was founded twenty-two years later.[2]

All companies went through rough water between 1643 and 1660. The East India nearly lost its monopoly, but Oliver decided that there were political reasons for retaining it: the Company stood for England in the East as no casual, free-trading, perhaps dishonest group of merchants could. To help it, and the African and the Fishery companies, an Act of 1662 relieved shareholders, in case of company losses, of all liability beyond the full nominal value of their shares. They were not to be bankrupted and sold up for their directors' folly. The Fishery Company died. The African brought gold for the 'guineas'; went through crises and reorganisations; practically failed; and was handing over to a new company without a monopoly in 1750. But the Hudson's Bay, chartered in 1670,

---

[1] See above, p. 193.   [2] See below, pp. 272–4.

has outlived the East India and, as a private corporation, even the Bank of England. Started by an adventurous group of Cavalier imperialists who were advised by two French Canadians who had fallen out with their own people, it had hopes of finding a route from the Bay into the South Seas. Its charter gave it most of what is now the interior of the Dominion, of which no one knew the geography; but its early trade consisted mainly in exchanging 'gunns' and hatchets for beaver skins with Indians living round the Bay. A 'full share' in the Company was £300, but as each £100 gave a vote, that came to be the working unit. No dividend was paid for fourteen years. Shortages of cash were met by 'adventurers', as they were still called, lending to the Company at fixed interest, an anticipation of the modern fixed-interest debenture issued in similar circumstances. A very small intimate affair in early years, the Hudson's Bay had only fifty shareholders even in 1720. It was rather like a modern private company; and except in the boom of the nineties its shares were not regularly quoted for more than half a century after it won its charter.

That boom of the nineties had complicated antecedents. The intense curiosity, the eager interest in all novel and useful notions, and in most beautiful things, which—coupled with a love of money—marked Samuel Pepys (1633–1703) were reflected, less brightly, in many of his contemporaries. It was they who founded the Royal Society and built St Paul's, in that 'century of genius' which produced Galileo and Newton, Spinoza and Locke. Lesser men, excited by an atmosphere of discovery, were 'joining their heads to understand the useful things of this life', as one of Pepys's correspondents wrote. They had also a full-blooded age's love of a gamble. Under Charles II, while Lord Shaftesbury in time spared from politics and law was straightening out the finances of the Hudson's Bay, Nicholas Barbon—son of Praisegod Barebon[es]—had turned from praise to insurance projects. Sir William Petty ranged from anatomy to land-surveying, population, money and banks. Water-supply, telescopes, pumps, new ways of making sword blades, new textile processes, the making of cloth waterproof, new lines of foreign trade, all had their enthusiasts. There emerged a special type of enthusiast—not for the Good Old Cause, though he might profess a tepid allegiance to it— but for all applied, profitable 'useful things of this life'. These came to be known as 'projectors'.

Among them William Paterson, generally called the founder of the Bank of England, represents the higher type. After commercial experience in the West Indies he dreamt of a trading settlement on the isthmus of Panama; and, being a Scot, promoted in 1695 'The Company of Scotland trading to Africa and the Indies' which was to settle on the isthmus and trade from it both ways. The isthmus belonged to someone else and the resulting Scottish 'Darien enterprize' was a tragic failure. In 1694 the Bank of England had been chartered, after Paterson had for some time advocated the establishment of something of the kind as mouthpiece of a committee of City men. When he had served it only seven months he fell out with his colleagues—having not then paid up the whole of his promised subscription—and had no more to do with it. In quite another field, he was a holder of shares for which he did not pay in the Hampstead Aqueducts Company: they were no doubt a 'projector's' reward for supplying ideas.

The 'Darien Company' was meant to crown a Scottish development which had preceded the boom in which it was floated. Since her compulsory union with England in 1654–60 Scotland had become economically more self-conscious. Until then there had persisted the simple economy of small, mono-polistic towns, united to defend privilege in the Convention of Royal Burghs, and on the land a little domestic spinning and weaving for market. 'Almost all articles of luxury, as well as most of the comforts of life'[1] were imported. What commercial wealth there was belonged to the few merchants of the east coast who brought these things in and shipped coal, wool, lead, fish, linen yarn and a little rough linen and cloth. The ac-cession of James VI to the English throne had been followed by a few economic experiments: the Convention had appointed 'ane agent' to reside in London in 1616; there were unsuccess-ful attempts to start the manufacture of soap and glass, and a more fortunate attempt to improve the cloth industry by settling a few Flemings near Edinburgh. Later, in 1641, the import of fine wool and of dyes and oil was freed from customs to help this infant industry. Then came war, victory, the Covenant, defeat, with Oliver crying 'now let God arise' before he charged at Dunbar, and Scottish prisoners shipped to the plantations.

A thorough official encouragement of infant industries sets in in 1681. Many imported foreign luxuries and comforts are

---

[1] W. R. Scott, *Joint-stock Companies*, vol. III (1911), p. 123.

prohibited—from gold thread to all linens and cottons; the formation of companies is facilitated; monopolies are freely granted. Between 1693 and 1703 companies are established—sometimes on small existing foundations—in the silk, baize, rope, sugar, paper, iron, hardware, gunpowder, saw-milling and pottery trades; the Darien enterprise is launched and the Bank of Scotland established.

Most of these creations fall into the boom years between 1692 and 1695, or after them. The situation of Britain in the boom was unusual. She had just got rid of James II, joined herself to the progressive and commercially-minded Dutch, enjoyed the excitement that goes with a safe, successful revolution. She was at war: there was a field for munitions and finance companies. Her foreign trade was suffering: develop home industries, said the projectors, and find an outlet for capital. The dividend of about 10,000 per cent yielded in 1687–8 by a company that salved a Spanish treasure ship off Hispaniola gave that fillip to imagination, enterprise, and greed which usually follows luck with the precious metals, at Potosi or on the Rand.

Plenty of treasure-hunting companies followed: these naturally were failures. There were copper and mining companies for which the new definition of mines royal had cleared the way;[1] there were saltpetre, leather, diving machine, pumping machine and fire-hose (Sucking Worm Engine) companies; brown and white and blue (wall) paper; plate and bottle glass; various kinds of munitions; water supply, including the Hampstead Aqueducts in which Paterson was associated with John Holland, the leading projector of the Bank of Scotland; various war-financing companies—and the two national banks. Altogether the number of companies in Britain rose from twenty-two in 1688, fourteen in England and eight in Scotland, to very nearly 150 by the end of 1695.

The speed with which the Bank of England capital was subscribed, about 1300 subscribers averaging over £900 each, shows how eager the public were and how easily tapped the flow of capital—when the name and the security both seemed good. Indeed, money went freely to bad names and very doubtful security, to be lost with them.

It was in this boom that Houghton, the pioneer journalist, started that quoting of security prices which later journalists

---

[1] See above, p. 233.

have imitated. After it (1698) Defoe published his *Essay on Projects*. There were a few survivors from it, besides the two banks. There were also a few important company creations under Queen Anne—including the Sun Insurance and the Company of the South Seas incorporated in 1711. Nine years later the boom of 1693–5 was repeated in the 'Bubble' of 1720, with its 175 new companies to tempt speculation, besides frantic dealings in the shares of the old ones. There were 'bubbles' for everything, coral fishery, garden improvement, perpetual motion, and insuring and increasing children's fortunes. Some insurance 'bubbles', however, proved useful and permanent. The crisis story of the South Sea Company itself is hardly part of general British economic history, though the consequences of its failure are a very important part. What it proposed, in brief, was to carry through a conversion of the national debt to a lower rate of interest in return for commercial privileges in the South Seas, the granting and exploitation of which were most speculative, because the coasts of those seas belonged to Spain. It had other amalgamating and monopolising ambitions which were never realised: it had wanted to absorb, or at least dominate, both the Bank of England and the East India Company—the amalgamated East India Company, because for a few years round about 1700 there had been an Old and a New Company, playing against one another for power, but well aware that amalgamation was the rational terminus to their rivalries. Amalgamation had come in 1709.

The Bubble was so crazily blown out—£100 South Sea stock once stood at £1050—that it was bound to burst; but in fact it was pricked in a way that is important in the history of joint-stock enterprise. At law, only a chartered company had corporate rights—a seal and a corporate personality. The South Sea had a charter, and so had all the old companies. Few of the new projects had; for years projectors had got into the habit of starting a company and hoping for a charter, or carrying on without one. Unwisely, the South Sea issued writs of *scire facias* against some of them—'make known by what right you do this'. They were deflated. And so was the South Sea.

In the end, after savage legal vengeance on its directors, suicides and confiscations of property, the South Sea—discreetly handled by Walpole—became little more than a holder of some of the government stock that it had undertaken to convert. For a few years it tried to trade, sending out whaling ships and inventing a gun for killing whales; but only one of its voyages paid, and they were abandoned.

The Bubble left Englishmen with a horror of new joint-stock enterprises and of 'stock-jobbers'. In 1734 Parliament passed an Act 'to prevent the infamous practice of stock-jobbing' which forbad 'all wagers, puts and refusals, relating to the present or future price of stocks'. This did not stop them; and though very few new companies were chartered, fortunes were made and lost by dealings in Government stocks, East India stock, Bank of England stock, and a few more—East India above all. When the young Pretender was at Derby in 1745, there was opportunity enough for timid people to sell and daring people to buy.

Scotland had not been much affected by the London Bubble. She was too poor, too cautious, and too far away. There were very few Scots in the London business world before 1720; not many until after 1745. Her hothouse-raised fine industries had been hit by the Act of Union;[1] but, after a few years' discouragement, she had turned to the development of her domestic linen industry. Linen and stockings moved in great quantities in Defoe's day into England, the colonies and the continent. Scotland, or rather the Clyde people, had seized the opportunity offered them by the opening of the English colonial trade. First they hired English ships from Whitehaven. The reputed date of the first Clyde-built ship to cross the Atlantic is 1718: by 1725–7 Defoe was assured that Glasgow sent 'near fifty Sail of Ships' to America every year, 'and are every Year increasing'—as they continued to do. He thought it the only city in Scotland that 'encreased and improved' in both home and foreign trade. It had no drains; nor had English towns; but Defoe thought it 'the cleanest and beautifullest, and best built City in Britain, London excepted'. It refined sugar, distilled spirits from the molasses, and manufactured plaiding and muslins and linen. Down the water—this Defoe had not heard—Paisley had just begun to make thread. The traditional date is 1725.

THE BANK OF ENGLAND; INSURANCE

The men who planned the Bank of England intended two things: first, to have a secure income from government, such as some continental 'banks' had which were really mere associa-

[1] See above, p. 238.

tions of state creditors; second, on this secure basis, to carry on private banking as it had developed in the hands of the goldsmiths.[1] They were rather shy of note-issue with its risks, but, as one of them wrote in 1697: 'The Custom of giving Notes hath so much prevailed amongst us that the Bank could hardly carry on Business without it'. However, they had so arranged matters that the ordinary note, the 'pay the bearer' note, the 'cashier's note' as it was called in early days—the cashier still signs it—was not mentioned either in the Act of Parliament that authorised the Bank or in their Charter. Yet they began to issue it at once.

Their establishment was due immediately to the country's need of funds in war time. They offered to lend their whole capital of £1,200,000, and the offer was accepted. The capital was promised in a few days and business started on 27 July 1694. According to an ancient pious custom now abandoned, the words *Laus Deo* stand at the head of the first page of their cash book. The only sort of 'bill' that their Charter spoke of was a solemn 'sealed bill', promising to pay. These were not to be issued to a greater amount than their capital. If this was exceeded, shareholders were to be liable personally for the Bank's debts. As it never was exceeded, their liability was in practice limited—as in a modern company—to the amount of their shares.

Jealousy of the new privileged institution was natural. But the rival scheme for a Land Bank in 1696 was a complete failure. The goldsmith bankers, after some tentative opposition moves, found that there was room both for them and it: some of them kept accounts with it in very early days—a small beginning of the process which in time, long time, well after 1750, made it the bankers' bank. It did all the private business that they did, deposit, discount and note-issue, with important semi-public business in lending to the East India, Hudson's Bay, and other companies, but its main business was with government. Each time that its Charter was renewed government bargained for better terms and the Bank made further loans. When government began to borrow 'short', on Exchequer Bills, it did so mainly through the Bank. In time, when more long-term loans were issued to the public, the Bank was asked to lend a hand; but down to 1750 it had no monopoly of this business. The South Sea and the East India, which

[1] See above, pp. 266–7.

like the Bank had lent to government under William III and Anne, held and managed some of that public debt which only became a permanent thing after 1700. Nor was there any rule that government departments should bank with it, until early in the nineteenth century. Eighteenth-century ministers kept their accounts, in their own names, where they liked; but most of them found it convenient as time went on to use that Bank which, as Lord North said in 1781, had by that time become 'a part of the constitution'. It was hardly this in 1750, but was becoming so from about 1724, after the South Sea failure. That was the year in which William Lowndes died, the great Secretary of the Treasury since 1695, who had worked the Bank into the constitution, so to speak, and had secured from Queen Anne the right to use as his family motto 'Ways and Means', a parliamentary term that he is said to have invented. So strong and important was the Bank, by that time, that foreigners, mostly Dutchmen, were finding its stock a safe and profitable investment.

Another type of joint-stock company had survived the crash of 1720 to become, like the Bank of England, part of the economic constitution of the country—the insurance company. Marine insurance was old, but individualistic. Following Italian precedents, merchants, meeting first in Lombard Street and then in Sir Thomas Gresham's Royal Exchange, would agree to share the risks on a vessel, just as they might share in its ownership, to 'underwrite' them. Elizabeth's all-seeing Council regulated their action and passed an Act about it: the marine insurance policy of to-day is based on an Elizabethan draft. But royal control of insurance faded out with other royal controls during the seventeenth century. By the reign of William III marine insurance was again a free activity; Lloyd's coffee-house was already in existence, and a well-known meeting-place for seafaring men, though it was not till after 1720 that Lloyd's became the headquarters of marine insurance in England.

There had been talk of a company for the work in 1662, but nothing came of it. After 1666, insurance against fire was naturally much discussed. Nicholas Barbon both speculated in buildings and opened an 'office' for insuring them, in 1667; it became a company in 1680. It had competitors and successors, semi-public or private, before the Hand-in-Hand started a long life in 1696. Ten years later the society started that became the Sun.

To pay a sum down to be boarded in a monastery for life was a medieval practice. This buying of a 'corrody' was a sort of insurance that had its risks for both parties. Against other risks—of a voyage or a pilgrimage—men also 'insured'. The ordinary risks of life no one knew in 1600, though work began later on the London 'bills of mortality', continuous from 1603. A passage in *Measure for Measure* suggests that seven years was then a popular expectation of life for a young man.[1] So when, late in the seventeenth century, insurance of lives or the accidents of life was taken up by projectors, it was always a gamble and often a fraud. There was a special insurance boom under Queen Anne, in 1709–11, during which more than seventy 'offices'—not companies—have been traced, from the Faithful Office kept by the Widow Pratt, to the Nuptial Office at Pilkin's Coffee House, that took marriage risks. None of these survived, but the Amicable, a chartered society of 1706, did—for more than a century and a half.

From the Great Bubble of 1720 two insurance companies emerged; both chartered; both designed to compete with private underwriters for marine business; both forced to turn to fire-insurance to get a living. They still survive—the Royal Exchange and the London Assurance.

ENGLISH PRIVATE BANKS; BANKING IN SCOTLAND

Private banking in England was almost entirely concentrated in Town during the whole period, although towards its close district banks were specialising out from mercantile firms in Bristol, Norwich, and elsewhere. The London banking firms were not yet all stable and their numbers varied a good deal: a list of 1740, taken from a London Guide, gives twenty-eight, and contains already long-established and still familiar names such as Child, Barclay, Hankey, Hoare and Martin.

Scotland, moving with remarkable speed, had a much smaller but well-developed banking system by 1750. Unlike England, she had three chartered banks—the Scotland, or Old, of 1695; the Royal, or New, of 1727, and that unique institution the British Linen Company which, founded to encourage the industry in 1746, began to issue notes a few years later. There were private bankers in Edinburgh in the forties; and late in the decade came the Banking Company of Aberdeen and the

[1] Act III, sc. i, ll. 74–7.

Ship, the first regular bank in Glasgow. Foundation was the easier because, while in England no non-chartered concern might have more than six partners, Scots law set no limits to the size of a co-partnery, so that considerable groups of relatively poor men could make a start which in England would have required a heavy previous individual accumulation of capital in commerce—or great risk.

'MERCANTILISM' AND THE NAVIGATION LAWS

By 1750 London was beyond question the leading commercial city of the West. Commodities apart, she had taken from Amsterdam what Amsterdam had taken previously from Antwerp, the first place as market for the precious metals, Mexican silver—the ingots and 'pieces of eight'—that came to her easily through her West Indian and North American colonies, and the new gold supplies that were coming from Brazil through her ally and good customer, Portugal. Of her merchants and their achievement Britain was exceedingly proud. A popular writer of 1747, a Scot domiciled in London, whose book giving an account of London's trades ran into several editions, when he came to the merchant wrote this:

> Other Arts, Crafts and Mysteries live upon one another, and never add one Sixpence to the aggregate Wealth of the Kingdom; but the Merchant draws his honest Gain from the distant Poles, and every Shilling he returns more than he carries out, adds so much to the National Riches and Capital Stock of the Kingdom. Wherever he comes... Wealth and Plenty follow him: The Poor he sets to work, Manufactures flourish, Poverty is banished, and Public Credit increases.[1]

The two main fallacies here are obvious, yet they are found in much less popular, more ambitious, writing; that all Arts and Crafts are unproductive of new wealth, and that sixpences, silver sixpences, are wealth in a special sense, even an exclusive sense. It was these fallacies, this over-estimate of the merchant, that Adam Smith was to lash later as the 'system [i.e. doctrine] of commerce' or 'mercantile system'. Unfortunately the word 'mercantilism' has often been used to cover very different notions and policies.

No doubt there runs through much of the thought of these centuries an exaggerated valuation of sixpences, the precious

[1] R. Campbell, *The London Tradesman*, 3rd ed. (1757), p. 284.

metals. It was inherited from man's earliest emotions and experience. Gold and silver were mystically attractive: they were also embodied value, embodied general purchasing power. That was not how men put it between 1500 and 1750, but it was true. And, as things were, nations that did not mine them could get them only through their merchants, by selling more other things than they bought, though for lack of sufficient statistics no one knew precisely how much they did buy and sell. A teaching grew up after Adam Smith that certain natural causes connected with price will guarantee to a nation all the treasure that it requires. In a smooth peaceful world, and in time, perhaps; but the men of the sixteenth and seventeenth centuries saw Spain gorged with treasure from the Indies; saw her lose it all; saw her reduced to a debased currency of alloyed metal. It did not appear that natural causes were strong enough to beat human folly.

In discussing 'mercantilism' in relation to national policy it is better to quote official documents and the recorded opinions of statesmen than popular writers and pamphleteers. Though the popular writer often shows how the wind blows, some of the remarkable pamphleteers who have excited modern writers, because they are 'ahead of their times', for that very reason do not. When, in the Preface to the Book of [Customs] Rates of 1608, King James's officials refer to 'such Marchandizes as serve for the setting of the people of our kingdome on worke (as Cotton wooll...) or such as serve for the inriching of our Kingdome (as Gold and Silver in bullion or plate, and all sorts of Jewels and Pearles)', it certainly looks as though they shared Campbell's second fallacy. But when the great Cecil wrote in 1581, 'it is manifest that nothing robbeth the realm... but when more merchandise is brought into the realm than is carried forth' he may only have been thinking of the need to acquire gold and silver for currency, and of the risks to his Queen's then very empty war chest if they were not acquired. More than two hundred years later Adam Smith said that only Tartar Khans and the King of Prussia kept war chests of treasure. Precisely. Half-civilised, half-grown and bellicose states did and must. Cecil knew well how often in the past an empty chest had stopped fighting, perhaps to a country's disadvantage: Gresham had kept England's chest a little fuller by tricky operations at Antwerp, bad for English trade. Cecil wanted 'more merchandise...carried forth', for good reason.

If it did not bring in treasure directly, it would provide purchasing power abroad.

The shrewdest official discussion of the matter was at the Restoration Council of Trade in 1660. The Council was instructed 'to consider...how it may be so ordered...that we may have more sellers than buyers...abroad'. (The instruction rings a bell, as they say, in the mind of the Englishman of 1949.) Reporting in favour of a free trade in gold and silver, and pointing to Holland who had one and prospered, they argued that England 'hath of its own growth, manufacture and produce always enough to oblige the importation of money and bullion upon all occasions, beyond any other nation whatsoever in Christendom'. She had the surplus exports that would bring the treasure as required. And so she had. There was no need to hoard treasure when people owed money or money's worth to her all up and down the world.

A few years later (1664) such a hoard was advocated in a book that became famous, written by a merchant-statesman: Thomas Mun's *England's Treasure by Foreign Trade*. But it had been written long before. Mun had died in 1641, aged 70; his first book had appeared in 1621, and probably *England's Treasure* was in manuscript before 1630. It contains the thought of an Elizabethan not that of a Restoration mind. Mun was a merchant, a director of the East India Company, and a member of James I's Standing Commission on Trade. His main business in both his books was to justify the very unpopular export of treasure by the East India Company. He agreed that England ought 'to sell more to strangers yearly than we consume of theirs in value'; but he argued that the treasure sent East might be counterbalanced by the re-export of the Eastern produce that his Company imported. That done, England with her other exports might draw in a substantial balance of treasure yearly.

He was most intelligent. He understood what are to-day called 'invisible exports'—the services for which a country is owed money. And he knew—as a man who had come of age in 1592 would have been a fool had he not known—that 'plenty of money in a kingdom doth make the native commodities dearer'. That was one reason for his advocacy of a hoard—keep the treasure from affecting prices, a policy familiar in the United States of the twentieth century. The other reason was the anxiety natural to an Elizabethan that England should have a full war chest ready for any 'day of Armageddon', any 'last great fight of all'. So far as his books tell, he was committed to neither of the popular fallacies of 1747, though no doubt he thought well of gold.

About the time that Mun's rather antiquated views were published, the acutest political mind of the Restoration, Shaftesbury, a coolly passionate imperialist, had written in a memorandum on commercial policy—'it is Trade and Commerce alone that draweth store of wealth along with it and that Potency at sea By shypping which is not otherwise to be had'. It is most unlikely that this cold, clear mind was thinking superstitiously about sixpences. He had in view the general wealth of the commercial Dutch, who got treasure without making rules about it, and their great 'Potency at sea'. He was interested in the colonisation of Carolina, and became in 1673 Deputy Governor of the Hudson's Bay which was trying to outflank the French in Canada—and made no profits while he was connected with it.

Many policies of these centuries which have sometimes been classed as 'mercantilist' were in fact policies of 'Potency', without any strictly commercial flavour. It was neither over-valuation of the merchant nor of the sixpence that made Henry VIII cherish his fleet; or Cecil nurse the munitions industries and institute 'fish [eating] and navy days' to encourage a breed of seafarers; or Charles levy ship-money; or Parliament hit at the Dutch with Navigation Acts in 1651 and 1660; or eighteenth-century statesmen reserve the big timber of Maine for the King's Navy, and develop that old colonial policy that was based on the assumption that Britain was to do the manufacturing, her 'plantations' the production of food, and tropical luxuries, and raw materials.

Whether the Navigation Acts and the laws associated with them that gave English, and after 1707 British, ships a monopoly of what would now be called imperial trade did much harm, in the long run, to Dutch 'Potency' in war or commerce has been doubted. In a history of Britain it need not be discussed. What of British 'Potency'? The law, by 1696, said that ships trading to the plantations should all be of British or colonial build. Yet it was precisely in the plantation trade that British and colonial builds had the best chance of prevailing;[1] and as colonial building progressed, they would probably

[1] See above, p. 235.

have prevailed in the eighteenth century, but for a few minor exceptions, law or no law. Ships' crews were to be three-quarters British: there is no evidence that there was ever much risk of their becoming half foreign. A list of the main goods which the Dutch had sometimes brought into England as middlemen was drawn up: these goods were now to be brought only in British ships or in ships of the country that produced them. A Dutchman was not to bring corn from Danzig or timber from Gothenburg. This hit some Dutchmen and helped some Englishmen. Its ultimate effect on British wealth as a whole may have been slightly harmful, for the Dutch were cheap and efficient carriers; on the British mercantile marine slightly helpful: no more can be said with safety.

No alien merchant was to settle in the plantations; but alien merchants might be, and sometimes were, granted letters of naturalisation. Further—by the Staple Act (1663), not the Navigation Act—all European goods were to go to the colonies via England. This helped various English ports and English traders and, in conjunction with the 'enumeration' clause, made England (after 1707 Britain) the buying and selling place for the 'plantations', as was intended. The 'enumerated' goods had to come here—they were sugar, tobacco, cotton, ginger, and various dyestuffs and dyewoods.

The rule about sugar, tobacco and cotton—the last mainly from the West Indies in this period—was immensely helpful to Bristol, Liverpool and Glasgow. Fortunes were made in Glasgow by buying American tobacco and selling it to the French government's tobacco monopoly—which already existed. To help the plantations—and make taxation of tobacco easier—tobacco-growing in England was suppressed with violence, by the troops. Again to help the plantations, foreign sugar was taxed three or four times as highly as British. Therefore, after a little loud grumbling, they settled down to an arrangement well thought out on those imperial lines which Dutchmen and Frenchmen followed even more strictly in their colonial policy than Britons did. When it suited them, citizens of the future United States evaded the law a good deal: their enormous coastline, which could not all be watched, and their growing mercantile marine, made this easy.

There was a foretaste of things to come after 1750 in an appendix to the savage law of 1699 directed against the Irish woollen industry:[1] the plantations were to export neither wool nor yarn nor cloth. This did them no harm. Their textile industry, such as it was, was still at that household stage—farmers in homespun and so forth—at which it long remained. They never thought of export to England. And if, in time, there should develop an opening for rough 'slave' cloth in the West Indies, English or Spanish, it would be able to go there, because no machinery was set up for enforcing the law. Stresses between Britain and the colonies began to increase during the thirties owing to British action;[2] but they did no great harm to the ship of state before 1750.

The resolute and brutal protection of native industries and native agriculture that developed during the seventeenth century, mainly in its second half, and was associated with what to-day would be called an export drive, may well have been connected, in the minds of some of those who supported it, with superstitious reverence for exports as such and the treasure that a surplus of exports may bring in. References to a favourable balance of trade often occur in the preambles of statutes and in parliamentary speeches. But, without any such explanation, the greed of landowners and their farmers, the greed of clothiers, coal-owners, miscellaneous manufacturers and above all merchants, with the very reasonable belief of these people, and of statesmen, that a growing export was necessary in an increasing and part-industrialised nation, are enough to account for the course of national policy. The law was made by landowners and merchants. Where it bore on Ireland, the savageries of Cromwell's campaigns, the memories of massacre by the Irish which in part explain them, that fear of Irishmen and of the Pope which lay deep and dark in the minds of the English and the Scots, must be called in to help explain 'economic' policies which were only in a secondary sense economic. What was wanted by the generation that believed in the Popish Plot, and heard of the Battle of the Boyne, was a weak Ireland. Whether particular policies made England stronger or not was less important than that they should make Ireland weaker.

---

[1] See above, p. 238.   [2] See below, p. 291.

COMMERCIAL POLICY AND THE CUSTOMS

The customs system which the early Stuarts inherited[1] contained, in its complexities, various protectionist elements, 'aliens' duties' and prohibitions; and it had been utilised to forward trade policies, to strengthen England or weaken her rivals, as it was supposed. But, having been devised for revenue, its most essential feature was that taxation of staple exports—first wool, then cloth, with many others—on which the crown had always relied. The export duty on wool had died with the trade; that on manufactures of wool remained important down to the Civil War. Gradually, parliamentary opinion came to favour the view, expressed concisely by a pamphleteer of 1695, that the ideal was free export of all manufactures and free import of all raw material, strict enforcement of the prohibition to export wool, and the discouragement of all manufactured imports—these all in the interests of manufacturers and merchants.

This policy had been approximated to during the intervening half-century; and, in the interest of landowners and farmers, the old fear that if foodstuffs were freely exported risk of famine might be increased was not allowed to interfere with the lowering of customs duties. In 1656, for example, export duties on a miscellaneous list of articles were reduced, a list that included cereals, meat, butter, candles, beer and lead. Lead, like wool, had hitherto been a commodity which it was thought desirable that aliens should not get too easily. But England had a surplus, and that being so the export arguments were allowed to tell. With the Revolution, reduction of export duties was replaced by a policy of repeal. In 1691 the export duties on pork, beef, butter, cheese and candles went; in 1699, the decisive year, those on all manufactures of wool, on corn, on meal, on bread, and a number of other things. The duty on coal went in 1709—provided that the coal was loaded on to British ships. Finally, in 1721, Walpole completed the process, or nearly so: the chief export duties that survived him were those on the coal shipped in foreign bottoms, on lead, on horses and on 'white' cloth. A fair amount of 'white' cloth still went out: the motive for retaining the duty was that of Alderman Cockayne a century earlier,[2] the wish to encourage the dyeing

[1] On the earlier history of the customs system, see above, pp. 174–7.
[2] See above, p. 251.

and finishing at home of all cloth whatsoever. As for the horses, the motive was no doubt military. Walpole associated with this free-export policy a reduction of import duties on various raw materials, partly with a view to discouraging the smugglers. Some goods which England could not produce at all were allowed to enter untaxed, notably raw silk.[1]

Meanwhile the policy of encouraging the export of corn by means of export bounties had been adopted, first experimentally then permanently, in the interest of landowners in the first instance but latterly in the hope, which did not prove vain, of so stimulating the growth of corn that the country might be assured of plenty even in bad years—when, if necessary, export might be stopped by Order in Council. No doubt, here also, the balance of trade was considered; for the early eighteenth century was the period in which the doctrine that it was necessary to legislate for a 'favourable' balance was most generally assumed, although the argument of 1660[2] that the country had such a balance in any case remained valid; there was never any real difficulty in importing what gold and silver currency needs and the outward shippings of treasure by the East India Company required. It was this situation which enabled Adam Smith subsequently to treat deliberate attempts to keep the balance favourable as unnecessary and superstitious.

The old corn policy had been one of intermittent control of export in the interest of consumers. Control under Elizabeth was local: if the west had a short harvest, the Western ports were not to ship corn. Later a general price test was applied: in 1624, for example, export of wheat was allowed when the price was below 32s. a quarter. In 1670 export was freed, the Government reserving the right to prohibit it if harvests failed. Then, in 1673, the experimental bounty was enacted, in connection with the vote of a property tax—'and to the end', the law ran, 'that all owners of land whereupon this tax principally lyeth may be the better enabled to pay, by rendering... corn more valuable...and that the nation in general may have her stock [capital] increased by the returns thereof'—an export bounty was offered of 5s. a quarter on wheat, 3s. 6d. on rye and 2s. 6d. on barley, when wheat was below 48s. a quarter, rye below 32s., barley below 24s. (The importance of rye here assumed is significant for agricultural history.) The

---

[1] See further on Walpole's tariff policy, pp. 290–1 below.
[2] See above, p. 278.

'mercantilist' argument about exports increasing national capital may have been only a flourish, but was evidently thought to have an appeal.

This bounty experiment lasted only five years (1675–80). Houghton the journalist thought that it cost the country over £60,000 a year. That was probably why an impecunious government let it drop.

In 1689 it was renewed. Export when corn was cheap, the preamble stated, had been 'a great advantage...to the owners of land' and to 'the trade of this kingdom in general'. (The 'mercantilist' flourish is not repeated.) The same bounties were offered again, subject to the same maximum prices— when wheat was below 48s. a quarter, and so on. As wheat was in fact generally below 48s. between 1689 and 1750, its export was steadily encouraged. It did not become heavy because neighbouring countries either normally supplied themselves or, as in Holland's case, bought cheap from the Baltic. As West European harvests are apt to move together, if French harvests were bad the price in England was likely to rise above 48s.; and long-distance corn shipping never paid.

It was in the interests of the English exporter of manufactures that the Scots were excluded from the 'plantation' trade between 1660 and the Union. They were not quite excluded. They might settle there: the plantations needed men. They might, by a law of 1663, ship 'servants and victual' there, 'servants' those indentured labourers, half-slaves—criminals, political offenders, and kidnapped innocents—who were too numerous at the time. Besides what was legally sent, Scotland's rough manufactures could not be kept out altogether: the stockings and linens and plaids were the things useful to freemen, half-free men, and black slaves in the plantations. With the Union, the whole growing empire was open to the Scot; and, after a pause, out into it all he and his ships and his goods went.

Fear and hatred and the same exporters' interest lay behind the brutal policy of 1660–1700 towards Ireland. Up to 1660 there had been no regular legal impediments to Anglo-Irish trade: there were no taxes on the entry of Irish produce or manufactures into England. The first Restoration Subsidy Act (of 1660) began the taxation of Irish woollens and other manufactures: Ireland had always had a woollen industry, and now it was improving—labour was very cheap. Next, in the interest of the English farmer and landlord, a series of measures in

1663–81 killed the shipment to England of Ireland's most 'natural' exports—butter, cattle and meat. This encouraged the Irish wool production and manufacture, an outlet for the energies and resources blocked by English policy. Ireland was, however, like Scotland, allowed to ship 'servants and victual' and horses across the Atlantic. At first she had been treated as English under the Navigation Act; but in 1670–1 it was decided that the 'enumerated' goods should never be landed in Ireland.

The consummation of England's policy came after the battle of the Boyne. Under the Act of 1699 Protestant English clothiers were to be saved from Irish Papist—and also non-Papist—cheap labour competition by the absolute prohibition of the export of Irish manufactures of wool to foreign countries and the plantations.[1]

Ireland had her few undesigned compensations. The law about the enumerated goods was much evaded: the tobacco with which the Irishman was learning to comfort himself did not all come in by way of England. And the English law which allowed the export of victuals made Irish ports, especially those of her south coast, the great victualling centres for Atlantic shipping—and that not only English. Irish salt butter, Irish salt meat, found their way into the stores of merchant ships under many flags. They were cheap and, as such things went, good. To the Irish, if they knew the facts, it should have been some satisfaction that they killed England's export trade in butter.

TAXATION AND THE NATIONAL DEBT; THE REGULATION OF THE CLOTH INDUSTRY

The gradual abandonment of customs duties on exports was a part of that broad and slow movement of policy which 'modernised' British public finance between Tudor and Hanoverian times. The Tudor monarchy was expensive and, under Henry VIII at least, extravagant. Splendour of the court; the building of new palaces; the proper and necessary cost of the navy and of munitions; a more elaborate administrative machinery, no longer run by clerics who were paid in benefices, and an organised diplomacy, all were costly—though diplomats were ill and irregularly paid, and local administration was thrown more and more on to unpaid Justices of the Peace and

[1] See above, p. 238.

on to parish officials, also unpaid. National finance remained in form the private finance of the crown: to the close of the sixteenth century the phrase 'the manor of England' is still met with. Queen Elizabeth's accounts in the year of the Armada illustrate the situation. She had her 'ordinary' and her 'extra-ordinary' revenue—and her borrowings. Apart from the last, the total came to £392,000. Out of this £148,000 was described as coming from 'Rents and Revenues', the Duchy of Lancaster, and the Court of Wards—ancient, landed, 'feudal' income of the Crown, the first item of which, the 'Rents and Revenues', included many very miscellaneous and traditional items. Also traditional, but fortunately for the Queen rather more elastic at a time of rising prices, were the customs. But to keep them elastic, it was necessary to add extra customs, 'impositions', or to put pressure on the farmers of the customs—since in England, as in other countries, such farming was common. The customs in that year paid the Queen £102,000; what the farmers got, what their profit margin was, is not shown.

Ordinary revenue was completed by a sum of £45,000; £22,000 from the first-fruits and tenths that Elizabeth's father took from the Church, and the fines levied on those who would not worship in her way; £22,000 miscellaneous, largely debts repaid; and a wretched £1000 from those fines imposed in courts of law which had been a *magnum emolumentum* for Plantagenet kings.

The 'extraordinary' revenue included £4000 in 'benevo-lences'; £5000 in prizes—a very poor yield compared with her share of Drake's plunder some years earlier—and, the main item, £88,000 from subsidies.

A subsidy was the parliament-voted Tudor equivalent of medieval taxes on property, from the Danegeld to that 'tenth and fifteenth' which had become fossilised and unprofitable, though still levied now and then.[1] Like them, the subsidy was nominally a tax on the annual value of land, or on moveable property—on land worth 20s. a year and upwards and on goods and chattels worth £3 or more. But, as often before, the valuation and revaluation of lands and goods proved too hard for what administrative machinery there was. Goods, even lands, ceased to be valued. A county was expected to yield so much and each 'subsidy man' to pay his share. After 1540–50 no attempt to hit the small man appears; subsidy men

[1] See above, pp. 175–6.

are the bigger fish. Even for them the tradition grew up that 'men must not rise in the subsidy-book although they rise in wealth'. That was convenient for them but hard on the Queen when prices were rising. In 1588 she extracted a loan by a threat of a real valuation, not 'such lowe and favorable rates as are now accustomed'. It was a most justifiable threat. But in the end Bacon was able to write that 'he that shall look into other countries and consider the taxes...that are everywhere in use, will find that the Englishman is most master of his own valuation and the least bitten in purse of any nation in Europe'.

No wonder that great men built splendid houses and lesser men rebuilt strong-timber manors in 'brick or hard stone'. Even the humblest, hard hit as he was if living by wages, had some reason to remember good Queen Bess; for as nearly as possible he paid no taxes. He was below subsidy level; he would worship as the Queen bid him and not be fined; hardly anything he ever consumed paid customs, though imported salt and salt fish paid a small poundage. No one taxed his ale or his cider: sugar and tobacco had not yet a place in his 'cost of living index'.

King James, coming south into what must have seemed to him an endlessly rich land, was unable to live in peace on an income that Elizabeth, by infinite contriving, had just managed to make suffice in war. King Charles, like so many of our least fortunate Kings—Henry III, Richard II, Henry VI—was a patron of art. For very sufficient reasons, he also wanted a strong fleet. Hence Ship Money and John Hampden. Charles' other financial expedients, being short-lived, fall out of the story.

Parliament and Oliver's advisers soon found that, either for waging civil war in a country or for governing it after victory, the old financial methods would not serve—especially when there were wars with the Dutch or with Spain. Confiscations and fines on 'malignants' did not go far. Besides, as has been seen, in 1656 some export customs were cut down in the exporters' interest;[1] and although, if exports grew, a lower duty might perhaps bring in as much as a higher, it was not likely to bring in more. But two important innovations of 1643 were promising. The first was the *excise*—a foreign tax with a foreign name, *accise* in French, *excijs* in Dutch. England

[1] See above, p. 282.

had long known about it and hated the thought of this tax on home-produced articles of consumption. In 1642 Parliament said that rumours of its contemplated introduction were 'false and scandalous'. Next year, on Pym's motion, it was introduced. Beginning with ale, beer, cider and perry, it soon spread to salt and butchers' meat. By 1645 hats, starch, copper and many other goods were added. Most unpopular with the public and in the army, and often varied in detail, the system nevertheless continued throughout the Interregnum—the main contribution coming from brewers' beer, not home-brewed, aided by low duties on salt and soap and some other things.

The more excellent invention of 1643 was the appointment of Commissioners to collect customs, or supervise the collection. Customs farmers came back in 1662; but they did not stay. The parliamentary innovation was seen to have been good. By 1671 customs farming in England had ceased, more than a century before it ceased in France. Excise had been collected by Commissioners from the start.

In direct taxation, Parliament relied on the Weekly or Monthly Assessment, a kind of running subsidy. An attempt at a revaluation of the subsidy-men made in 1649 was a failure. The disturbed state of property, with fines and confiscations, rendered the years that followed unfit for so difficult an administrative reform.

The Cromwellian government, with its civil and international wars, was very expensive. It has been said that Charles II was restored to a bankrupt inheritance. He would have had financial difficulties, if he had been never so economical. Parliament kept him very short of 'ordinary' revenue and grudged 'extraordinary' supplies. When feudal tenures were abolished, and with them such 'feudal incidents' as wardship, they had in fact already faded away. About £50,000 from lands was all that remained to the crown. It had the customs. To help, Parliament perpetuated the excise on alcoholic liquors. It also gave the crown, in 1662, 'hearth-money'—2s. on every hearth, except the very poorest. This replaced the subsidies, now seldom voted—and hit people further down the social scale. Both they and those with big houses disliked the 'chimney-men' who came to count the hearths. The tax gave England its first statistics of houses, but was so unpopular that it was dropped in 1689—to be replaced six years later by the window-tax, no more popular in great houses but less burdensome on the cottages. The window-tax survived till 1851.

Parliament under William and Mary and Anne had to finance long wars, and the loans for long periods that were introduced to pay for them—in place of the hand-to-mouth royal borrowings of Tudors and Stuarts. For this the excise was found dangerously convenient. A loan would be raised and the interest charged on the fund to come from some particular tax: in time, the loans themselves came to be called 'the funds'. The Bank of England was nicknamed the Tunnage Bank, in its early days, because the interest to be paid it was charged against a duty on ships' tunnage, the tunnage fund—soon dropped. Ordinary articles of consumption were found easier to tax. One after another they were made to contribute, as they had been by the Long Parliament and its successors under Oliver—malt and hops as well as beer; salt and soap and leather and coal and paper and candles. By 1715, the excise yielded £2,300,000, the customs £1,700,000 out of a total national revenue of £5,500,000 (compare the Queen's income of 1588).

The balance came mainly from what had come to be called the Land Tax. In the nineties of the seventeenth century, that decade of bright ideas and projects, various experiments for raising money had been tried. The most interesting was a graduated so-called Poll Tax—beginning at 6*d.* on indoor servants who received less than £3 a year, and so upwards. The most permanent was the Land Tax. Originally called an 'Aid', it was meant, like the Tudor subsidy, to hit wealth in general —1*s.* (later 4*s.*) in the pound on yearly income from lands and houses; from salaries; on income from merchandise and goods generally on the assumption that they yielded 6 per cent—the rate of interest then usual—on their capital value.

Once again, administrative difficulties proved too great. By 1698 the tax had become an 'apportioned' tax: each county was told to raise a certain share of the £500,000 or thereabouts that 'a shilling in the pound' was expected to produce, whether that meant 1*s.* in the pound of residents' income or not. In effect this 'aid' became the Land Tax that it was called; and though now and then the tax-paying capacity of townsmen was tapped a little, the squires' view that they and not the 'moneyed interest' paid it was not far wrong. For fifty years, when the 'landed interest' attacked official or military extravagance, or the new national debt that was going to ruin England, the Land Tax was generally in that 'interest's' mind. Their fears about the debt, which Adam Smith shared, were not a mere faction cry. Charles II had 'stopped the Exchequer', and the King of France failed three times to keep his word to his creditors between 1710 and 1730.

Walpole (1721–42), by keeping out of war, did succeed in reducing the debt—both the capital amount and the interest paid. In 1727, for example, he converted a large block of 5 per cent stock into 4 per cent. Peace and prosperity were driving down the rate of interest which investors could reasonably expect. In 1737 Sir John Barnard, the man who had promoted the Act of 1734 against speculation in stocks and shares,[1] came forward with a plan 'to take advantage of the present rate of interest for the more speedy lessening of the national debt'. He wanted all the debt put on to a 3 per cent basis. As what 3 per cent stocks existed were actually at or above par, this seemed attainable. Barnard, however, did not win immediately; and in the forties Britain was again engaged in a long war, during which its confidence was shaken by the Jacobite rising of 1745. But with the return of peace in 1748, what would to-day be called a cheap money policy again became possible. Already, when the Bank of England charter had been renewed in 1742, the Lords of the Treasury had beaten the Bank down to a general 3 per cent on its consolidated loans to government, now amounting to £3,200,000. This chapter of financial history closes in 1751, when, after three years of peace, Henry Pelham at the Exchequer grouped together, consolidated, a list of distinct government borrowings—some already on a 3 per cent basis, some now reduced to it—into the 'three per cent consolidated annuities'. These were the original Consols, the 'three per cents', the 'old Consols', which remained the typical form of British debt, to which successive Chancellors tried to assimilate the more expensive forms that wars necessitated, right through the next century and more—until in 1888 Goschen converted the whole of the old '3's' into '2½'s', 'new Consols', 'Goschens'. Sir John Barnard, who was still an M.P. for the City when Pelham arranged his 'consolidation', must have been content.

It was once the fashion to say that Walpole 'laid the foundations of free trade'. He did adjust the tariff in a way of which

[1] See above, p. 272.

free-traders subsequently approved, by getting rid of nearly all export duties and reducing some import duties.[1] He made technical improvements in the 'official values' at which customs duties were levied. But all this was on a basis of administrative common sense, not on any basis of economic doctrine: Walpole was the last man to act as a doctrinaire. That 'excise scheme', which he was forced to drop when the London mob was encouraged by some inventor of slogans to yell 'no slavery, no excise, no wooden shoes', was really an excellent administrative device—for increasing the revenue, which explains its unpopularity. The taxation of certain commodities had all been done via the customs. Customs were collected only at the ports and smuggled goods dodged them. There were excise men everywhere, to supervise the taxes on malt and candles and so forth. Walpole had transferred collection of duties on tea, coffee and chocolate to the excise early in his ministry: it had paid. The scheme that he had to drop applied to wine and tobacco: it involved merely compulsory warehousing of these goods and collection of duties on them by excise officers as they left the warehouse. The fight turned on tobacco: the tobacco merchants were well organised; the opposition in parliament wanted to down Walpole; and he gave way.

Imperially and internally his ministry had no flavour of free trade. It was in the thirties that the American colonies were forbidden to export hats—not a great grievance—and were ordered to get from the British West Indies all the molasses from which they made the rum with which they bought the slaves—an imperial policy pleasing to the well-organised 'West India interest', and much evaded by the New Englanders. Rice from the Carolinas had been 'enumerated', obliged to come through Britain, since 1705: as a concession it was allowed to go direct to places south of Cape Finisterre in 1730. But the Admiralty monopoly of colonial naval stores—especially the great timber for masts—which also dated from 1705, was enforced as strictly as was practicable.

In internal matters Walpole maintained the regulative, protectionist policy that he inherited, if perhaps with a dash of scepticism and his characteristic letting of sleeping dogs lie. He had been a member of the government which had introduced the 'Calico' Bill of 1720[2] to please the worsted manufacturers. He reduced no existing tax, and abolished no prohibition, on

[1] See above, pp. 282–3.   [2] See above, p. 239.

imported manufactures. He never thought of revising England's treatment of Ireland's woollen industry.[1] He retained various measures of forced consumption introduced in the interests of the home manufacturer—the rule about burial in woollen shrouds;[2] the rule that every ship should carry full sets of home-made sails; the rather ridiculous little rule that all button-holes should be bound at their edges with home-made thread. Nor did he attempt to revise the complex, antiquated and by his day ineffective jumble of laws which were supposed to rule the country's main wool-manufacturing industries.

From the thirteenth and fourteenth centuries England had inherited the 'ulnage' system of inspecting and sealing market-able cloth, as a guarantee of length and quality, and an occasion for taxing it. 'Throughout the fifteenth and sixteenth' a 'be-wildering maze of legislation' was supposed to regulate 'every detail of dimension for every variety of cloth', forbidding processes and prescribing processes.[3] National, that is county, searchers supplemented the town searchers of the gilds for this largely extra-urban industry. But there was infinite disobedience and neglect, and under James I moralists were wailing about the fraud and bad workmanship that the maze of laws was supposed to prevent.

In the seventeenth century the 'ulnage' system continued, with the taxation of cloth, but 'searching' became more and more difficult as the industry became more diversified. How was a searcher to judge a fabric not mentioned in any law? Men devised, and even experimented with, county corporations to control the local industry. Little came of these, nor of such schemes as that by which, under the Restoration, Leeds tried to exercise urban control over a rural industry.[4]

'Ulnage' then barely existed: cloth, broad cloth, still paid for its own inspection—but as a source of revenue to some great man who farmed the tax. The last ulnage farm was to the Duke of Lennox and his widow, 1664–1724. He was not interested in processes and quality. In Yorkshire at any rate clothiers bought bundles of his seals and attached them to their cloths.

Very elaborate Acts of Walpole's day for the West Riding of Yorkshire, which was rapidly gaining a lead in the cloth industry, handed over enforcement of the law to the County

---

[1] See above, p. 238.   [2] See above, p. 239.
[3] Herbert Heaton, *The Yorkshire Woollen and Worsted Industries* (1920), p. 130.
[4] See above, p. 254.

Justices and their searchers; for broad cloth in 1725, and for narrow cloth in 1738. A serious attempt seems to have been made to work these statutes; but by the sixties they had broken down. The current of individualism and industrial freedom was then running too strong for them; but it cannot be said that Walpole had done much to clear its channels.

THE GUINEA AND THE GOLD STANDARD

Nor had Walpole any direct and conscious responsibility for an economic change effected without noise, without legislation, and with very little public recognition during his ministry—the practical adoption by England of the gold standard: its formal adoption only came three-quarters of a century later. Gold had circulated in England for centuries, but silver—the normal currency metal—had dominated monetary and price history. It was silver primarily that drove up prices in the sixteenth century. The Stuart kings, following ancient practice, had coined a fair amount of gold—but their gold coins were always being rated and re-rated in relation to the silver. Henry VII had struck the first golden 'sovereign', meant to be a 20s. coin like its nineteenth-century namesake. James I had struck golden 'unites' which were soon rated above 20s.; others, rather lighter, kept better to that rate. But a proclamation of 1661 rated the heavier of the unites at 23s. 6d., the lighter at 21s. 4d.: a man had to date, or weigh, his gold coin before changing it.

Charles II's 'guinea' was based on the lighter unite. It settled down at a weight and fineness which remained constant for nearly 150 years. Nominally it was again a 20s. coin; but the silver coinage was deteriorating so fast, by clipping and other forms of fraud, that by 1695 the guinea commonly passed for 30s.

Then came the great recoinage of the silver of 1696–8, in connection with which the guinea was rated down in stages to 21s. 6d. It should have been lower—in view of the weights of the coins when new and the relative values of gold and silver in the world's markets. This Sir Isaac Newton pointed out in a famous report of 1717. On the market value basis about 20s. 8d. was the right figure.

Parliament, however, rather naturally voted for that 21s. at which the guinea remained for the rest of its life. But at 21s., twenty-one new shillings were worth rather more, as metal, than a new guinea. They tended to be melted or exported, only worn silver remaining in use. In course of time much of it became very badly worn: by 1760 average shillings were down to about five-sixths, and sixpences to about three-quarters, of their full proper weight. That, however, did not matter, because a rich country made growing use of the gold. As small change, silver, even when badly worn, would do. So early as 1730, Conduitt, the Master of the Mint, wrote that 'nine parts in ten, or more, of all payments in England are now made in gold'—the more convenient as well as the 'nobler' currency. The Bank of England in the thirties was buying gold right and left; keeping an 'Account of Bullion for the Mint', and having its gold coined in great blocks of 80,000 or 100,000 guineas at a time. At law, a man could still pay large debts in silver. In practice he did not. It might have been bad for his social or commercial reputation, had he tried. The bank-note and the cheque were now available for very large payments; for the rest the guineas, not many of which were as yet badly worn, were what men liked and used.

THE POOR LAWS

Though the centuries before 1500 had their 'social problems', it is not to them that for 'social legislation' an inquirer into 'social legislation' turns. The greatest problem of all was that insecurity of life which no one expected to solve, except by self-defence when men were its cause, or prayer when it was an Act of God. But as society was to a great extent crystallised into distinct and fairly sharp-edged units—manor, parish, town—some customary or planned provision against the more familiar recurring insecurities had developed within them. The custom by which a villein's widow might hold the tenement without paying an entry fine, *dum bene et caste se gesserit*, seems to have been general on the manor; just as it was usual for a widow to carry on her husband's craft or shop in a town. If the villein widow married again, the holding passed to the children. Of non-villein land, free or rent-paying, the widow had a right to the yield of a third, 'as her dower'. She was both a familiar and a Scriptural type; and, so far, the duty of caring for her was not neglected.

In some districts, this principle of 'dower' might extend to an aged or infirm tenant in villeinage. He would surrender his holding to his son, retaining a few acres and a *receptaculum*, small cottage or couple of rooms, in which he and his old wife would end their days. A Pepiz (Pepys) is found doing this at Cottenham, Cambridgeshire, in 1347. Even when the incoming tenant is not a son, the outgoer may get 'dower' for his old age. How widespread such excellent arrangements were we do not know. We know them best in a very different connection, and far later—the dowager's house on a great estate, the Small House at Allington always assigned by the reigning squire Dale of the Great House to a poor or widowed Dale.

Where no such formal arrangements existed, it was assumed —as it was everywhere until recent times—that the able-bodied housed and supported the aged of their families. To the sick, lonely and destitute the alms of the Church were due, if not always adequately paid. There were social-religious gilds, both in town and country, which might help them. And, particularly in the larger towns, there were scattered endowed almshouses and hospitals—St Bartholomew's, St Thomas's, St Cross. There were also a few leper hospitals, for the most utterly outcast class of all.

In an imaginary society all made up of land-holding villagers and urban craftsmen no more might be needed. In the fairly stable rural society of eighteenth-century Scotland there was no more. Parish ministers and elders were responsible for the destitute; the village idiot was licensed to beg; no one actually starved.

But between the crystals, and more and more where crystallisation was incomplete or breaking down, there were fluid elements: people without lords, outlaws, people without land, men in the Greenwood, wandering beggars—impotent, fraudulent, or 'sturdy'—vagrant harlots, thieves, 'Egyptians', strictly proletarian townsmen. The picturesque literature about 'upright men', the 'sturdy', 'priggers of prancers' (horse thieves), 'counterfeit cranks' who shammed sickness, and the rest, that the printing-press let loose in Tudor times, hardly proves, though it may suggest, that all these became exceptionally numerous; though the proletarian townsmen did.

One outlet for the incurable wanderer was officially closed by the Reformation—pilgrimage. Perhaps inability to start off in the spring for Canterbury or Rome or the shrine of St James of Compostella encouraged wanderings to Guinea or the Spanish Main: even a poor man could ship as a deck hand.

The legal tradition inherited from long before 1500 was to treat irregular vagrants as the criminals that they often were: the outlaw had always been a 'wolf's head': in medieval Germany there was a royal right of *Wildfang*, of capturing 'wild' men for slavery or at least serfdom.

Early Tudor legislation was mainly of the old criminal sort. Alleging that violent 'beggars' were going about in 'great routs and companies', it threatened them with the stocks and with floggings until their backs should be 'bloody'. That was in 1530–1 and 1535–6. Vagrant children, when the Justices got at them, were to be arrested and prenticed to some honest work. As newly-made Head of the Church, Henry, or his advisers, also decided to overhaul the machinery of parish relief for the unfortunate innocent poor. Begging-licences might be issued—as they still were in Scotland far down the nineteenth century. There were to be parish collections for the poor: the parson was to keep accounts. The only direct unaccounted 'charity' was to be the giving of 'broken meats'.

Not only was Henry now Head of the Church—there had been much unemployment among the scattered textile workers in recent years,[1] and prices were beginning to rise. It is noticeable that experiments in systematic poor relief were first tried in towns—London, York, Bristol and others—where proletarians who had lost roots in the country were in a great majority. The number of these was probably swelled by new uprootings due to the agrarian changes of the time—but this movement is easily exaggerated and cannot be measured. In any case, it is only a possible one among a score of causes that favoured the unwholesome growth of Tudor London.

Experiments made in the towns were often adopted as part of national policy. London had begun the licensing of beggars —a thousand of them—in 1517. But the nation never followed the remarkable experiments tried at Coventry in 1547 and at Norwich in 1570: censuses of the poor with their occupations, the size of their families, and their needs, which anticipated such modern inquiries into life and labour as those of Charles Booth in London and Seebohm Rowntree in York. Government generally assumed that parishes knew all their poor—no doubt a sound assumption for the rural parish and the small town, but hardly sound for Norwich or London.

Reformation attacks on religious foundations certainly did

[1] See above, p. 250.

harm. All the suppressed parish gilds were religious; and in many country places the 'gild house' or the 'church house' had served as a poor-house. In London the hospitals, also religious, suffered badly: Bishop Ridley is found making an effort to reorganise St Thomas's in 1552. A year later, the Crown handed over the ancient Palace of Bridewell to the City authorities as a centre for relief, employment and discipline— a sort of mixed poor-house and, in later terminology, house of correction. 'The weaker sort'—women, children, and perhaps old men—were to be set to card and spin. 'The fouler sort' were to be put to heavy disciplinary work. Such a comprehensive institution was likely to be the failure that it proved. In later years the Bridewell authorities specialised in harlots.

There was always the problem of finance; but for this there was something to work on; an old tradition, traceable to at least the early fourteenth century, of levying a parish church rate, for maintenance or repair. Marshland parishes, in south Lincolnshire or Romney Marsh, had also been rated for work on the dykes: *villata de Pynchebek est in periculo submersionis;* we do not know who ought to do the necessary work, so all must contribute. That is in 1375. Towns were accustomed to pay their share of subsidies on a property basis. So, as early as 1547, London is found using that basis to raise a poor fund. In 1556 Cambridge follows.

In the shifting years of the mid-century, years dominated by religious action and reaction and by those political uncertainties and misfortunes which wrote Calais on Queen Mary's heart and were not good for trade; in these years the Council and Parliament were hesitant and tentative. There was not money enough coming in through the reorganised and again reorganised Church to relieve the poor adequately: the Councils issued exhortations. Parish collectors were 'gentellie' to ask: the response was insufficient. The Justices were 'charitably' to 'perswade and move' their neighbours: they were not moved enough. Finally the Justices were to assess them, and by 1563 had power to imprison those who did not pay what was now, where demanded, a plain legal poor rate.

Government found it necessary to define and redefine that 'vagabond' class to which criminal treatment was applicable, as opposed to the class of the 'deserving poor' which should be helped. The 'Egyptians' had been first dealt with by Act of Parliament in 1530. Subsequently, the vagabond class was made to include, besides obviously criminal types, 'bearwards', strolling players, and scholars of the universities who begged without a licence—from the Vice-Chancellor. It might also be made to include secret agents of the Church of Rome and political undesirables generally. It was so made in 1569, at the time of the revolt of the earls, when a vigorous flogging campaign was directed against backs either socially or politically undesirable.

The early seventies that followed this campaign were difficult and hungry. Their industrial unemployment is registered in the Norwich census. One direct result was the law for the poor of 1572, intended to organise and generalise provision for them. It contains the vagabond clause; it makes the compulsory poor rate binding on all parishes; and it instructs the unpaid and overworked justices to see to the appointment, year by year, of parish overseers of the poor—also unpaid. In 1575-6 the thing is carried further. The Justices are empowered to spend public money on stocks of raw material to 'set the poor on work'. (Where they did so, it was generally wool or flax to be spun for the market—which, *ex hypothesi*, was not brisk when unemployment drove many poor people to seek relief.) Every county is to set up a House of Correction for the undesirable poor, 'the fouler sort'. The county gaol was merely a place of detention: a man was not made to work there. In the House of Correction he was meant to work.

There is a pause; and then in that unhappy closing decade of the century, with its exceptionally high food prices, its dragging war with Spain, and the resulting interference with the 'vent' of English manufactures, the English Poor Law is made into a code that was to have a very long life. The best brains of the time were behind it—Burghley and Archbishop Whitgift, Bacon and Coke. They considered a long list of proposals, bills tabled in the Commons, and drew up the Act of 1597-8 which both Houses approved. Parish administration was to be in the hands of church-wardens and overseers; the poor rate was to be universal; poor children who came on to the hands of the overseers were to be apprenticed to a trade; girls until 21, boys—like other apprentices—until 24; the 'impotent' were to be supported in one way or another; and those capable of it were to be 'set on work' as under the earlier law.

As if to underline the difference between the deserving and the undeserving poor, the flogging of vagabonds and the control of the county Houses of Correction were dealt with in a separate Act.

The code was designed as an experiment. It was voted for three years; but was re-enacted in all essentials in 1601; was subsequently renewed, and finally made permanent. But it might not have acquired effective permanency had it not been supervised and kept in running order by the Council of the early Stuarts with its bias—in this case healthy—on the side of paternal government. There was an important inquiry into the working of the law in 1630, followed by the issue of a Book of Orders, the equivalent of a modern Home Office circular. The Houses of Correction, whose general establishment was enforced, were at first worked more as training places than as gaols—though in the long run they acquired a penal character. Before the Civil War the whole system was in fair working order except in the North and North-West, and in Wales. Parts of Wales were almost untouched by it; and more than a century later there were Welsh counties in which no rate was 'laid'. True, Welsh conditions were often near to what English conditions had been before the Poor Law was devised—and what Scottish conditions remained.[1]

Provision for the deserving and destitute poor took various forms. Sometimes a regular poor-house was provided for them. At Aylsham in Norfolk, under James I, they were lodged in 'one great house whereof there was no use but to keep certain rotten stuff that was used to the setting forward of a superstitious and ungodly game': it sounds like one of the parish gild-houses, fairly common in East Anglia, with 'ungodly' ceremonial relics for festivities and processions—perhaps those 'hobby-horses, dragons and other antics' brought out for the festival of 'my Lord of Misrule' that an Elizabethan Puritan had denounced: he had seen the horror himself.

Aylsham is a little market town. In the village proper a regular poor-house was seldom established. A few cottages might be assigned to the struggling poor, or they might be allowed to run up rough huts for themselves on the waste. It was easiest of all to feed them or give them small pensions, if they had houses over their heads. In some towns serious attempts were made at industrial training, as in the early county Houses of Correction. At Hitchin in 1618, a man was hired from St Albans to give instruction in the making of 'curious

[1] See above, pp. 215–6.

wool work and excellent yarns'—in a vacant barn; later a man from Ware who understood flax-dressing. Hitchin was one of eight Hertfordshire towns that tried to teach men out of work how to make the baize that was becoming such an important industry to the east, in Essex.[1] The barn was replaced by a 'town house' or 'house of maintenance'. After the Inquiry of 1630, overseers at Hitchin are also found busy apprenticing 'the poorest children', as overseers were in many other places.

A form of 'relief' found fairly often in wool-working districts was the hiring-out of pauper labour cheap to a clothier—an obviously unsatisfactory arrangement, both socially and economically.

Civil War, with Justices of the Peace fighting on opposite sides, was as bad for the administration of the Poor Law as for that of the older Labour Law. London filled up with beggars. A London parish, especially one outside the City, was not like Aylsham or Hitchin. You could not easily help the out-of-works of Bethnal Green by teaching them to make baize; they were very likely weavers already. No 'one great house' would hold the destitute of Shoreditch. In a society fermenting with religious and social ideals, the society of the Fifth Monarchy men and the Diggers, there was a spate of reforms planned but little effective reforming.

Inevitably under Oliver vagrancy of every grade became more abundant. There were demobilised soldiers; miscellaneous seekers of work; and so down to the camp-following harlots, the thieves and the footpads. But no one has yet found real evidence for a rhetorical passage in the preamble to the Restoration poor law of 1662, which speaks of the unrestrained wanderers who will 'endeavour to settle' in a parish 'where there is the best stock, the largest commons and the most woods ...and when they have consumed it then to another'. No doubt rich parishes attracted tramps, but this rhetoric suggests locusts.

This Act of 1662 formally authorised every parish to move on, within forty days, any immigrant who seemed likely to become a burden to it. There was nothing new in the policy. Flogging and expulsion had always awaited the vagabond by definition. There are plenty of recorded cases of moving on before 1662: no parish could be expected to accept permanent liability for every poor person who might choose to come into it,

[1] See above, p. 241.

though every parish was bound to give temporary help to wanderers properly certified—shipwrecked seamen, for example, making their way home. But, with a growing population and the extra streak of hardness that seems to enter public life in the Restoration Age, this policy of moving on all who had not a 'settlement' in the parish might very easily be abused; it certainly was often a cause of great misery.

The educational policies did not disappear. After the Civil War Aylesbury had a house in which children were taught trades and people set to work on 'the town stock'. There, as in other places, almshouses met the needs of some at least of the 'impotent' poor, the sick and broken down. Hitchin kept up its training schemes, but had not much success with men: it set them to beating hemp or breaking stones, much as tramps were set to earn their nights' lodging in the 'casual wards' of the late nineteenth century. Hemp-beating became a regular task for loose women in Bridewell, as shown in Hogarth's *Harlot's Progress*.

Towards the end of the century relief in doles of money for the decent poor seems to have been gaining ground in most places. It was easy to pay the rent for a parishioner short of work; to dribble money out to the diseased and the destitute; to supplement the earnings of some aged spinning woman, or to have her wheel repaired at the cost of the parish. 'It is rare to see any provision of a stock', a contemporary writes. But it was in the boom-year 1695 that John Bellers, a Quaker 'projector', thinking not of gain but of human welfare, published his *Proposals for raising a College of Industry of all useful Trades and Husbandry* that was to have 'a stock', was to solve problems of poverty and safeguard the social future.

Nothing came of it for a very long time. The sort of opinions that carried most weight and were most representative had that hard strain in them. There was much talk about the idleness of 'the poor'; no doubt there were poor men who were idle. It was suggested that dear food was not a bad thing; was a cure for idleness. A serious and influential writer lumped together the wage-earner and the dependent pauper as people who ate 'their employer's bread'—as if it was the employer who created the bread. At the same time—in the late seventeenth and early eighteenth century—the practice of supplementing wages out of the rates was spreading, not as a regular thing but in emergencies—when the wage-earner's capacity was impaired by disease or some physical disability, or when he had managed to keep a large family alive. The children usually came often; but like those of their Queen, Anne, they very often died. The English birth-rate was seldom below 30 per 1000: in 1730 it was 32. (To-day it varies between 15 and 19.) But the death-rate kept close behind it, and sometimes, as in 1730, got in front. It was between 1740 and 1750 that the gap between the two curves began to widen—leading to that greatest known change in the course of population which makes the years about 1750 a watershed in economic and social history.

Hard as opinion and practice were, the greater towns were taking steps to house at least some of their poor—in newly built poor-houses, or workhouses as they were sometimes called, in the hope that they would provide training as well as accommodation. The usual method was to get a special Act of Parliament to authorise the experiment of dealing with a whole town rather than a parish, which was an evidently unsuitable unit in urban conditions. London Work House in Bishopsgate Street, opened in 1698, tried to do what an experimental House of 1647 had failed at. Half a dozen others, including Bristol, Hull and Liverpool, also date from William and Mary's reign. Under Anne came the great house at Norwich—eventually capable of housing more than a thousand souls. This served the whole city as the Bishopsgate house could never hope to do. Outer London retained its parochial arrangements, and the greater parishes—Bermondsey St Mary and Deptford St Paul, for instance—eventually started houses of their own.

A beginning having been made, an Act of 1722 gave general authorisation for parishes or groups of parishes to establish similar houses and to apply what became known in the nineteenth century as the workhouse test: anyone who refused to enter the house might be refused public assistance. But before 1750, indeed throughout the century, both the provision of such houses and the application of the test were exceptional. Parish grouping, outside towns, was not attempted for a long time. About forty houses are recorded as existing by 1775, including those set up before the Act of 1722. How generally the test was applied is not known; but it can, at most, have affected only a small section of those in need.

To what extent, in town or country, the whole system of the Poor Laws, as administered under King George II, served to relieve unemployment, underpay, or absolute destitution is a thing not to be calculated, hardly to be guessed at. The law was harshly administered; but that was a hard age, in which women were still flogged, seamen flogged to death, and criminals in France broken on the wheel. The English law was, in any case, the best, almost the only, thing of its kind in Europe. In 1789 when the French peasants were sending in their grievances, their *doléances*, parish by parish, among some lamentable descriptions of beggary and of day-labourers starving, there are constant demands for an organised poor law on a parish basis.

The parish, the *commune*, was the foundation of all French rural life; and so it had been of English. But the Act of 1722 recognised the probable advantages of joint action among parishes, although it was not until after 1750 that this policy was tried in country districts. At what date the words 'parochial' and 'parish pump' were first used to carry a sneer need not be discussed: certainly the sneer had often been earned before 1750. The farmer, or whoever he might be, who took his unpaid turn as country overseer of the poor, very easily learnt to think in terms of keeping rates down, keeping potential paupers out, and saving himself trouble.

One result was the discouragement of cottage building, even here and there the encouragement of the pulling down of that kind of half-derelict cottage in which vagrants and potential paupers tended to herd. There was still on the Statute Book an old, well-intentioned Elizabethan law that required every new cottage to have four acres of land about it. This law might be used, sometimes is known to have been used, against the kind of 'squatter' who 'set up a cottage in the night time on the waste in Finchley...without four acres of ground laid to it'.[1] (What sort of a cottage would go up in a night on 'the waste in Finchley'?) Cases under the Act are fairly common in Middlesex down to 1720, though the law is not regularly enforced; but after that, as might be expected in the London area, the Justices ignored it if satisfied that a new cottage was needed and was innocuous. Under George II the law was 'virtually a dead-letter'[2] there; but in more rural counties, its existence in the background would be a useful argument in the mouth of anyone who did not want to see the parish's liability for more people increased by provision of more housing. In such areas

[1] E. G. Dowdell, *A Hundred Years of Quarter Sessions* (1932), p. 82.
[2] *Ibid.*

there was very little building of cottages in the first half of the eighteenth century.

Nothing illustrates better the zeal of parish authorities to keep down their liability for the poor than the interminable litigation about settlements—has, or had, the family of Hodge a settlement in Nether Wallop? If they have not, and have come there, 'pass them on' until they get to a place where they have. A chance family of O'Flahertys or Macdonalds would, in theory, have to move to the English frontier; but then few Scottish or Irish families were adrift in England before 1750— though there were individuals, especially Irishmen making for London.

Everything goes to show that the law did not interfere appreciably with the mobility of the single man who was looking for work, a mobility which all the circumstances of the later seventeenth century, especially the Fire of London, had favoured. The overseers did not fear him and unless there was a local opening he would not want to stay. It was on destitute families and wretched half-vagrant women and children that the hand of the rural overseer lay heavy: sometimes they were driven out to die.

No explanation is needed for the drift to Town, where overseers did not know people's pedigrees and skilled or casual work might be hoped for. Outer London that had escaped the Great Fire was full of old tumble-down timber houses and of lanes and alleys where stood newer jostling ill-built stretches of so-and-so's 'rents'. There was Gin Lane and all the marshy insanitary ground by the waterside, east and south and even west. Parish authorities in London gave some doles, housed some of the destitute, and were eager to apprentice those poor children for whom they could not deny responsibility to 'no matter what master, provided he lives out of the parish', as a writer says in 1738. There was all possible difference between this apprenticeship and the educational apprenticeship still almost universal in the skilled trades and mercantile occupations of London. The parish would pay, something, to get a boy or girl off its hands. Usually this would be into some 'mean' trade or, in the case of a girl, very often into 'the art of housewifery'—as a domestic drudge to a woman who had over her an absolute control. A boy might be a helper in a stables, a pot-boy, or a chimney-sweep; and when his master had a craft worth learning, he might not be taught it or his master might hire him out to someone else. There was misery enough in the system at its best, apart from the far too numerous cases that came into the courts of criminal ill-treatment of apprentices. The courts did what they could. When a case came before them and gross neglect or ill-treatment was proved, they would discharge the apprentice from his obligation to remain and serve a bad master, or if a girl, to stay with a mistress who starved her. But what proportion of the cases of neglect and ill-treatment that was not quite criminal, or even of those that were, ever got into court, in the ill-governed and imperfectly-supervised London of the eighteenth century? What became of the girls apprenticed into 'literal slavery' until the age of twenty-one with the milk-sellers? They were not often those charming young persons in bright frocks cut low at the neck who appear in coloured prints of 'the Cries of London'. Theirs would be other crying.

INDEX